ANXIETY IN RELATIONSHIP

The Scientific Therapy to Cure and Overcome Insecurity, Depression, Jealousy, Separation Anxiety and How to Transform Couple Communication to Achieve Happiness in Love

Scarlett Williams

Text Copyright©

All rights reserved. No part of this guide may be reproduced in any form without permission in writing from the publisher except in the case of brief quotations embodied in critical articles or reviews.

Legal & Disclaimer

The information contained in this book and its contents is not designed to replace or take the place of any form of medical or professional advice; and is not meant to replace the need for independent medical, financial, legal or other professional advice or services, as may be required. The content and information in this book has been provided for educational and entertainment purposes only.

The content and information contained in this book has been compiled from sources deemed reliable, and it is accurate to the best of the Author's knowledge, information and belief. However, the Author cannot guarantee its accuracy and validity and cannot be held liable for any errors and/or omissions. Further, changes are periodically made to this book as and when needed. Where appropriate and/or necessary, you must consult a professional (including but not limited to your doctor, attorney, financial advisor or such other professional advisor) before using any of the suggested remedies, techniques, or information in this book.

Upon using the contents and information contained in this book, you agree to hold harmless the Author from and against any damages, costs, and expenses, including any legal fees potentially resulting from the application of any of the information provided by this book. This disclaimer applies to any loss, damages or injury caused by the use and application, whether directly or indirectly, of any advice or information presented, whether for breach of contract, tort, negligence, personal injury, criminal intent, or under any other cause of action.

You agree to accept all risks of using the information presented inside this book.

You agree that by continuing to read this book, where appropriate and/or necessary, you shall consult a professional (including but not limited to your doctor, attorney, or financial advisor or such needed) before using any of the suggested remedies, techniques, or information in this book.

Table of Contents

Introduction Part 1 17

Chapter 1: Understanding Your Anxiety in Love 21

Understanding Why You Feel Anxious, Insecure and Attached in Relationships 25

Chapter 2: Unconscious Behavior Caused by Anxiety 30

Over-Analyzing 32
Fear of Being in a Serious Relationship 33
You Have a Bad Temper 35
Being an Extreme Pleaser 36
You Beat Yourself Too Much 37
You Lack Confidence 37

Chapter 3: Different Types of Anxiety in Love and How to Overcome Them 39

Anxiety Can Negatively Influence Relationships 39
The Key to Tension Is Just How Couples Handle It. 40
What Can You Do? 40
How to Reduce High Couple Conflicts 45

Chapter 4: Recognizing Your Anxiety Triggers 48

Fear of Collapse 48
Fear of Being Vulnerable 49
Fear of Not Feeling Important 51
Fear of Failure 52
Fear of Entering into Intimacy 54
Past Experiences Ended Badly 55

Chapter 5: Love Yourself to Love Your Partner 57

Do You Know Your True Value? 57

Reasons Why You Are Unique 58

Chapter 6: Ways to Recover Communication with Your Partner 67

Chapter 7: How to Strengthen the Relationship with Your Partner 77

Chapter 8: How to Help Your Partner to Overcome Anxiety 87
Loving a Person with Anxiety 87
Specific Disorder Interventions 90
Social Phobia 94
Post-Traumatic Stress Disorder 94
Make a Plan for Relieving your Partner's Anxiety 94

Chapter 9: Exercises and Remedies to Overcome Anxiety 96
A Healthy Relationship Is a Good Relationship 96
The Six Stages of a Relationship 100
The Six Human Needs in Relationship/Marriage 101
Why Couples Argue 102
How Communication Works in Relationship 103

Chapter 10: How to Create Healthy Interdependence 106
Keeping the Spark Alive 106
Understand the Meaning 107
Time to Disconnect 108
Make and Maintain Eye Contact 109
Something New 109
Spend Some Time Apart 110
Starting a Conversation 110
Laughing Together 111
Impress Your Partner 112
Making Changes 112

Kiss 113

Chapter 11: Observing Your Thoughts 115
Causes of Mental Clutter 115
Practical Tips on How to Declutter Your Mind 118

Chapter 12: What Are My Personal Goals? 124
Do We Have Shared Interests and Goals? 126
Do We Have Conflicting Personal Interests and Goals? 128

Chapter 13: Secret Strategies for Handling Insecure Partners 133

Chapter 14: Communicate to Your Partner 142
Good Communication 143
Importance of Good Communication in Relationships: 144
Signs of Poor Communication in a Relationship 146
Keys to Good Marital Communication 149
Communication in Your Marriage 151

Chapter 15: Make a Reflection and Self-Care 153
Take Time for Yourself: Self-Care 154
The Importance of Stillness 155
Journal Effectively 157
Grant Yourself Grace 158
Allow Yourself to Be Loved 159
Did You Know You Were Made for Love? 160
Opening Up to Love from Others 160

Chapter 16: Creating and Maintaining Relationship 163
How Do We Relate With Each Other? 164
Using Positive and Motivation Words during Conversations 165
How Do You Keep Connected and In Sync With Each Other? 166
How Deep Is Our Emotional Connection? 169

Chapter 17: Reminding Yourself of Your Positive Traits 174
Adopting a Positive Attitude 178
Boosting Self-Confidence 179

Chapter 18: The Role of Attachment in Relationships with Anxious Individuals 183
Types of Attachment 185
Attachment Problems in Anxious Adults 189

Chapter 19: Benefits of Guided Meditation 192
Mental Health Benefits 192
Decrease Depression 193
Reduce Anxiety and Depression 193
Performance Benefits 194
Better Decision Making 194
Improve Focus and Attention 194
Relieve Pain 195
Avoid Multitasking Too Often 195
Physical Benefits 196
Reduce Risk of Stroke and Heart Disease 196
Reduce High Blood Pressure 197
Live a Longer Life 197
Relationship Benefits 197
Improve Positive Relationships and Empathy 198
Decrease Feelings of Loneliness 198

Chapter 20: Retraining the Mind 200
The Cognitive Model of Anxiety and Depression 201

Chapter 21: Solutions for Anxiety in Relationships 209
They Forgive Your Past 211
Acknowledge Yourself, the Great and the Awful 211

Start to Rehearse Self-Approval 212
Stop Comparing Yourself 212
Figure Out How to Be Trustful at the Time 213

Chapter 22: The Purpose of Relationship 218
Find the Purpose of Your Relationships 219
Figure out how To Be in Love with Love 221
Be Independent and Connect from the Heart 222

Chapter 23: Setting a Goal for a Healthy Relationship 225
What to Look for in a Partner 226
Nurturing a Relationship, You Feel Secure In 229

Conclusion Part 1 233

Introduction Part 2 241

Chapter 24: Understanding Your Anxiety 245

Chapter 25: The Various Types of Anxiety 253
Generalized Anxiety Disorder 253
Obsessive-Compulsive Disorder 254
Post-Traumatic Stress Disorder 255
Panic Disorder 256
Social Anxiety Disorder 258
Phobias 260

Chapter 26: Anxiety in Different Types of Relationships 262
Signs That Anxiety Is in Your Life 263
Getting Rid of Relationship Anxiety 265

Chapter 27: Principal Frequently Worries 273
Practice Relaxation and Self-Care Techniques 274
Panic Attack 274
Causes 275

Chapter 28: Signs that Anxiety is Affecting Your Relationship 278
- What Causes Anxiety in Relationships? 278
- What Thoughts Perpetuate Anxiety in Relationships? 281
- Essential Inner Voices about Relationship 281
- How Does Anxiety in Relationship Affect Us? 282
- Signs That Anxiety Is for Your Life 284

Chapter 29: The Management of Anxiety 287
- Strategies for Anxiety Relief 287
- Realistic Thinking 287
- Seeking out a Therapist 288
- Worst Case Scenario Roleplay 290
- Play out a Situation to the End 291
- Strategies for Improving Quality of Life 292
- Understanding Body Language 292
- Studying Emotional Intelligence 293

Chapter 30: Steps to Overcome Anxiety in Relationships 295
- Slay Those Dragons and Find Love and Contentment 295
- Effects of Earned Security 297
- What to Aim For 297
- Recognize Your Triggers 299

Chapter 31: Tips to Help Reduce Anxiety Levels Using Exercise 302
- Realistic Perspective 302
- Hard Work 303
- Quality Time 303
- Alone Time 304
- Differences Are Good 304
- Trying to Change 305
- Acceptance 305

Learn to Communicate 306
Be Honest 307
Respect Matters 307

Chapter 32: Cultivating New and Healthy Relationships 310
Allow Vulnerability 310
True Beauty Comes from Within 311
The Family 311
Selflessness 311
Enjoy Being in Love 315
Tips for a Long and Happy Relationship 315

Chapter 33: Build a Healthy, Long-Lasting and Loving Relationship 320
Change Naturally 320
Keep the Connection Alive 321
Show Love through Actions 323
Be Honest 324

Chapter 34: Build Connection 328
Connection 328
Let Them Know What You're Going Through 328
Set Boundaries: Outline Your Expectations 329
Learn Your Love Languages 331

Chapter 35: Dating, Relationships, and Finding Love 338
A Culture of Patience 338
The Fear of Rejection: Practicing Failure 339
Managing Expectations 342
Improving Communication in Social Situations 344
The S-Words 344

Chapter 36: Disagreements and Arguments 347

Why Do We Disagree?... 347
What Issues Do We Disagree On? 350
How Do We Reconnect and Maintain Intimacy After Resolving Conflict? 354

Chapter 37: Rebuilding Trust Once It's Broken 357

Chapter 38: How to Appreciate Your Partner and Accept Them 365

Chapter 39: Healing from Toxic Relationship 373

Chapter 40: How to Heal from Emotional Anxiety 381
How to Heal the Scars 381
Recognize the Decision is yours 381
Have the Conversation... 382
Avoid Placing Blame or Guilt 384
Remain Calm and Compassionate 385
Be Firm 386

Chapter 41: Managing Stress and Anxiety to Prevent Anger Outbreaks 389
Identify Your Stressors... 389
Avoid or Confront Your Stressors.. 390
Psyche Yourself about Your Stressors 390
Focus on Positive Thoughts... 391
Spend Some Relaxation Time 391
Manage Your Thoughts 391

Chapter 42: Overcoming Fear and Anxiety 394
How Can You Help Yourself?... 396
The Link between Excessive Fantasizing and Overthinking....... 398

Chapter 43: Effects of Emotions in Your Daily Life 403
How Emotions Help You to Survive and Thrive 406

Help Build Stronger Relationships 407
They Affect Decision Making 407
They Improve Your Health 407
They Motivate You to Take Actions 408
Emotions Help You to Avoid Danger 408
They Help You to Understand Other People 408
Enhance Understanding 409
They Build You as a Strong Leader 409
They Help You to Apologize When Wrong 409
They Help You to Cope with Difficult Life Situations 410
They Boost Your Creativity 410
They Help You to Accept and Appreciate Yourselves 410

Chapter 44: How to Break the Cycle of Anxiety 413

Chapter 45: Treatment for Anxiety 422

Chapter 46: Affirmations for Success 430

Affirmations for Finding Success 431
Positive Thinking Affirmations 431
Confidence Affirmations 433
Dedication and Hard Work Affirmations 436

Chapter 47: Practicing Cognitive Behavioral Therapy 442

Axing Anxiety and Depression 442
Beliefs That Keep away Fear 443
Exposing Yourself 444
Preparing Your Exposure Plan 445
Being Realistic on the Likelihood of Bad Events 446
Bringing Bad Activities Back into Perspective 446
Surfing Physical Sensations 447
Relaxation Strategies 449

Chapter 48: The Solution to Relationship Anxiety 451
Distinguishing Thoughts and Emotions 454
Awareness of Thoughts 455

Conclusion Part 2 460

PART 1

ANXIETY IN LOVE

Introduction Part 1

Are you constantly anxious in your relationships, worrying that your partner does not love you enough and will leave you? Have you been told you are too sensitive, too clingy, too demanding? Do you feel blocked, suffer from insomnia, nausea, or experience an irregular heartbeat?

These are classic signs of anxiety and stress, and many people get trapped in relationships that stop them from achieving the life and the love they deserve, going around in circles and never resolving any of their problems. You begin to feel as if you are doomed to loneliness and a loveless life, but the good news is that you can rewire your brain to feel happiness in a relationship and stop feeling like you are walking on egg-shells all the time. You can stop being afraid. You can enjoy your relationship.

The author of this has helped thousands of individuals and couples alike to understand their relationship strategies, based on neuroscience. Also, to give them simple but effective advice based on neuroplasticity and behavioral exercises to promote healing from past relationships and to build healthy, exciting, and satisfying relationships.

You will be able to look at yourself objectively, understand how your childhood, your past relationships, and your brain influences your choices and behaviors. You will learn how to tame your thought processes to become clearer, more objective, and able to sustain wonderfully satisfying relationships with people and able to build a strong, lasting bond with a romantic partner.

It will open up your understanding of what jealousy is and why you may be experiencing this feeling. You will understand why jealousy is not considered abnormal and why underlying factors can materialize into jealous feelings. You will learn practical, real-life examples to effectively gain control and eventually overcome your jealousy while keeping your relationship intact. You will also learn to battle insecurities and low confidence so you can feel great and secure about yourself and your relationship again. So why wait?

I have personally battled with jealousy silently for many years. I continued to think I was in control until my jealousy started to get the best of me, and I decided to seek help. I realized I had been mistaken for a long time thinking my partner was the cause of my jealous feelings. I did not know I was the one with the problem. It has been a long journey to recovery, but I can finally say I kicked the green-eyed monster out of my life.

You will emerge a stronger, more confident person from this experience, one that can instantly recognize a good relationship from a bad one and that is capable of cultivating the lasting love you crave.

Dive in right now to start you on your journey to long-lasting love and healthy relating and leave the misery and stress and anxiety behind forever!

Chapter 1: Understanding Your Anxiety in Love

Anxiety can impact your relationships negatively, especially if you spend a great deal of time worrying and thinking about everything that could go wrong or has already gone wrong with the relationship. Here are some questions that may run through your mind when you are too anxious in a relationship:

What if they don't love me as much as I love them?

What if they're lying to me?

What if they're cheating on me?

What if I'm not good enough in the future for them?

What if they find someone else more attractive?

What if their family doesn't love me?

What if they die?

What if my anxiety ruins our relationship? (Anxiety about anxiety)

What if we break up?

What if they bail out on me?

It is normal to have some of these thoughts, especially in a new relationship. However, when thoughts like these come to your mind frequently, it might be a sign of anxiety issues or an anxiety disorder. The intensity with which you constantly ruminate over the questions listed above and other questions that are similar determine how far gone you are into an anxiety problem. It will also determine how insecure you are in your relationship.

These anxious thoughts are manifested in diverse physical ways and present as symptoms such as shortness of breath, insomnia, and anxiety or panic attacks. You may discover that whenever you think this way, you trigger a panic attack in which your heart may begin to beat fast, a hard lump forms in your chest, and you begin to shake all over your body. These are the physiological signs that you are suffering from an anxiety disorder.

Some symptoms of intense anxiety disorder can include:

- A feeling of restlessness
- Tensed muscles
- Difficulty concentrating or remembering
- Procrastinating or having trouble making decisions
- Worry that leads to repeatedly asking for reassurance
- Inability to get enough sleep and rest

Inasmuch as relationships are very beautiful and pleasurable, they can also breed anxious thoughts and feelings. These thoughts can arise at any stage of the relationship. If you aren't in a relationship yet, the thought of meeting the right person and being in a relationship can already generate anxiety for you, which you must deal with.

Insecurity is an inner feeling of not being enough or feeling threatened in some way. We've all felt it at one time or the other.

It's quite normal to have feelings of self-doubt once in a while, but chronic insecurity can ruin your success in life and destroy your romantic relationships.

Severe insecurity steals your peace and prevents you from being able to engage with your partner in a relaxed and authentic way. The resultant actions arising from insecurity may include jealousy, false accusations, snooping, lack of trust, and seeking reassurance and validation. These attributes are not conducive to a healthy relationship and can push your partner away.

Most people believe that insecurity stems from the actions or inaction of their partners. The reality is that most insecurity comes from within you. You build insecurity when you negatively compare yourself to other people and judge yourself harshly with your inner critical voice. A lot of the insecurities in your relationship are based on irrational thoughts and fears that you are not good enough and that you are not capable of making someone else happy. But these aren't true!

When you start to notice that uneasy feeling of being insecure, one thing you can do is to begin taking stock of your value. Insecurity makes you focus on something you feel is lacking within you. In most balanced relationships, each partner brings different strengths and qualities that complement each other. In order to conquer your insecurity, take stock of the value you offer to your partner. Personality and a great character are important qualities to the overall health of a relationship.

Building your self-esteem is also crucial to surmounting any insecurity you face in your relationship. It is important that you feel good about who you are on the inside in order to not constantly seek validation from someone else. You are complete within yourself and you must let your independence and self-worth shine brightly through your deeds and actions. When your well-being depends on someone else, you give them the key to your joy, and you empower them. This may be quite unhealthy for your partner to bear and certainly does not work well for a relationship. One way to build your self-confidence is to silence your inner critic and focus your mind and attention on positive qualities. Look in the mirror and speak positive affirmations to yourself - looking yourself in the eye when you do this makes a greater impact than simply telling yourself in your head that you're worthy of love.

You should also be able to maintain your sense of self-identity and be able to cater to your personal well-being. If before the relationship you were doing a great job of tending to your physical, mental, and emotional needs, this should not stop now just because you are in a relationship. You should maintain your independence and not allow yourself to turn into someone who is needy or attached. Being an independent person who has a life and identity outside of the relationship also makes you a more interesting and attractive partner. Your life must continue to move forward and make considerable progress when you are in a relationship. Being in a relationship is not the final phase of your life, and you should continue to be driven and achieve more goals, which can further endear you to your partner.

Some ways to maintain your independence include cultivating and nurturing great friendships, making time for your own friends, interests, and hobbies, maintaining financial independence, constantly improving yourself, and setting high standards for your dreams.

Understanding Why You Feel Anxious, Insecure and Attached in Relationships

Worry, stress, and anxiety about your relationships can leave you feeling lonely and dejected. You may unknowingly create a distance between yourself and your loved one. Another grave consequence of anxiety is its ability to make us give up on love completely. That is rather devastating, because love is a very beautiful thing. It is important to really understand what makes you so anxious in a relationship and why you feel so insecure and attached. I will take you through some of the reasons in subsequent paragraphs.

Falling in love puts a demand on you in countless ways - more ways than you can imagine. The more you cherish a person, the more you stand to lose. How ironic is that? This intense feeling of love and the powerful emotions that come with it consciously and unconsciously create the fear of being hurt and the fear of the unknown in you.

Oddly enough, this fear comes as a result of being treated exactly how you want to be treated in your relationship. When you begin to experience love as it should be, or when you are treated in tender and caring way, which is unfamiliar to you, anxiety might set in.

More often than not, it is not only the events that occur between you and your partner that lead to anxiety. It is the things you tell yourself and feed your mind with regarding those events that ultimately lead to anxiety. Your biggest critic, which is also the "mean coach" you have in your head, can criticize you and feed you with bad advice which will ultimately fuel your fear of intimacy. It is this mean critic that suggests to you that:

"You are not smart, he/she would soon get bored of you."

"You will never meet anyone who will love you, so why try?"

"Don't trust him, he's probably searching for a better person."

"She doesn't really love you. Get out before you get hurt."

This mean coach in your head manipulates you and turns you against yourself and the people you love. It encourages hostility, and you soon discover that you are paranoid. You begin to suspect every move your partner makes, and this reduces your self-esteem and drives unhealthy levels of distrust, defensiveness, jealousy, anxiety, and stress.

You soon discover that you are reacting to unnecessary issues and uttering nasty and destructive remarks. You may also become childish or parental towards your partner.

For example, your partner comes home from work and does not have a good appetite, so they politely turn down dinner. Sitting alone after some time, your inner critic goes on a rampage and asks, "How can he refuse my food? What has he eaten all day? Who has been bringing food to him at work? Can I really believe him?" You may begin to act cold or angry, and this can put your partner off, making them frustrated and defensive. They won't know what's been going on in your head, so your behavior will seem like it comes out of nowhere.

In just a few hours, you have successfully shifted the dynamics of your relationship. Instead of savoring the time you are spending together, you may waste an entire day feeling troubled and drawn apart from each other. What you have just done is initiate and enthrone the distance you feared so much. The responsible factor for this turn of events is not the situation itself - it is that critical inner voice that clouded your thoughts, distorted your perceptions, suggested bad opinions to you and, as a result, led you to a disastrous path.

When it comes to the issues you worry about so much in your relationship, what you don't know - and what your inner critic doesn't tell you - is that you are stronger and more resilient than you think. The reality is that you can handle the hurts, rejections, and disappointments that you are so afraid of. We are made in such a way that it is possible to absorb negative situations, heal from them, and deal with them. You are capable of experiencing pain and ultimately healing and coming out stronger. However, the mean coach in your head, that inner critical voice, more often than not puts you under pressure and makes reality look like a tragedy. It creates scenarios in your head that are non-existent and brings out threats that are not tangible. Even when, in reality, there are real issues and unhealthy situations, that inner voice in your head will magnify such situations and tear you apart in ways you do not deserve. It will completely misrepresent the reality of the situation and dampen your own resilience and determination. It will always give you unpleasant opinions and advice.

These critical voices you hear in your head are, however, formed as a result of your own unique experiences and what you've adapted to over time. When you feel anxious or insecure, there is a tendency to become overly attached and desperate in our actions. Possessiveness and control towards your partner set in. On the other hand, you may feel an intrusion in your relationship. You may begin to retreat from your partner and detach from your emotional desires.

There are some critical inner voices that talk about you, your partner, and your relationships. These inner voices are formed out of early attitudes you were exposed to in your family, amongst your friends, or in society at large. Everyone's inner critic is different; however, there are some common critical inner voices.

When you listen to your inner voice, the resultant effect is an anxiety filled relationship, which can mar your love life in many ways. When you give in to this anxiety, you may stop feeling like the strong and independent person you were when you first started the relationship. This can make you thin out and fall apart, which further induces jealousy and insecurity. Attachment and neediness set in, and these put a strain on the relationship.

Chapter 2: Unconscious Behavior Caused by Anxiety

1. Become Clingy

Under certain circumstances, anxiety feelings can make us act desperate and bug our partners. Anxiety can make a person to stop feeling as independent and strong and he/she did before getting into the relationship. Consequently, he/she may find him/herself falling apart easily, acting insecure, becoming jealous, or avoiding those activities that require independence.

2. Control

Our human nature demands that when we feel threatened, we attempt to control or dominate the situation. If we feel threatened in a relationship, chances are, we will try to regain control of the situation. What we fail to realize is that the feelings of threat are not real; rather, they are as a result of the inner critical voice that is distorting reality.

When taking control, we may start setting rules on what a partner should and should not do, who to visit, talk to, interact with, et cetera. This is a desperate attempt to alleviate our feelings of anxiousness and insecurity. This controlling behavior can breed resentment and alienate our partners.

3. Reject

If a relationship is making us to feel worried, a common and unfair defense mechanism is rejection. We start to act aloof, that is, aloof. We become somehow detached and cold. This ensures that if the partner suddenly leaves, we will not feel pain. In other words, new are protecting ourselves by beating our partners to the punch. These actions of rejection can either be subtle or overt. Either way, they are a sure way of creating distance between two partners by stirring up insecurity.

4. Withhold

In some cases, instead of explicitly rejecting our partners because of anxiety, some people tend to withhold from them. For instance, when things have gotten very cross and a person feels very stirred up, he/she retreats. People who use withholding techniques to deal with anxiety in a relationship hold back either a part of their affection of a whole segment of the relationship altogether. Withholding might seem harmless since the partner is not facing rejection of clinginess and control but note; it is one of the gentlest and quietest killers of attraction and passion in a relationship.

5. Retreat

Anxiety leads to fear and being afraid of a relationship you are in can be really stressing. To avoid such stress, a large number of people choose to retreat, that is, giving up on the real acts of love and replacing it with a fantasy bond. By definition, a fantasy bond is a false illusion that replaces the real feelings and acts of love. In this state of fantasy, a person focuses on the form instead of substance. He/she gives up on the real and vital part of the relationship and still stays in it to feel safe. In a fantasy bond, people engage in many destructive behaviors such as withholding or engaging in non-vital activities. The resulting distance leads to the end of a relationship. As much as the retreat will protect you from feelings of fear, it will give you a false sense of safety and you will lose a lot of precious time living in a fantasy. What most people fail to realize is that at the end of the day, they will have to face reality.

Love is a beautiful thing, but truth be told, it has its own demands and consequences. Honestly, love is a very complicated thing.

Over-Analyzing

This is the urge to overthink things, and even literally look for weaknesses or negative aspects. There is a sating that goes, over-analysis causes paralysis. Here is the thing; there is nothing wrong with using logic. In fact, it is okay to be critical or skeptical at least until you figure things out. The ability to think about things thoroughly before accepting them can help you to tell fiction and reality- what is a mere delusion and what is the reality.

However, there is an issue/downside to overanalyzing a relationship. You will never be satisfied with the answer. Everything that is said on done is subject to scrutiny and more cross-examination. A good example of over-analysis and its consequences is when a person n starts to overthink things and consequently creates scenarios in his/her mind, hence basing their actions on imaginary events that have not happened yet.

Picture this; you are on a first or second date. Your clothes, shoes and language give a good first impression. Everything about the prospective relationship looks bright. However, once the partner arrives, you start bombarding them with a bazillion questions about their past relationships. "Have you been in another relationship? How many exes do you have? Why did you leave them? Was there cheating involved? Who initiated the breakup? Are your parents still together? Do they have a good relationship?"

On the brighter side, it is totally fine for a person to express his/her worries about love and being hurt. However, it is absolutely wrong to ask a person some questions that are too personal in the name of protecting yourself. It is wrong on all levels to force someone to recall some things that might be painful for them. Do not ask people questions that make the person feel interrogated. And if you find that you cannot stop yourself from asking these questions, then that might indicate that you are suffering from relationship anxiety. You cannot control your fears about relationships and commitments, therefore, looking for ways to validate your reasons.

Fear of Being in a Serious Relationship

How long can two people take before deciding to be in a serious relationship? There is no specific timeframe. It all depends on the people involved and how well they know each other. Some take three dates, others one month while others might take years before being ready.

If a person has relationship anxiety, his/ her answer to every request for commitment will be "Never" "I am not ready." Regardless of whether the person is in love or not, he/she will not commit to the relationship. The real reason for this lack of commitment is the deep-seated fear at the back of the individual's mind. This person is afraid that he/she is going to end up alone, all over again. Therefore he/she avoids those situations that might set him/her up for betrayal.

Falling in love involves facing real risks. It is about allowing yourself to feel vulnerable. The hard part of love is placing a massive amount of trust in someone else and allowing him/her to mold our hearts. You cannot be 100% certain that the person will actually take care of you. You are not yet sure if the person is the one for you. So, anxiety will make you think "If I am not 100 per cent sure about this person, is there need seriousness?" Then rationalizing a little more, you will get an answer like" If you do not get committed, you will not get hurt" Now, that is an illusion brought to you by anxiety.

In real life, this is what is happening; you are feeling afraid thus reluctant to commit to a person. Consequently, you will never learn through experience. If you are always turning away the chances of love. How will you know the real deal that might help you deal with the relationship anxiety?

You Have a Bad Temper

The most awful thing about relationship anxiety is that it affects the two people in a relationship. In fact, it hurts you and your partner, unfairly. No matter how much the sober person expresses his/her love to the partner suffering from relationship anxiety, this feeling will make him/her look for ways to make the other to feel terrible. For instance, a person can tell you that he/she loves you and relationship anxiety will make you say something like "Do not worry, you will stop." or another bitter thing.

So, what makes you so angry when a person tells you that he/she is in love with you? It is the fact that your brain never allows you to take time off from your dark thoughts. You know very well that these thoughts are irrational but cannot just get past them. They terrorize you every day, no matter what you do. The fear of losing constantly ruins your good moods. Simply, you are mentally exhausted and cannot think rationally. Any minor inconvenience will make you go berserk.

If your partner fails to do things according to plan or says something that does not augur well with what you have determined is appropriate, you start feeling like the relationship is strained. More like someone is pushing the other to make things work. And once you feel bad about the relationship, you start to say painful things or even fight physically. AN understanding partner will forgive you and move on. But remember this; a day will come when that partner gets tired of dealing with your negative energy and raging temper. And when he/she decides to leave, you will develop more relationship anxiety complications.

Too much attachment

Attachment may be positive, but here is the thing, anxiety can make you needy. You will not only be ill-mannered but also, clingy. Why, you might ask, because you are paranoid about the relationship. You are afraid that the slightest silence will evolve into a full-blown painful breakup. That is very unlikely to happen, but, in this irrational state of mind, it seems very much possible.

How can you tell if your attachment is based on relationship anxiety and not real love? First if you are attached simply because you are monitoring your partner, then that is anxiety. If you are oversensitive to cues that might indicate the slightest chances of being abandoned, then you might be having relationship anxiety.

Note, it is very good to remind your partner that you love him/her/your partner to start questioning your real intentions. In fact, it is very sweet to ask for hugs and kisses randomly. But overdoing this can be point-blank annoying.

Being an Extreme Pleaser

Always going that extra mile to impress a partner can be an indicator of relationship anxiety. We have to admit that it feels good to have a partner that arranges for surprises for you. It also feels nice to see the look of happiness and surprise when we do something unexpected for our partners. Giving each other surprises and going the extra mile for each other is very romantic. However, such efforts and sacrifice can be very dangerous if you have relationship anxiety. You might end up doing endless things just to maintain the perfect image for your partner. You might be so afraid that your partner will lose interest in you that you become obsessed with impressing him/her.

You Beat Yourself Too Much

Anxiety causes doubt. You might be the best partner in the best relationship but still, you will feel invalid. You might be doing everything in the relationship but still feel lie it will never be enough. Instead of seeing the good things in front of you, you opt to focus on those things that make you feel bad. You do not have the time to enjoy what you already have.

In the real sense, it could be easier for you to be happier, but your brain tells you that life does not work like that. You believe that happiness is a fake and short-lived experience. The problem is that insecurity will start to push your partner away. Then you will have your fears coming true because he/she will gradually lave.

You Lack Confidence

Sometimes, a person may experience relationship anxiety because of a lack of confidence. Before getting into a relationship, it is important to check on the level of your self-esteem. Having low self-esteem does not mean that you should not get into a relationship, but it is very important to know the status of your heart. Know the state of your mind, heart and soul before getting into a relationship.

Chapter 3: Different Types of Anxiety in Love and How to Overcome Them

Tension prevails in partnerships.

All pairs experience anxiety. Occasionally stress and anxiety originate from troubles at the office or with household and or friends that we carry over into our partnerships. Stress and anxiety can likewise arise from the couple's issues, such as an argument, distinctions in wants or requires, or sensation ignored.

Anxiety Can Negatively Influence Relationships.

Although tension prevails, it can be harmful to relationships. Usually, individuals suppress or keep their anxiety to themselves, which makes it tough for their companions to comprehend what they are undergoing and to supply assistance.

Not managing stress can develop a negative cycle where partners "catch" each other's weight. This happens due to the fact that tension is transmittable-- when our partners are stressed out, we become worried. Think back to a debate that escalated rapidly. You could have "caught" each other's stress and anxiety during the discussion, which made you both feel even more frazzled and made you say things you would not have or else stated. Pairs obtain embedded this unfavorable cycle as well as may be too stressed out to take care of the underlying issue(s).

The Key to Tension Is Just How Couples Handle It.

Couples need to determine as well as speak about what creates their anxiety and what they require when they feel stressed. Although it could be tough to talk about what is producing tension, especially if it is brought on by something within the partnership, it is helpful for companions to speak about their needs and also for partners to supply assistance. Those couples that are most effective in dealing with stress tackle it together. They produce a sensation like they remain in it with each other as well as are a team.

What Can You Do?

Check-in with each other and also pay attention first before you supply options. Ask your partner(s) what you can do to help as well as to make their day smoother. Hug more frequently. It appears weird but embracing for at the very least 30 secs after work each day can assist your bodies to line up and calm each other down. Keep attached throughout tension. Discussing your stress and also having a supportive companion to see you through it makes you as well as your partnership is stronger. Most of us have demanding experiences from time to time because tension can come from numerous sources. Funds. Household stress. Work. Relationships.

And it can have a genuinely distorting effect on our practices. It can make us feel genuinely reduced and also not want to speak to people - with a propensity to close ourselves away and also keep our feelings on the inside.

As well as it can be tough to be self-aware when it pertains to your feedback to tension, very commonly, it can seem like these means of expression are a little outside of your control. Many people find themselves avoiding speaking with others as well as becoming taken out without somewhat knowing they're doing it or unexpected themselves by becoming all of a sudden snappy, cranky and unreasonable.

To offer a little viewpoint on this, our coping mechanisms in these kinds of circumstances are frequently affected by what we experienced maturing. If our parents didn't reveal treatment quickly, we might have become rather experienced at looking after ourselves - indeed, we might have needed to - and so this reaction can kick back in instantly as an adult. Likewise, we commonly duplicate the practices of our moms and dads and also their responses to tension when we're younger.

Just how tension can impact connections

It's not difficult to see why either of these behaviors would affect your relationship adversely. If you're ending up being withdrawn, your partner is most likely to feel pressed away. And also, if you get stylish, they may feel injured or come to be defensive. What can be truly bothersome, though, is that they may intend to help, as well as think that their efforts are being rebuffed. This can feel like an actual rejection, as well as can result in them becoming withdrawn or snappy themselves. Thus, the problems of stress can snowball as one companion begins to act in an adverse or unconstructive method, so may the various other.

Additional including in this is the truth that they may not become aware of why you're functioning as you are. It might not be quickly evident that it's a tension that's causing you to state unkind points or be unresponsive when talked with. They may feel it's something they have done. This can undoubtedly be mad and also annoying - both for the hurt created and also complication about why it's happening.

Without some type of intervention, the void caused by this kind of circumstance can get bigger and also more significant. And the more you seem like your partner - that, once more, may just wish to assist - gives tension themselves, the much less likely you'll want to try to close that space.

Commonly, the most effective method to proceed in situations such as this is by utilizing a strategy that enables the person experiencing the stress to remain in fee of how much they claim. Very frequently, the very best first step is to say: 'Exactly how can I help simply?' These places firm strongly with experiencing individual problems and are much less likely to make them feel under

And if your companion is open to talking, then the very same emphasis - on them, and their firm - ought to continue to use. Once more, there can be a lure to right away begin to provide remedies or to get them to 'attempt to see the silver lining' - yet, in a feeling, these can be demanding feedbacks in themselves. They can seem like reasoning's, or as if you're disregarding their experience as one that's quickly fixable. Sometimes, this is precisely the feedback that the cagey person was afraid: one that demands they accede to it, as opposed to one that correctly absorbs precisely how they're feeling, and what they believe.

Instead, it can be a lot more practical to sympathize and also to ask inquiries simply. Very frequently, when we're discovering something challenging, what we want isn't a solution, but just a person to be there with us and provide emotional support. Providing this - even if it implies sitting silently together or simply embracing - might be all they require to begin to seem like the scenario is in control.

Tension can be useful.

Experiencing tension doesn't always indicate your relationship is going to suffer. Instead, your assumption of stress and anxiety-- such as seeing it as a challenge that you can overcome-- is necessary. By watching pressure as a chance to share as well as open with each other, relationships end up being more potent since pairs find out how to browse tension and construct resources to much better deal with future stress and anxiety. Partners discover what they need from each various other and reveal one another that they are looked after, valued, and understood. Having a companion who is there for you as well as reacts to your needs aids your body to manage stress and anxiety better and also makes anxiety feel much less extreme.

Stress

Does that word define your life today? If so, you're not the only one. Most of us experience stress and anxiety. It might be something significant: a new relocation, a health and wellness worry, a harmful partnership. Yet frequently it is something small: a hectic week at work, a youngster house ill on a day loaded with meetings, the post-work/school thrill to put supper on the moment, the last-minute demand from an employer. These tiny everyday inconveniences can add up and also have huge repercussions overtime for our partnerships. Why? Tension in other areas of our life's spills over right into our connections. The work-life problem is a leading source of stress today. Also, research has revealed over and over again that we bring anxiety and even pressure from work and other areas of our lives home with us, hurting our partnerships.

When people are stressed out, they end up being more taken out and also sidetracked, and even less caring. They likewise have much less time for recreation, which leads to the alienation between partners. Stress and anxiety additionally draw out people's worst attributes, which may influence their partners to take out as well, because who wishes to be around someone when they are acting their worst? Gradually, the relationship comes to be more superficial (less we-ness as well as participation in each other's lives), and also couples happen to be a lot more withdrawn, experiencing more problems, distress, and alienation in the partnership.

Stress and anxiety likewise influence our physical as well as psychological health as well as areas extra strain on the relationship. Stress can specifically be bad for couples who remain in rocky relationships since these couples tend to be a lot more strongly affected by daily occasions (good as well as bad) than couples in more steady relationships. However, also for healthy and balanced, stable relationships, tension can create people to see troubles in their relationships that aren't there.

A pair who usually connects well might see their communication break down over an especially challenging week, and also, as a result of the tension as well as sapped sources, they feel like there are real interaction troubles in their relationships. Likewise, a pair which is usually caring may have little love when stressed and also, therefore, pertained to believe that they have an issue with respect as well as time together, instead of identifying it is just the anxiety. These misperceptions can create discontentment with otherwise healthy connections as well as lead people to try to solve the incorrect trouble (interaction, affection) rather than identifying as well as resolving the actual source of the concern (stress).

How to Reduce High Couple Conflicts

The problem belongs to all connections. In an intimate partnership, where the risks are top, as well as sensations, run deep, the problem is unavoidable. Nonetheless, the problem can wear at the fabric of a connection if it is regular or if it crowds out love, love, and also support.

The best study on the dispute in couples was done by John Gottman, the master pairs' study. In one research study, Gottman took an example of high conflict pairs as well as separated them right into two therapy groups. One team discovered problem resolution skills as well as the other group focused on enhancing what he calls the "marital friendship." Pairs in this 2nd group worked on structure trust, goodwill, and also compassion in their relationships. Gottman found that couples who reinforced their relationship reduced the problem to a much better degree than those who discovered dispute resolution skills.

So, what is the message from these two sets of research? If you want to reduce disputes in your partnership, focus on increasing the favorable instead of lowering the negative. Look for opportunities to improve your relationship with your partner. Look for methods to reveal affection and support. Search for chances to produce goodwill and also depend on it. Be kind. Be empathic.

As anybody that has been in a romantic connection understands, differences, as well as battles, are unpreventable. When two individuals spend a great deal of time together, with their lives intertwined, they are bound to disagree every so often. These disagreements can be big or tiny, ranging from what to consume for dinner or stop working on finishing a job to debates about whether the couple needs to move for one companion's profession or choosing youngsters' spiritual training.

Chapter 4: Recognizing Your Anxiety Triggers

Fear of Collapse

This is a sudden fall. It might occur due to peer pressure from close friends who are obvious in one's life, and mostly they always come with shocking words which can cause one to collapse and sometimes eventually die. It can also be caused by a lack of support from one's partner; good support encourages and strengthens love because it is also a bond that fulfills true love. Part of the support includes finance, food, and even closeness to your partner. For the best outcomes, one should avoid peer pressure and negative people.

Just like any other photophobia fears, fear of collapse freezes the heart. Your heart becomes ice-cold, you are constantly thinking that this relationship is going to hit the rock any time, and if you do not do something about it, it will end up destroying your relationship. To recognize this fear, you will see the following.

Suspecting a motive

When your partner tries to show you kindness, for example, take you out for a drink or buys a beautiful dress, all you think of is there must be something he wants, or he has done that is why he is behaving the way he is.

- Trust Issues

You cannot trust anything your partner says, you must go ahead behind his back to find out if he was saying the truth or talking about the exact thing.

- Sticking to the Old Ways

You only want to do things according to the times when you felt like it was working. You do not want to change and experience something new.

- Doubt

You are always in doubt, asking yourself every now and then if it is going to work and still convincing yourself that it might not work.

- Clingy

When you see your partner distancing himself or pulling away, you start being so clingy even after he tells you that he needs some space. It is good to give someone space, this does not mean he is leaving. Being clingy only shows that you have a fear of collapse

Fear of Being Vulnerable

Vulnerability is not always a show of weakness. If you are vulnerable, it only means you trust easily, people can get to you faster; they can understand you better, understand your likes, dislikes, and boundaries and be able to watch their steps when they are with you. It gives you an upper hand, unlike you thinking that it pulls you down. To face your fear of being vulnerable, you will have to point the following signs to know if indeed it is the fear of being vulnerable:

- Not Opening-up

You do not want to open up to your partner because you think he will see you as weak. You prefer to suffer in silence. For example, you have a problem with your parents' home that needs financial help, but you can't tell your partner because you think he will see you as weak. You feel he will think that you are working too, and you must be weak to get help from him.

- Avoiding Conflict

Each time there is a problem in the relationship, like a situation that is more likely to lead to a heated argument or other conflicts, instead of handling it, you let it pass by sugar coating it with fancy dinners, cocktails or even movies so that it won't be a topic of discussion anymore.

- Overprotective

You do not want your partner to understand what is going on in your life clearly. You have put up a shield that should be ventured through. There is a no-go zone in most of your doing even the least important things because you are afraid that if he finds out, he will capitalize on it and you will be seen as weak.

- Overthinking

You are constantly asking yourself a thousand and one questions every time you think of your partner knowing something about you. You are thinking so much about what he will say, how he will react, how he will see you, and so many others.

- Lashing out at Your Partner

This is a defensive mechanism. You do not your partner to go ahead and understand a certain thing about you, so the only way to make him stop and never be interested again is to lash at him. This will keep him at bay from anything that concerns you.

To avoid this in a relationship, partners should be faithful, honest, loving, caring, and stop exposing themselves to that possibility. Lovers should also respect their partner's gargets/devices such as phones for them to acquire peace of mind.

Fear of Not Feeling Important

This is a situation where someone feels not useful to his or her partner. The fear comes in when your lover does not involve you in his or her activities; the partner remaining silent in the house, infrequent communication, frankness, not having sex with your partner whereby sex is the only action that can bond the relationship, Unfaithfulness among the couples. It really hurts due to unexpected changes in the relationship. Some problems might persist; one has to adapt the situation while getting a time of viewing the other partner, in the proses of viewing your partner one should also be patient to give a room for any change.

- Too Sensitive.

You are taking things too personally. Your partner makes a comment, and you think it is aimed at looking down upon you. For example, your partner "honey I think your dress will look better if ironed a little bit". You take this statement super personal, and you start sulking about it because you think that he meant you are useless wearing an un-ironed dress. You start thinking on behalf of him.

- Making a Catastrophe Where It Is Not Needed

You start making a mountain out of an anthill. Your partner calls to say he will be late for dinner and you go to a no speaking spree for a week. Don't you think you are exaggerating things here? He called to inform you early, why are you sulking and not speaking? Because you are suffering from the fear of not being important

- Perfection

Everything you touch or do; you want them to be so perfect in that he will see you as the most important person. You do not want to give him any reason to comment or think otherwise. You are afraid to make a mistake because you think he will see you as useless.

- Panic Attacks

Every time you are looking at your phone to see if he has texted you. If you find that he has not texted, you start panicking. You start feeling less important. You start feeling that you are not among the things he values in his life.

- Doubting Your Every Step

You always doubt what you are doing. You are not sure if it will be good for him so that he can see you as an important person. You are not sure he will like the idea because you want to be the most important thing that has ever happened to him.

Fear of Failure

Fear of failure comes in a person when one does not succeed in his or her plans and oaths of their bond. This makes one be totally discouraged to love another partner; it is caused by things like long sickness, hunger, bad company and idleness, lack of job opportunities. This leads the partner to feel bored, and the true love disappears, the partner seemed to be losing the loved one. To avoid that fear and stress, you should not make it personal, seek advice, share your problem, and let it go.

- Expecting Him to Fix Everything

You are expecting him to be a hero, a Mr. Spider man. You want him to save every situation there is. You want him to walk in your mind and do everything you are thinking of, but if this is not happening, and then you think this relationship is bound to fail.

- Aggressive Response to Passive Questions

The fear of failing is telling you that this must be heard loud and clear and never be repeated again, and you answer aggressively to a simple passive question that he asked. The aggressive response only instills fear in your partner or anger or mixed ideas, and this might ruin your relationship.

- Feeling That the Partner is Un-Reliable

Feeling that you are investing a lot in this relationship than he is, you think he is not reliable; he is not supporting you in anything that matters to you. You feel and think that he is unstable, and he is going to lead this relationship in the wrong path. You think that he is slowly digging the drainage to drain the relationship each time he tells you he is not in a position to attend your exhibition. This is the fear of driving you, and it is important to handle it.

- Having Thoughts That He Will Leave

Each time you are seated, you picture him leaving. You are afraid that he is going to walk out of the door any minute. This all the fear of failures doing, maybe he has no plan of leaving, and it is the fear driving you.

Fear of Entering into Intimacy

If you are asked why you keep on dodging the idea of intimacy you have no answer; this only communicates one thing. You are afraid to get into it. For you to understand that you have this fear, look at how you will know that you have it room in your head.

- Incompatible Schedule

Each time an intimacy topic is brought up and planned when to happen, you say your schedule is not compatible with his.

- Lame Excuses

You are always giving excuses that do not make sense. Like, I just do not feel like it, I do not think it is the appropriate time, and when asked when the appropriate time is or why you do not feel like it, you completely have no answer.

- Am Not Worthy Enough

A feeling of unworthiness has engulfed you. You think he deserves better and that is a more reason as to why not to enter into intimacy. This is all wrong, it is only in your mind and it needs to be corrected.

- Feeling Shameful

Why would you feel shameful to a partner you have been with for a long time? It is not shameful; it is the fear of intimacy.

Past Experiences Ended Badly

Past experiences leave wounds, which causes fear based on their experiences. If you want to realize that you are suffering from this fear, the following are the manifestations:

- Getting Very Angry

A small thing that doesn't need all your anger makes you so worked up because it reminds you of the same thing before.

Always on guard for betrayal signs

You are always waiting for that moment for him to betray you. You are in his phones, diary laptop just looking to find any sign.

- Constantly Thinking That People Will Hurt You and You Need to Protect Yourself.

You are thinking of putting up an out of bounds sign on your face for people to keep off.

- Thinking That Each Time You Get Close to People You End up Being Hurt.

The last time you were hurt because you loved and were so close, this time you are thinking your closeness to another will get you hurt again.

- Thinking That No One Ever Comes to Your Aid When You Need Help. No One Is Ever There for You.

You stood alone in the pain as it tore your heart and you probably are thinking since no one came to your aid, no one is ever going to come and help you when he finally breaks your heart.

Chapter 5: Love Yourself to Love Your Partner

Do You Know Your True Value?

A lot of us look down on ourselves, and we fail to give ourselves the credit that we deserve. We might indeed have gone through experiences that may now affect the way that we look at ourselves. We might have gone through a lot of hurt and abuse and even a very challenging childhood. But these circumstances do not have to continue to define you and hide the unique qualities that make up the real you.

Reasons Why You Are Unique

Just in case you are not convinced about how unique you are, here are some significant reasons proved by science, why you should start seeing yourself differently.

- **Your unique genetic composition is the only one there is and will ever be**: Research has shown that humans are somewhere between 90 -99% different genetically. Such a big difference isn't it? This is to say no one is exactly like you genetically (even if you have an identical twin) and no one can ever be like you completely no matter how hard they try. Why try to compare yourself with or even become someone else when there is only one of you in existence? You simply can't be them, and they can't be you.

- **Your personality is unique**: A person's unique personality is made up of their temperament, thoughts, attitude, behavior, character, and beliefs. No two people will have the same combination of these qualities at every given time. Your personality is how people see you and how they often try to describe you – meticulous, quiet, outgoing, selfless, funny, proud, humble, loud – these are all components of a person's personality, and yours is a unique one.

- **Your experiences are unique**: Your entire life experiences, as well as your day-to-day experiences, are what make you a unique person. There are no two people who have had the same experience throughout their whole lives. Even if you live together, work at the same place, maintain the same schedule, you will find that your point of view of these experiences differs. So, your life experiences are unique to you.

- **Your purpose is unique**: You should believe that you have a unique purpose in this world. You don't have to live the life that someone else has lived. You don't have to be your father or your mother – you should be yourself instead. Even if you follow in their same footsteps you will still find that you cannot produce the same achievements, something will differ from the other, and this difference speaks of the uniqueness of your life and who you are. You have such a unique purpose in life; therefore, you should pursue it and embrace it and not live someone else's life.

Building an Unbeatable Self Confidence That Will Defeat Jealousy Always

The matter of self-confidence is very important when talking about jealousy because a reduced self-confidence can bring about jealous feelings. If you suffer from low confidence, then you are bound to get jealous at some point.

- **Self-confidence can be learned**: Some people have described themselves as not being confident naturally, and they have stuck to that belief from childhood, where it now causes problems with jealousy and the likes in their relationship and life in general. The truth is that even if you are genetically inclined to be withdrawn and shy, that doesn't mean you should have low self-confidence. You can learn to be confident in yourself gradually, and in time you will see the changes confidence can make to your entire life. There are so many people today that were initially not confident in themselves but have grown from that stage into living their dreams and achieving their goals with high confidence. So, if your jealousy is due to an injury to your confidence and is affecting your relationship, believe that you can learn to be confident again no matter your experience or genes and indeed start learning!

- **There are no losers, only winners**: Never see yourself as a failure or a loser at anything you do even if it doesn't work out a hundred times. Life is not a competition, and there are no losers. You are a winner if you choose to see yourself that way and behave like that as well.

- **Life is a process and you can get there as well**: So, you are not where you feel you are supposed to be, so what? And you have tried and failed so many times. We have all failed at something as well, so you are not alone. Some people can't cope with failure and others can't stand the fact that those they consider their mates are getting ahead of them in life, so they turn these feelings to jealousy and anger. You need to understand that life involves process, and the fact that you have failed ten times doesn't mean that you cannot succeed on the eleventh try. Also, the fact that you feel you are behind in life doesn't mean that you cannot reach where you want to be eventually. There are a thousand and one examples of people who have made it great in life but failed initially.

- **There is room for everyone to shine**: Just like the moon and the sun, they shine their light differently, and they don't compete with each other because they know their uniqueness. That is how you should see the world. No one is taking your opportunity or your job. If you didn't get that dream job and someone else got it, you should believe that the job perhaps wasn't for you and you can get another opportunity. Don't imagine the competition and become jealous when someone like that makes a pass at your partner. There is room for everyone to shine our lights as brightly as we desire.

- **Start loving yourself**: It is surprising how some people can love a partner so much and show themselves no love at all. You should start loving the person that you are and treat yourself better. Do things for yourself and be selfish sometimes – it will make you feel great. Treat yourself to something special on occasion. Something that is just for you – a nice spa, an expensive meal, a new dress, anything that screams 'treat!' Start doing things not for others but yourself as well, and you will notice how good it makes you feel. Look at yourself in the mirror when you are all dressed up to go and tell yourself how beautiful / handsome / gorgeous / sexy / adorable you look. You don't have to wait for someone to say those words to you so you can feel good about yourself. Learn to start loving your unique self and see the boost in confidence that it will bring.

- **Stop doubting your abilities**: The worst thing you can do to your confidence is to question yourself. People will doubt you at least until you can prove them wrong, but when you start doubting your abilities, then there might not be an opportunity to prove anyone right or wrong. Even if no one believes in you, you should still believe in yourself – that is how a lot of people have kept going until they succeeded – by believing in themselves. Whatever it is that you want to embark on, you need to tell yourself that you can. The more you keep feeding your mind with a positive thought, the more your confidence will improve, and you will get better at whatever you try. You can't depend on what people say to give you the confidence that you need, you need to be the first and only coach of your life.

- **Start doing the things that you used to love**: Are there activities you used to love doing but have lost interest in because of how your life has changed? A great way to revive that confidence is to return to some of the things you loved doing like playing a sport or a musical instrument, fishing, skating, singing, dancing, traveling. Whatever it is, start again if it makes you happy – even if you weren't so good at it, this could be an opportunity to get better and do what you love.

- **Try out new interests**: Perhaps you have been passing by a dance school and wondering what it would look like if you enrolled in a class. Or you have recently been interested in playing a musical instrument and have held yourself back because of what your partner or friends might say. You should take that positive step now and try out one or two interests that you have nursed for a long time. It is never too late to try out something new – unless you are physically limited. So how about trying something and if you like it, then continue doing it – you will see that your confidence continues to grow as you make such bold steps.

- **Work on you continuously**: Working on yourself is very important to building a high self-confidence. These are areas that you can start improving. For instance, if you haven't felt confident about your body and have always been threatened when someone with a great body makes a pass at your partner, then why not decide to achieve that great body that you want as well? Remember that you will be doing this for yourself and not for anyone else – it is to make you feel great and confident again. So hit the gym and start working hard to achieve that great body that you want. Perhaps it is something about your appearance or your language that kills your confidence. You can learn how to improve these things as long as it makes you feel more confident. Go get it!

- **Re-assess your company**: One cause of low confidence without even knowing it is the kind of company that you keep. Do your friends look down on you or tell you that you are not good enough for a role or something you want to try? Do you have friends that laugh or mock you when you fail at something? These are confidence killers, and you should avoid them as soon as possible. Great friends should be able to encourage you to reach your dreams and not kill your confidence. So, what kind of things do you hear from your friends? Does it help you grow your confidence? If it doesn't, then you are better off without them. You should stick with friends that are confident and do not see you as a threat to their progress as well. Friends who are secure in themselves and can inspire that in you as well are friends indeed.

- **Take good care of yourself**: Just like I said about loving yourself, you can't love something that you do not care for, so start taking care of yourself. Scientists have shown that taking good care of you can reflect in your overall demeanor and confidence. Pay attention to your hygiene. Take showers regularly, put on clean and appropriate clothing, apply pleasant scents, and pay attention to your hair care. Take care of your living space as well and keep it clean and tidy. Just saying – look great and feel great as well. When you start to feel so good about your body and environment, it will begin to reflect in your confidence eventually, so try changing up a few things and see the difference it will bring you.

- **Strive to be a better version of you**: Make it a habit of taking regular appraisals of yourself. Where are you now and who do you want to be in one year or five years? Always strive to improve yourself and keep becoming a better version of yourself. Remember that it's not about becoming someone else or competing, but it is all about yourself and building a secure and confident you!

Chapter 6: Ways to Recover Communication with Your Partner

Ask for Clarification

Perception is different from communication. One can pass on a message, but what matters is how it is received. Therefore, clarification is essential, so that information can be received the way it is intended. One way to ask for clarification is to restate what has been said. In case the message was misperceived, the speaker will correct it. It also ensures that one pays attention and encourages the speaker to open up more.

Maintain Neutrality

Emotional intelligence is essential when communicating; one must be informed of their biases and opinions so that the art of active listening can be developed.

When communicating, it is essential to remain grounded. Getting defensive will impede the communication process. As much as people hate critics, one should be open to it, and understand that they are bound to be criticized from time to time.

Listen

Let someone finish their train of thought before butting in and giving one's opinion. Moreover, one should listen entirely and take time to digest the information before evaluating the information provided. It is common for people to get distracted and start thinking of what to respond to before the speaker finishes what they are saying. It is paramount that one has to avoid this type of distraction because it prevents them from genuinely listening to the other person.

Silence

Bouts of silence when communicating allow time for one to digest the information given, it also provides room for evaluation of knowledge and time for a person to identify their biases, and how they might be affecting the listening process. Thus, silence should be used as a tool to sharpen the listening process and promote communication.

During a volatile interaction, silence can be an instrument that is used to bring tensions down. It can also be used to diffuse a conversation that is not productive. It enables parties involved to assess the chat and assess whether it is still within the objectives set.

Use Encouragers

Use prompts to encourage the other person to open up more. The prompts should be minimal so that the listening process is not impeded. Examples include 'oh,' 'uh-uh' and 'then?'

Prompts indicate to the speaker that the listener is following what they are saying and is genuinely interested in what they have to say. Thus, it encourages them to open up more. The listener also pays attention to what is being said because they take an active role in the conversation by encouraging the other person to open up more.

Reflect

Reflection enables the listener to take in the speaker's words. It also helps to connect the body language and other nonverbal cues to verbal communication. Thus, instead of just restating the information, one should take time to reflect the message, and take into account emotions, their background, and why they have the opinion that they have.

Reflection also enables one to make linkages with the information given. At times, one can make a comment, which can be connected to another piece of information.

Reflection is the right way for one to identify their bias, and how it affects the communication process, and decide how to do away with it.

Use 'I' Messages

During active listening, putting feelings into words helps the speaker be objective. When communicating, one might not be aware of the body language they are projecting. This is especially true if they are talking about something sensitive to them. Thus, putting feelings brings objectivity to the conversation.

Validate

Be nonjudgmental to the way the speaker is feeling and validate their emotions. Listen with empathy and understand why they think the way they think. At times, people get extreme emotions from trivial things, and it is okay, as people are entitled to feel, however, they think about issues that affect them.

Validation does not mean that one has to open up about their experiences. The goal is to listen and respond that their feelings are seen, and it is okay to have such feelings. In the communication process, this helps a person open up more.

Redirect

Sensitive topics can lead to aggression, raised voices, or anger. These are emotions like any other, and a person is entitled to them. Thus, instead of making someone feel bad for their feelings, it is better to redirect and talk about something that is not as sensitive.

It can be a brief discussion of a neutral topic, so that the tensions drop, then reverting to the question under discussion after that. If the speaker does not calm down, one can redirect and talk about something else entirely.

Avoid Suing Communication Blockers

Communication blockers make the speaker unable to pass on their points effectively. Thus, they should be avoided at all costs.

'Why' questions make people defensive because they feel like their validity is being questioned. Thus, they should be avoided.

Giving quick reassurances, before a person finishes expressing their point is not advised, because it they will not pass on the information effectively

Another communication blocker is advising the speaker. The goal is to listen and not advise someone unless the speaker asks for advice. Therefore, refrain from giving advice and actively listen.

Digging for information is another communication blocker. People are intelligent and can tell when a person is genuinely listing to them or is digging for information. Once they realize that the listener is doing for information, they clam up and stop communicating. Thus, for effective communication, avoid digging for information, in the pretense of active listening.

Be courteous

Have good manners when communicating. It indicates that the message is essential, and one is more likely to talk more to someone with polite behavior.

Statements like "excuse me', 'pardon me' should be used appropriately, and as stated before, they should be used sensibly to avoid frequent interruptions. They also indicate that someone is following the conversation actively.

Ask Questions

To start a conversation, it is best to start by asking questions. The type of questions that are proposed as a conversation opener has to be neutral. This means that sensitive topics such as religion, politics, and gender have to be steered clear of. Asking questions ensures that a person considers the feelings of the other person first, and quickly learns their opinion on topics that are not as neutral.

Avoid Judgments

Every person on earth has a bias, and this is especially true when it comes to sensitive topics. Thus, to enact emphatic communication, one should avoid judging. One should listen keenly, and refrain from judging the other person at all cost. The other person in the relationship should feel like they are being listened to, and their point of view is being understood. Simply put, when communicating with someone, the listener should be able to walk a mile in the other person's shoes and understand their point of view. In case there are arguments, they should be presented in a manner that is not judgmental.

Pay Attention

There is nothing as unnerving as talking to someone who is not actively paying attention to the communication process. It makes a person lose interest and not open up as much as they want to. Thus, secure communication should be achieved by paying attention to the person speaking, be it in a group or a private setting. Distractions such as noise, phones, and other gadgets should be done away with, and the speaker is given undivided attention. It will enable the listener to identify the feelings of the speaker by reading the body language and respond accordingly.

Refrain from Giving Unsolicited Advice

A popular pitfall to emphatic communication is giving advice or sharing one's point of view, even when the speaker has not sought it. At times, all a person wants is to be listened to. Giving advice that has not been asked for impedes this process, and the person will not be able to communicate their feelings effectively.

Thus, for empathic communication to occur, refrain from giving advice, unless the speaker directly asks for it. Additionally, sharing one's opinion on a subject is good. However, it communicates to the speaker is that the listener is self-centered and does not consider the feelings of other people. At times, giving advice can generate resistance from the other party, and they stop communicating what they wanted to pass on.

Silence

Silence is powerful, especially in a conversation. It makes sure the listener can take in what has been said, and digest it, and give time for summarization. It helps the listener understand what the other person is trying to say and give room for the other person to organize their thoughts.

Short bouts of silence can be used to enact emphatic communication because they are a way for the listener to understand what the speaker is saying. It also gives room to a person to do away with their biases and get the point from the other person's point of view, according to their background. Thus, silence during a conversation should not be seen as awkward, but a practical way to ensure empathic communication.

Managing short instances of silence is a skill that takes time to master. Thus, the listener should practice it so that they do not become awkward or indicate the end of the conversation.

Raise Attention Levels by Self-Detachment and Decreasing Self-Centralization

Seeing a point from someone else's point of view or experience is hard and has to be learned. Thus, to increase attention, one has to detach themselves from their experiences and biases and pay attention to the other person. It helps a person be in the moment, and solely understand what is being said at the moment.

Read the Speaker

People might communicate one thing and mean the other. It happens to the nest of us, especially when we are nervous, or afraid of judgment. However, body language does not lie and will always betray what the speaker wants to say. This is why the listener should read the speaker.

Take Action

Emphatic communication is meeting the needs of the other person. Thus, after being communicated to, one should take action and meet the other person at the point of their needs. It does not have to be the right action, but any activity that would help them overcome their situation.

A person might communicate that they do not seem to get a hold of their finances. An action that can be taken is teaching them simple methods of saving, referring them to someone who can help them.

The most important part is their opinion has to be sort on which option is the best and let them make that decision for themselves.

Understand That Perception is everything

Psychology states that empathy involves communication and perception. Communication can occur at any time, but perception is very important, especially when one wants to build an emphatic connection.

People often understand what they want to, depending on their experiences and background. Thus, what is being communicated might not be what will be understood. Stephen Covey once said that "Many do not even listen with the intent to understand; they listen with the intent to reply." Ideally, many people are either speaking or are listening with the intent to reply. Therefore, conversations are like monologues because they are from one person's point of view.

Chapter 7: How to Strengthen the Relationship with Your Partner

1. Start Trusting

Learn to consciously get into the habit of trusting people more. Choose a trusting disposition over a distrustful attitude. Unless you have absolutely concrete evidence about someone, take their word for it. Going around snooping, stalking your partner and behaving like a suspicious maniac only harms your relationship further. Rather, if there really is no reason to be suspicious other than a feeling of insecurity or jealously, let it go.

2. Write Your Deepest Feelings and Thoughts

Journaling is known to be one of the most effective techniques for bringing to the fore your deepest feelings and emotions. It helps you discover multiple layers of your personality to achieve greater self-awareness. It also facilitates the process of an emotional catharsis for venting out pent up feelings. For instance, you may constantly harbor feelings of insecurity because you were raised by neglectful parents or you may never feel you are "good enough" because you were raised by parents who had extremely high and unreasonable expectations from you.

People who have been neglected in their childhood often feel they aren't worthy enough to be loved. This in turn causes them to think that their partner is seeking someone more worthy or deserving of love than them, which creates feelings of insecurity.

3. Regulate Your Negative Feelings and Emotions with Mindfulness

Mindfulness is a great way to calm your nerves and manage runaway emotions. Tune into your physical and mental self by identifying your feelings, thoughts and emotions by taking deep breaths. Try and detach yourself from overpowering negative emotions such as jealousy and insecurity. Every time you find yourself overcome with thoughts of jealousy or insecurity, practice mindful meditation.

4. Be Frank and Accepting About Your Feelings

Discussing your insecurities with your partner will help you create a frank and open communication channel. Rather than doing and saying crazy things to your partner, be upfront and share your feelings. Say something similar to "I apologize for bothering you regarding your friendship with ABC, but it is not my lack of trust in you. I simply feel insecure about it."

5. Avoid Suffocating Your Partner

Start relaxing a bit by letting go of your desire to imprison your partner. The harder you try to imprison someone against his/her own will, the more forcefully they'll try to escape your domineering behavior. Let your partner have the freedom to spend time with his/her friends, talk to their attractive colleague or do other things that otherwise make you feel threatened. Once they realize how secure and confident you are about the relationship, they will automatically be drawn to you. A secure and self-assured partner can be extremely irresistible.

6. Create Boundaries as a Couple

Sometimes people behave in a certain way without even being aware that their actions negatively impact loved ones. You may find your partner indulging in flirtatious behavior often, but he/she may believe it to be a part of their fun personality. They may not even be aware of the damage being caused to you or the relationship. For them it may be a harmless display of their charm and wit.

Setting boundaries early in the relationship will keep you both on the same page as to what is appropriate or acceptable behavior and where to draw the line. You both can mutually discuss and arrive at the "non-negotiables" in your relationship. Is harmless flirting alright with both of you? What about kissing on the cheek? Dancing with a member of the opposite sex? Once clear boundaries are established, your partner will be less likely to behave in a way that can upset your or incite feelings of insecurity. Talk issues through, look for a common ground and once everything is clear – learn to trust your partner unless there is compelling evidence to believe otherwise.

7. Go to the Bottom of Your Insecurity and Negative Emotions

It can be really hard to objective assess why you feel pangs of insecurity each time someone compliments your partner, or he/she speaks warmly with his/her colleagues. It can be highly tempting to blame another person for your emotions. However, getting to the root of your insecurity by being more self-aware is the foundation to free yourself from its shackles. Take a more compassionate and objective look at the origination of your insecurity. Think about the potential causes for feelings of insecure.

For instance, if you find yourself being increasingly insecure of your partner, know why you feel it. Is it because you don't want to lose him/herDo you suffer from a false sense of self-entitlement that your partner's time belongs only to you? Do you feel what you feel because of a sense of inadequacy that constantly makes you think "you aren't good enough?" Once you identify the underlying reasons causing feelings of jealousy and insecurity, it becomes easier to deal with your behavior.

8. Switch Off from Envious and Insecure Mental Chatter

Tell yourself to mentally shut up when you find yourself engaging in self-defeating jealous self-speak. You can use several techniques to achieve this. It can be using a stop or "x" sign whenever negative thoughts begin to pick momentum in your mind. Condition yourself to stop unexpected thoughts with practice sessions using visual and mental reinforcements. Try saying stop really aloud when you find yourself embarking on a destructive insecurity self-talk journey. This way you will embarrass yourself more and realize how ridiculously you are behaving. The idea is to train your brain into thinking that it isn't alright to come up with insecure self-talk.

9. Avoid Judging Other People Based on Your Past

Ever notice how suspicious people are always suspicious of others? Or liars think everyone around them is lying? Our perception of people and their motives is often a reflection of who we are. Stop using your past or present behavior as a yardstick for perceiving your partner's actions. For instance, if you have a history of being involved with married men/women, do not assume that no married man/woman can ever be trusted and start mistrusting your spouse. Just because you did or are doing something does not mean he/she is indulging in it too.

10. Discard past Relationship Baggage

A strong reason why you are always paranoid about your current partner cheating on you can be traced back to an earlier relationship. You may have had an ex-partner horribly cheat on you with your best friend. The betrayal may have had such a severe impact that you view every relationship in a similar distrustful light.

Painting everyone with the same brush can be a disastrous mistake in any relationship. There is a solid reason your earlier relationship did not last, and you should leave the garbage of your earlier relationship where it belongs – in the trash can.

11. Question Yourself Every Time

Each time you find yourself feeling even remotely jealous; question the underlying feeling behind the complex emotion of jealousy. Is the insecurity a consequence of my anger, anxiety or fear? What is it about this situation that makes me jealous? When you question your jealously critically, you are a few steps away from taking constructive steps to convert a cloud of negativity into a bundle of positivity.

12. Insecurity Is Not Always an Evil Monster

It may sound contradictory to everything we've been discussing about insecurity, but truth is insecurity may not always be harmful. Sometimes, a tiny amount of it may actually do your relationship a whole lot of good. How? It can sometimes motivate you or your partner to safeguard your relationship. If expressed in a productive and wholesome manner, insecurity gives you the much-needed impetus to protect your territory. Insecurity helps you assume the role of a protector for your loved one and/or relationship, and this can be good if it doesn't scale extreme heights. Be smart enough to realize when jealousy goes from being a relationship protector to a relationship destroyer. You choose whether it is a boon or bane for your relationship.

13. Remind Yourself of Your Strengths Periodically

Each of us possesses unique strengths that set us apart from others. Keep reinforcing to yourself how wonderful you are through positive affirmations and visualizations. You will find yourself feeling less insecure when you are aware of your positives. The more self-assured and confident you are, the less affected you will be by other people's actions. Know where your strengths lie, keep doing things that make you feel great about yourself and believe that you are worthy of true love.

14. Focus on Productive and Positive Ideas

Rather than obsessing over who your partner is cheating you with, try to develop interests outside of your relationship. Do not make it the nucleus of your existence even if it means a lot to you.

15. Imaginary Fears Do Not Necessarily Mean It Will Actually Happen

We need to understand that our insecure hunches do not necessarily mean the act is actually occurring. Just because we fear something is going to happen doesn't mean it will happen. A majority of the times our fears are totally unfounded, and not even remotely close to coming true. Just because your partner is somewhere else, and you fear he/she is with someone else doesn't really mean he/she is actually proposing relationship on a date. Understand the difference between thoughts and actual events. The make-believe imaginations of our destructive mind are often far from reality.

16. Be Generous

Spend more time giving and helping others. This will not just make you feel great about yourself but also help you develop a greater understanding of how you add value to others' lives and how they would be grateful to have what you have. Volunteer within your local community by helping folks read and write English or preparing meals for the less fortunate or even assisting a friend who is struggling to finish college.

17. Stay Away from Insecurity Triggering Situations

Be aware of situations that trigger elements of jealousy and insecurity in your behavior and avoid these situations whenever you can. For instance, if you are a person who can't help experiencing pangs of insecurity each time your partner mingles with members of the opposite sex, avoid dating a person who generally hangs out with the opposite sex and is extremely popular with them. This will invariably lead to friction unless you work a common ground.

18. Focus on the Positives

So, you witnessed your partner flirting with one of his friends. Big deal? Not really. Keep in mind that you both have a history of intimacy and an incomparable closeness, which is why you are together in the first place. There's a unique spark about your togetherness that cannot be matched by others. Just because someone pays their friends a few compliments and displays warmth doesn't necessarily mean they want to be with him/her for life. Sometimes, people just flirt to lighten the mood or break the ice or make the other person feel good about himself/herself.

Remember the really positive and unusual things about your relationship every time you are overcome with feelings of insecurity/jealousy. Remind yourself of your wonderful moments, of everything your partner has told you about why he/she fell in love with you, and the loving things you have done for each other.

19. Do Not Be a Party to Relationship Games

People often try to feel great about them by purportedly getting their partner to feel insecure. Do not fall into the trap. Displaying any signs of insecurity will only encourage your partner's behavior. Tell your partner firmly that indulging in a jealousy/insecurity inducing behavior only demeans him/her and won't make him/her feel any better about him/her. Even if you feel jealous, try to keep a stoic and unaffected demeanor, which should eventually stop these excruciatingly uncomfortable, attention-drawing tactics.

Chapter 8: How to Help Your Partner to Overcome Anxiety

Loving a Person with Anxiety

This part is dedicated to partners of people who struggle with anxiety. Relationship and love demand that we get involved in our partner's life and this means we always have to be supportive and loving. If you have a partner with one or more types of anxiety, you are already aware of how it can influence not just the relationship, but your life too. Anxiety comes in many forms, and there is no magic pill that can help. Anxiety is also an individual experience that can differ in many ways. The list of things we can do to help our partner when they are having an anxiety attack differs from person to person.

Acute Anxiety

Acute anxiety happens out of the blue. It can be caused by different things, certain situations or other people you and your partner meet. It happens suddenly, and there is no time for planning and taking it slow. You need to be able to react in the moment and to know how to assess the situation. Understand what is happening, what your partner is going through, and come up with the right way that can help neutralize the anxiety. There are four steps you can take to be supportive and helpful in case of acute anxiety:

1. Be calm, be compassionate. If you are not, you won't be able to support your partner needs at that moment. If

you give in to anger, frustration, or your own anxiety, it won't help. It can even make things worse. You also need to remember not to give in to your partner's anxiety and accommodate it. In the long run, this is not helpful. Instead, offer understanding, not just solutions.

2. Assess your partner's anxiety. What level is it? What are the symptoms and signs of an anxiety attack? An anxiety attack can hit with a different strength each time. You need to be able to recognize it to choose actions appropriate to the given situation.

3. Remind your partner of the techniques that helped with anxiety attacks. Whether it is breathing or exercise, your partner is probably aware of their success in neutralizing anxiety. But in the given situation, maybe he or she needs reminding. Once they are on the right path of dealing with anxiety, your job is to provide positive reinforcement. Give praise and be empathetic once your partner executes techniques that will help with an anxiety attack.

4. Evaluate the situation. Is your partner's anxiety attack passing? If it is, be supportive and encourage your partner to continue whatever he is doing to lower his anxiety. If it stays at the same level, or increases, you should start the steps from the beginning and come up with different techniques and strategies to help your partner with an acute anxiety attack.

Chronic Anxiety

To address chronic anxiety, you might have to try out exposure therapy, as it is considered the golden standard of treatment by many people. Usually, it takes the guidance of a professional therapist to try with exposure therapy. But, if the level of your partner's anxiety is not severe, you might feel comfortable enough to try it on your own. In this case, you have to act as a guide and learn how to be a supportive person for your partner.

You have to start with the least challenging situation and progress slowly and steadily towards more challenging ones. If anxiety isn't decreasing in the first challenge, it's not time to go to second.

For example, let's say your partner has a fear of heights. He or she wants to overcome this fear and be able to climb the buildings last floor. How will exposure therapy look in this case?

1. Tell your partner to look out the window from the ground floor for exactly one minute.

2. Climb to the second floor together with your partner. Remember that you are not just an exposure therapy guide; you also need to act as a support. Make them look out the window from the second floor for one minute. In case of anxiety showing up in its first symptoms, remind your partner to do breathing exercises to lower its impact.

3. Once your partner feels better, they should try looking out the window again.

4. If no anxiety presents itself, you should leave your partner's side. They need to be able to look through the same window, but this time without you.

5. Climb to the third floor and repeat steps three and four. When your partner feels ready, continue to the fourth floor, sixth and so on. If your partner's anxiety is too high, don't hesitate to stop. The first session doesn't need to take longer than 30 minutes.

6. Each new session needs to begin with the last comfortable floor your partner experienced. You don't need to always start from the ground floor, as your partner progresses, feeling no anxiety when looking through the window of the second, third, even fourth floor.

7. Take time. Your partner will not be free of the fear in just a few days. Be patient and continue practicing exposure therapy in this way until your partner can achieve the goal and climb the last floor.

8. The goal of exposure therapy is not just to get rid of fear and anxiety. It should also teach your partner that he or she can control and tolerate discomfort. Your partner will have an opportunity to practice anxiety-reduction techniques in a safe and controlled environment, with you in the support role.

Specific Disorder Interventions

Under the guidance of a trained therapist, the two of you will learn how to approach it in the best possible way. Your partner's therapist might ask you to join in a few sessions, and he will teach you how to better help your partner in situations that elevate anxiety. If your partner is not diagnosed, but both of you suspect he might have a certain disorder, advise your partner to visit a doctor. Self-diagnosing can lead to mistakes, and you will make wrong choices in how to approach your partner's anxiety.

Panic Disorder with Agoraphobia

If this is your partner's diagnosis, you two probably already have a pattern of behavior that is designed to accommodate your partner's anxiety. You probably follow your partner to social events, and you are the one who is in charge of running errands outside of the house. This accommodation is counterproductive in the long run. You are showing that you care, love, and support your partner, but it prevents him or her from experiencing a full life. Your partner needs to learn how to overcome anxiety. You may approach panic disorder with exposure therapy, so your partner becomes less dependent on you:

1. Choose an errand that your partner thinks he can handle himself. It can be shopping, going to a doctor appointment alone, walking a dog, etc.

2. Plan what errands are more challenging for your partner and add them to the list. Write them down as "to be accomplished in the future." It is important to work slowly but keep a clear vision of what needs to be accomplished.

3. Work together on slowly accomplishing the first task on your list. If it's going shopping alone, accompany your partner a few times, so they are accustomed to the environment. When he or she feels confident enough to

go alone, let them. Encourage and support their decision.

4. Once your partner accomplishes the task, be there to discuss his experience about it. Listen carefully and address any issues that might arise. Encourage your partner and keep track of his progress.

Obsessive-Compulsive Disorder

When it comes to OCD, what you can do for your partner is not to engage in his behaviors. Also, encourage him not to give in and repeat their compulsive behaviors. If you give in and comply with your partner's OCD, you will not be helping. Although it will surely elevate the tension made by your partner's OCD, complying will reinforce the fears. For example, if your partner asks you to go to the kitchen and make sure all appliances are off, you shouldn't comply. But you should also not argue or call your partner irrational. It is ineffective, and it will only deepen the anxiety.

Discuss with your partner how is it best to approach anxiety and agree on a strategy. This is where a professional therapist will be of most use to both of you. A professional can guide you through this conversation and help both of you feel comfortable discussing the delicate topic of your partner's disorder.

You will need to learn how to change from saying things like:

"I will not go to the kitchen again, you are imagining things, and being irrational" to "I appreciate your concern about the kitchen appliances, but we agreed that the best thing we can do is to help you learn how to manage the feelings you are having right now."

Your partner will agree for their own benefit that the best thing you could do is stay by their side, not check the kitchen, and help them work through the anxiety. This can be done with breathing exercises that will help your partner calm down. In time, your partner will show less fear. The OCD will decrease, and you will feel less frustrated.

Generalized Anxiety Disorder

The behavior of people with GAD is similar to that of people who have OCD. They have fears about certain things, and these fears are not comforted by reassurance. GAD usually creates concerns that we all have. It can be about finances, health, and school. But people with GAD will overblow the proportion of these fears, and they will influence their daily life. If your partner is diagnosed with GAD, you are aware of how simple problems we face every day can sound like total catastrophes. Your partner probably assumes the worst possible end of certain situations.

It often happens that people with this affliction develop a constant feeling of inadequacy. They believe they are not good enough for their partners, and that they never will be. When this happens, they usually try to overcompensate and make everything perfect so their partner can love them. On the other hand, some may feel that there is nothing they can do and that there is no point in trying. They underperform reinforcing their feelings of inadequacy.

Social Phobia

Social phobia comes in many forms. It can make going to work a very difficult task, or it can make maintaining relationships impossible to achieve. A therapist uses the technique of testing the hypothesis of a patient. This is a very successful way of bringing realization to the patient that their fears and anxieties do not have a foundation. A therapist can teach a person with social phobia the basic communication skills to prepare them for situations they might encounter in their endeavors to overcome anxiety.

Post-Traumatic Stress Disorder

PTSD is caused by experiencing a traumatic event, and it can affect every aspect of a relationship. If your partner is suffering from PTSD, he or she will react to certain triggers that will remind him of the traumatic experience. In the case of PTSD, anxiety attacks can happen both spontaneously and routinely. Often people who have PTSD become disconnected from their partners when anxiety hits them, they become unresponsive to their partners, or they don't even recognize them for what they are.

Make a Plan for Relieving your Partner's Anxiety

Now you know potential techniques you can use to reduce your partner's anxiety. Use this knowledge to create a plan, make a list of practical actions and ineffective actions for when your partner experiences anxiety attack. It is important to remember what to do in situations that trigger anxiety, but it is also important to know what not to do.

Chapter 9: Exercises and Remedies to Overcome Anxiety

A Healthy Relationship Is a Good Relationship

A healthy relationship makes both partners feel safe. Only when there is a basis for protection will individuals and the couple grow and mature. Intimacy is possible only if people feel safe enough to be vulnerable. Any conflict without it threatens the whole relationship.

It is possible that some of the people I see in counseling will end their marriages. Some certainly should never have happened at all. These are the couples who were unable to establish and maintain their partnership with others. Some of them married for all the wrong reasons: to get out of a parent's house for money, or just because everyone else expected them. Many combat verbal, physical, or emotional violence. In-such situations, it is vital to ensure the protection of individuals first. Only then should a couple think about trying again.

Nonetheless, most of the couples I saw in practice do not battle the repercussions of marriage without love or violence. They have come for advice because they long for the link they once had, or they don't function. "We can't communicate" means "we're not communicating," and it often does not feel sufficiently comfortable for one or both of them to be 100% connected.

Loving alone isn't adequate. Security depends on attitudes and behaviors, which foster emotional connection and deep mutual respect. If one felt insecure, distrustful, or challenged emotionally, marriage would obviously not work in the long-term. It may last — for many reasons, people remain in unsatisfactory relationships. But it's not going to be personal.

A marriage-should be a safe place for every partner to be loved, respected, and seen and to have a strong sense of cohesion. A good marriage is one where each partner regularly works on the following security elements:

- **Security**

Safety depends on ensuring that the other person is committed to the promise of commitment and does everything he can to fulfill this promise. Every wedding has rough patches. Each marriage has periods when the partners feel out of sync. Commitment to commitment ensures that the issues are dealt with by both parties. They're not disengaging or bailing. We don't allow themselves to lay blame. Each of them has a duty and works hard to fix their role in that gap between them.

- **Trust**

Confidence is a gift that we give to someone we love. It's a fact in a healthy marriage. Everybody knows that the other person would never do anything to break their hearts. You treat it as a precious commodity because you realize that once destroyed, it is challenging to recover trust, couples who are last couples who do not betray the faith. Since trust is so vital for security and because circumstances can be misread, either I leap to conclusions about treason. Instead, they speak through one of the partners when they feel betrayed.

- **Honesty**

All partners must be frank with each other in order to trust. Since neither of them has anything to hide, phone and computer passwords are exchanged. Their investments, actions, and relationships are real. You understand that a couple is a team of two, and each of them needs the integrity of the other to function.

- **Mutual respect**

In healthy marriages, the partners appreciate and love the other person, and often say so. We respect the opinions, goals, thoughts, and feelings of each other.

- **Fidelity**

Fidelity means various things to various people. It is not beneficial to say that when you think about it, you both, of course, have the same thing in mind. A happy couple has spoken openly and honestly about how they interpret "cheating" and their expectations of each other. You make a mutual agreement that you intend to uphold.

- **Platinum Rule**

It is a good rule, but the Platinum rule takes things a step further: "Treat someone as they want to be handled." It means taking the time to consider and to do what most respects and pleases your partner even if you don't want that to be.

- **Emotional accessibility**

The partners are emotionally involved in successful marriages. All frequently show love. They both share their thoughts and emotions and are open to their mate. If a conflict occurs, no one shuts down mentally. Alternatively, they meet and support each other while working through anything that is disturbing.

- **Clean fighting**

Sure. Yes. Sometimes everyone loses it. But one can be upset without the other individual being weakened. Calling, bullying, intimidating, threatening to leave, or throw out the other person are aspects of dirty struggles. Those who deal with a dispute by physical or emotional violence never settle it. Usually, the situation is much worse than it had to be.

Sanitary couples know how to fight with dignity. I don't blame them. Instead, they speak from their own feelings and experiences.

Last marriages are founded on health. Without the relationship, no member of the couple will relax. Every person thereby becomes a better version of themselves, and marriage becomes stronger and more intimate.

You must be both interested in good contact in your partnership. This needs you to be genuinely interested in what your partner says and responds in kind. You should also show your feelings plainly, for a stronger relationship. This lets him know exactly what's happening to you, which fosters a deeper connection and a better relationship. Nevertheless, this relationship is not a static object. It moves through its ups and downs through the different stages. What are these stages? Let's take a look. Let's take a look.

The Six Stages of a Relationship

According to life and organizational strategist Tony Robbins, the six (6) phases of a partnership are clearly defined.

1. Love and Passion

This is the step when your partner is the only thing on your mind. The chemistry between you is correct, and you are invested in your partner's success. All your acts are designed to lose yourself and help you achieve them.

2. Not Enough Romance

You both love one another, but you sense a void deep within. You wish your partner could fill this, but you can't.

3. The relationship of convenience

The romantic dimension has dissipated in the third stage as the relationship progresses. This is not so much devotion, not so much passion. You cannot, however, separate yourself because you have other ties to keep you from doing so. You're living with the family (when you have children) or because it's too difficult to get rid of mutual financial obligations and responsibilities. "You may live together with your partner, and you may be happy, but there's no profound emotional involvement. Whether you focus on work, hobbies, family (other than your partner), friends, etc., most of you are probably in Position Three. What is challenging is to believe your partner is a right person— not lovely enough to get excited, not bad enough to quit.

4. Planning your escape

In stage 4, the relationship brings you no pleasure. In reality, you still think of how wonderful life would be if you weren't with your current partner.

5. Don't want to be in a relationship

In the fifth stage, you want to communicate with someone.

6. You're not in a relationship, and you don't want to be in one

You've given up relationships now. You don't want to let anyone come close to you. You've had a bad experience, and you don't want to ruin it. Which level do you feel at the moment? Write it down. Write it down. Sensitivity is the first step towards any positive change.

The Six Human Needs in Relationship/Marriage

Here is a breakdown of the six human needs:

    1. **Certainty:** You must make sure in your relationship you are relaxed, i.e., you have enjoyment free of pain. However, for some people, particularly those who long for spontaneity, it can be monotonous and boring, to make sure that everything is perfect.

    2. **Variety:** It is the need for variance and variety ety "spice things up" and keep things more exciting in the relationship. You want variety and tasks that exercise your emotional and physical scope.

    3. **Significance:** It feels good to know that you are important, special, necessary, and desired.

4. **Love / Connection:** This is the need or need for a deep connection with another human being and a sense of true belonging.

5. **Growth:** "If we stop growing, we die," it was said. It is important in every facet of life-spiritual, emotional, and intellectual-to continue to grow.

6. **Contribution:** This is the ability to go beyond one's own needs. As Tony Robbins says, "All things in the world benefit or are destroyed outside itself." Whether it's time, money, energy (or all three), it's all worth it and makes you feel like a whole person. Which of these six human needs are your first and second motivations? What's your partner like? Problems arise when in our relationship, we do not meet the primary and secondary needs of each other. Now that you know the phases and human needs in a relationship, I hope you have found out where the partnerships and interests (as well as your partners) fit into the scheme. Let us take a look at the things that one or both of you most likely do.

Why Couples Argue

There are lots of reasons why couples fight and argue about differences in-laws, quality time spent together, or jealousy. Let's look at those. Let's look at those.

1. **Sex:** There is typically a disconnection at some stage in this type of intimacy. Perhaps your partner is not as open as you are in your bedroom or

vice versa. You may not also be happy that you feel you deserve.

2. **Money:** Couples fight for money, too. Your costumes might not represent your partner's. Such discrepancy also leads to tremendous disagreements, which can even end the relationship.

3. **Kids:** Children are another major topic that creates a divide between couples. The preference of parenting style, in particular. You may be strict in your parentage, but your partner is more relaxed. If children gravitate to the lenient parent, the harder parent may feel tired of being the "bad guy." This could then lead to discord and a sense of being left out or unbearable. Even before the rugrats are born, fights will begin. You might, for example, like your grandma to name your child, but your partner may prefer to use "northwest" as a certain celebrity couple did. You may have differing opinions, even though you are not parents, on whether or not you both want children, what religious or cultural system they are taught, or how you want them to be educated. All these communications must be answered as soon as possible.

How Communication Works in Relationship

Many in troubled relationships say,' We don't talk anymore.' They probably mean that they don't communicate any more effectively. The truth is that people still connect. Sometimes two people who treat each other quietly interact with each other.

The five traditional forms of marriage communication:

1. Emotion
2. Touch
3. Spoken or written communication
4. Context of the situation
5. Non-verbal physical expression (facial expressions, expressions, gestures, behavior, etc.)

It is easy to concentrate only on words, but only a fraction of the information pairs share.

Chapter 10: How to Create Healthy Interdependence

Keeping the Spark Alive

The initial phase of a relationship is quite beautiful. There seems to be a natural spark between you and your partner, undeniable chemistry, which cannot be explained. If you have been in a long-term relationship, for as long as you can remember, then you know what I'm talking about. Let us think about your relationship as a rom-com movie. So, you met your partner à la rom-com movie style, have lived through your first fight, and maybe even your hundredth (unscathed I hope), and now, you are nearing the end of the movie where the screen fades to black, the end credits start to roll, and unfortunately, the rom-com ends. Now, reality sets in. There are schedules to follow, work to be done, errands to run, a house to be maintained, and several nights when you need to burn the midnight oil. How do you maintain the spark in the relationship after the honeymoon phase ends? This is a question a lot of couples struggle to answer.

Before learning about ways in which you can keep this spark alive, let us first understand why this spark fades away. There are different reasons for it, ranging from long distance to any growing resentment over small issues. One simple truth you must accept is that even in the strongest of relationships, romance dies down if you don't actively work on it. Think of romance as a muscle.

Understand the Meaning

Before you can work on keeping the spark alive, you must understand what this means to you. No two human beings are alike, so the way you interpret what it truly means to be loved and appreciated will be quite different from what your partner feels. We all tend to speak different love languages. So, it is quite likely that the way you show your love is different from the way your partner shows it. You most probably expect your partner to express their love or appreciation in the same way you do. If this doesn't happen, you might start harboring feelings of resentment and even frustration. If you truly love your partner, and have sufficient trust and faith in your relationship, remind yourself that it is perfectly alright to ask for what you want. If you find yourself often hesitating while doing this, you might as well turn it into a fun game.

For instance, think of a very specific thing that you and your partner must work on at the beginning of the week. Talk about it and come up with a super-specific task. It might be something as simple as complementing the way you look, purchasing flowers for a partner, or maybe even planning a surprise date. Maybe your partner wants to spend more quality time with you or wants some form of positive feedback for all their effort. You might be thinking, what difference will it make, if it will last only a week? Well, you're right to think like this.

Time to Disconnect

These days, the right to disconnect has become rather popular, and rightly so. Plenty of companies across the globe have started incorporating the policy of the right to disconnect in their work agreement. This right essentially allows the employees to avoid answering any calls or responding to emails related to work post their regular work hours. Well, it is time to start exercising this right of yours. In fact, by disconnecting your personal life from professional life, you can effectively improve your relationship. Make a habit of spending time with your partner without the interference of any gadgets. It is quite unlikely you'll be able to give your undivided attention to your partner if you constantly keep checking your phone. Not just you but encourage your partner to do the same. Most of us are so engrossed with technology these days that we forget about reality while living in virtual reality. Put your phones away, start a conversation, connect with each other, or maybe even have a meal together. Indulge in activities you both enjoy and love rather than staying glued to the bright screens of your mobile phones.

Make and Maintain Eye Contact

Not to sound like a cliché from a movie but maintaining eye contact is perhaps one of the most romantic gestures a person can make. In any romantic movie you might have seen, the hero always maintains eye contact. There is something quite engaging about maintaining eye contact. Making grand gestures to show your affection is quite romantic, but this isn't possible on a daily basis. After all, life isn't a musical where you can keep serenading your partner with a song and dance routine on a daily basis. So, it is time you start working on coming up with simpler ways to show your love and affection. Whenever you make eye contact with your partner, it produces oxytocin. Oxytocin is a feel-good hormone that triggers feelings of love and warmth.

Something New

If you want to keep the spark alive, then you must keep trying new things together. Having a routine can give you the feeling of security, but when you try something new, it brings a sense of excitement. Excitement is quite important for the survival of a relationship, especially in a long-term relationship. You might think about traveling together or even taking up a hobby class together. Come up with different activities you and your partner can indulge in together to break free of your usual routine. It will also help bring a fresh perspective to the way you see your partner. You might even discover things you like that you never knew you did before. There are plenty of activities to try, so get on board, and make a list of different activities you would like to try with your partner. If you keep doing this, I'm pretty certain you might just end up falling in love with your partner all over again. Isn't that an enticing benefit?

Spend Some Time Apart

Do you remember the age-old saying - absence makes the heart fonder? Well, the same is true for distance, and distance starts to make the heart grow fonder. The excitement of seeing your partner after a while is indescribable. When you spend too much time together, you tend to get used to being around each other, and this is one most of the couples tend to fall in a rut. Maybe even spending an hour away from each other every day works. If you and your partner both have day jobs, then you're already spending a lot of time apart, so coming home to each other is quite exciting and relaxing at the same time.

Starting a Conversation

You will obviously talk to your partner on a daily basis. However, when was the last time you ever actually had a conversation with your partner? I don't mean talking about any to-do lists, shopping, kids, or any other issues. Instead, you must have a real conversation where you share emotions with each other; a conversation related to your future, understanding what is going on in each other's mind, and establishing a strong connection. Start a conversation where you can reconnect and understand each other's needs. If most of your daily conversations are related to questions like, "How was your day?" or "Well, this is what we have to do tomorrow," and this is how your usual conversations are, then it is time to dig a little deeper.

If you are unsure about doing this, then here is a simple conversation starter, "What is the one thing you are scared to try, but you really want to?" Or "What do you like the most about our relationship?" By doing this, you can have deep and meaningful conversations with your partner. It is believed that to compensate for every negative experience you have, it takes five positive experiences. For instance, to get over a simple negative experience like an argument or a disagreement, a majority of your conversations must be engaging, fun, and exciting. If most of your conversations are rather mundane or end up in arguments, then it is not a sign of a healthy relationship. In fact, a relationship like this isn't going to lead you anywhere good.

Laughing Together

There is a popular saying which goes something like this, "Laughter is the best medicine." You might have heard this several times. However, did you ever take a moment and think about it? Well, laughter certainly is the best medicine there is. When you laugh, your mind releases feel-good hormones, which immediately elevate your mood. Once you are in a better mood, everything seems to look better. Laughing together is the simplest way to keep the spark alive in any relationship. Talk about all those times where you have a personal joke to share or an incident wherein you know one day you will look back upon them and laugh. If you are in it for the long haul, then there are certain things you must let go. Talking about any funny incidents from your past, or bringing up any happy memories, will make your partner feel good too. There is nothing that will bring two people closer together the way shared memories do. If these memories trigger happy thoughts or emotions, then there is nothing like it.

Impress Your Partner

If you are in a long-term relationship, then it's quite likely that your partner has seen you at your best and the worst. Likewise, you have seen your partner at their best, as well as their worst. During the initial stages of a relationship, both partners usually try to make an effort to impress the other person. You probably used to dress up for date night, plan ahead, come up with grand gestures of romance, or even a surprise departure. After a while, these things certainly dwindle down. Well, if you want to keep the spark alive in your relationship, then there is one thing you must never stop doing, and that's making an effort. It always pays off to make some effort. Never stop trying to impress your partner. It helps keep things exciting and fresh.

Now, it is quintessential that for this tip to work, you both must be on the same page. If you keep trying to impress your partner while your partner doesn't do anything, your efforts will go to waste. Spend some time and talk about this. If your partner often compliments you on your looks, tries to impress you or, always tries to do you proud, then it certainly calls for some extra effort from you every now and then.

Making Changes

If you want your partner to become more romantic, then at times, it can feel like you are constantly nagging them to give you more. Instead of doing this, think about all the things you can do for your partner. If you are with a person you truly love, then they will start noticing all the effort you put in and will automatically feel like making an extra effort themselves. It is okay to be a little generous with your love and affection. If you do love your partner unconditionally, then prove it. If all these things don't work, then you can start thinking about the way you both used to behave during the initial stages of the relationship.

Kiss

Being a teenager in love is a wonderful feeling. Do you remember the first time you kissed someone? Wasn't it incredibly exciting? With age, the way you express yourself physically in a relationship also changes. However, there is one thing that must never change. Ensure that kissing is still an important part of the physical relationship you share with your partner. I'm not referring to kissing in general. It's not about waking up in the morning and giving a quick back to your partner or kissing your partner to greet them.

Chapter 11: Observing Your Thoughts

We live in a world that requires us to act on many things. Besides overcoming daily stressors, we should learn how to develop the right habits that prevent us from worrying and thinking negative thoughts. The strenuous environment and the hustle and bustle we have to face often fills our minds with clutter. It often reaches a point where our minds can't stop thinking. You may become overwhelmed with thoughts which leave your mind in a total mess. Does this sound like you? If yes, then your mind is waving a white flag at you and may require some decluttering.

Causes of Mental Clutter

In an ordinary case, when cleaning your home or office, you will start by identifying the items that are causing clutter. Likewise, before decluttering your mind, it is important that you start by identifying the causes of mental clutter. The importance of doing this is that it guarantees that you can effectively deal with clutter in the long run. You will be more aware of the factors that contribute to clutter in your mind and work to avoid them.

Overwhelm

Naturally, if you are overwhelmed with things, then it will lead to disorder in your mind. As a result, it will be daunting for you to establish a reasonable way of dealing with your issues. This causes clutter. Fortunately, you can overcome this by acknowledging the fact that you can't handle everything at once. This means that you should break down your tasks into smaller, yet manageable mini tasks. Handle these things one at a time. At the end of the day, you will realize that there is a lot that you have accomplished without feeling overwhelmed.

Over-Commitment

Committing yourself to finish certain activities on your to-do list is a good thing. Nonetheless, when you can't say no to other assignments, it means that you are over-committing yourself. Handling too many things will only lead to frustration. This is because there is a probability that you might fail to deliver. Learning to say no is an essential attribute of living a productive life. Saying no shouldn't be considered a bad thing since you're committing yourself to work productively on what you can manage. So, avoid over-committing yourself and taking on more than you can handle.

Fear

If you're afraid to let go of what has happened in the past, then are likely to strain your mind. The habit of holding on to things and thoughts often consumes us. Instead of working productively, your mind will keep ruminating on the past. This is pure clutter. Why should you put yourself through this torture when you can simply learn to let go?

Emotional Overload

Maybe your mind is filled with unwanted thoughts and feelings that keep draining energy from you. For instance, you might be dealing with a looming family crisis and it ends up affecting your productivity at work. If this is what you are going through, then it is best that you find time to deal with the issue. Ask for a leave of absence and free your mind from having to think over this matter repeatedly.

Lack of Time

Time will always be a prevalent issue. In everything that you do, you will often feel as though you don't have enough time. The reality is that there is enough time to handle all the important things in your life if you prioritize and plan effectively. Therefore, you shouldn't use the excuse that you lack time. The only issue here is that you may not know how to effectively manage your time. Organize yourself and prioritize what needs to be done first. This way, you will have more time to handle pending tasks on your to-do list.

Procrastination

If you are a victim of procrastination, then it comes as no surprise that your mind is always in a state of overdrive. After a while, you will feel overwhelmed that you cannot complete everything on time. The problem began with the decision to procrastinate.

A Major Change in Life

Another reason why your mind might be filled with clutter is because of a major change which has occurred in your life. Frankly, sometimes we have to acknowledge the fact that change is inevitable. People fail to embrace change in their lives. As a result, they spend too much time doing what they used to do instead of changing. When faced with such predicaments, it is imperative that you evaluate what's going on in your life and strive to change.

Familiarity with the causes of mental clutter is the first step towards successful mental decluttering. Once you are aware of what causes clutter in your mind, you can develop practical solutions of how to get rid of them. It is worth bearing in mind that in most cases, there are multiple reasons why your mind is cluttered. So, open up your mind when trying to identify the factors that cause your messy mental state.

Practical Tips on How to Declutter Your Mind
Set Priorities

Sometimes we fail to realize that a life without goals is a boring life. Living a goalless life is like wandering in the forest forever without a map. You don't have a particular destination that you want to reach. What's worse, you don't even know how to maneuver through the forest. Similarly, life without goals has no meaning. Your daily activities will be consumed with people and activities that don't add value to you. You will live in your comfort zone since there is nothing that you're actually targeting to achieve.

Setting priorities is a good place to start when looking to declutter your mind. This requires that you sit down and identify things that matter the most to your life. List down these goals and work to ensure that your actions are in line with the set goals. Setting priorities create structure with your to-do lists.

Keep a Journal

Keeping a journal is a great strategy to help organize your thoughts. People tend to underestimate the power of noting down their thoughts every day. Journaling helps you rid your mind from things that you might not be aware of. It enhances your working memory and also guarantees that you can effectively manage stress. Similarly, the habit of noting down your daily experiences in a journal helps you express your emotions that may be bottled up within you. Therefore, you create space to experience new things in life. The effect of this is that you can relieve yourself from the anxiety that you might have been experiencing.

Learn to Let Go

Decluttering your mind can also be made easier if you learn to let go. Holding on to things in the past adds little or no value to your life. In fact, it only affects your emotional and mental wellbeing. The mere fact that you cannot let go implies that you will find it daunting to look ahead. Your mind will stagnate, and this will stress you out. If you were a bird and you wanted to fly, what would you do? Without a doubt, you would want to free yourself from any burden that weighs you down. Apply this to real life and free yourself from any emotional baggage that you might be holding on to. Whether it's your failed past relationships or failed job opportunities, just let go. There is a greater reward in letting go since you open doors for new opportunities in your life.

Breathe

Breathing exercises would also be helpful in clearing clutter from your mind. There are certain forms of meditation that depend on breathing exercises to focus your attention on the breath. So, how do you practice breathing exercises? Start by taking a slow deep breath. Pause for a moment before exhaling. While breathing in and out, focus your mind on how you are breathing. Concentrate on how your breath goes in and out of your nose. It's relaxing, right? Practicing breathing exercises more often relaxes your mind. Besides helping you to relax, it boosts your immune system in profound ways.

Declutter Your Physical Environment

If you live in a messy house, then there is a good chance that you're more likely frustrated. This may be because you find it difficult to find things you need. For instance, you end up wasting a lot of time looking for your car keys before heading to work. This affects how you start your day. You will be stressed that you arrived late and that there are numerous tasks waiting for you. Therefore, decluttering your physical space will also have a positive impact on your mind.

Learn to Share Your Thoughts

There is an overall positive feeling when you sit down to share your feelings with someone you care about. Instead of holding back your tears and emotions, sharing your feelings with your loved ones can clear emotional clutter from your mind. Have you ever wondered why you can think more clearly after sharing your sad feelings with another person? There is power in sharing your thoughts and feelings with other people.

Curb Your Information Intake

The information that we consume affects the quality of the decisions we make. Unfortunately, the information we consume is sometimes unimportant to our lives. It only fills our minds with clutter, and this prevents us from thinking clearly and making the right decisions.

Spare Some Time to Unwind

More importantly, to declutter your mind, you should consider taking a break. You might believe that taking breaks is unproductive, but the truth is that your productivity can be given a huge boost when you take breaks more often. Giving yourself some time to unwind helps you recharge. As a result, you end up doing more in less time. This is what effectiveness and efficiency are all about. They both account for your productivity.

The Importance of Decluttering Your Mind

Decluttering the physical space around you will help you create more space for more important things. In addition, such tidiness will also have an impact on your mind since everything will be organized and you will know where everything is.

A Decrease in Stress and Anxiety

Clutter will stress you out. Feeling like your mind is messy may make you feel tired since there is a lot to do yet so little time. Similarly, mental clutter will also make you feel unconfident. You will rarely be confident about your abilities. Repeatedly, you will notice that you second-guess everything that you do. All this is happening because your mind can't think straight. There is a lot that it is focusing on and therefore, finding practical solutions to the little things ahead of you may seem impossible.

An Improvement in Your Productivity

Clutter can prevent your mind from achieving the focus it needs to handle the priorities that you have set for yourself. For instance, instead of waking up early and working on an important project, you might find yourself paying too much attention to the emotional burden that is weighing you down. Frankly, this thwarts your level of productivity. You are unlikely to use your time wisely, which affects your productivity.

Eliminating unwanted thoughts and emotions will help you focus more on what is important. You will find it easier to set priorities and work towards them. You will wake up feeling motivated and goal oriented. In the short run, you will notice an improvement in your efficiency. Over time, you will realize that you're more effective than ever before since there is more that you can do in less time.

Enhanced Emotional Intelligence

There are numerous situations in which we allow our emotions to affect how we perceive things in life. In addition, these emotions cloud our judgment and we end up making conclusions that are not valid. In most cases, this occurs when there is a lot on our minds that we have to handle. The result is that we fail to deal with these emotions in an effective manner.

Chapter 12: What Are My Personal Goals?

Goals are aims and objectives an individual strives to achieve.

Ones goals direct the path one's life take; every life altering, and life shaping decisions are taken with one's goals and aspirations in mind.

In the "getting to know each other" process, partners ought to ask questions about each other's goals and objectives because it gives individuals an insight into the kind of life an individual wish to live. Goals, aspirations and objectives are more than just career choices; although one's goals may include career choices, in relationships context, it is mainly focused on lifestyle and lifestyle choices.

In the same way that an individual's family and society they belong to influences behaviors and personality traits, one's family and society they belong to also influence their goals and aspirations.

For example, an individual who experienced lots of hardship during childhood due to the low financial capabilities of his/her family might aspire to be wealthy so his/her own children do not have to go through the same hardship as they did.

In the context of relationship, an individual that did not experience any feeling of affection either from his/her parents or between them, may be determined be different from what he/she experienced during formative years and strive to create intimacy and deep emotional connection between his/her self and their partner.

An individual's short-term goals and long-term goals can be used to determine certain aspects the individual's personality. Short term goals as the name implies are goals and aspirations that cover a short span of time. These goals are easily attainable and, in most cases, do not require a lot of effort.

An individual's short-term goals cover mundane areas of the individual's life.

Long term goals are attained through reached through short term goals. These usually take years to reach and when they are realized; incite mien changes in an individual's life.

Our goals and aspirations are like a blueprint of how we want our life to go. It includes everything we hope to achieve in an entire lifetime.

An individual's goals and aspirations also encompass his/her relationship hopes and aspirations.

When partners understand each other relationship goals, it gives them an insight into what his/her partner hopes to achieve in the course of the relationship, whether he/she hopes to build intimacy or not, whether he/she yearns for true emotional or not, it shows what partners are willing to give in a relationship and what they hope to get in return; their aims and objectives in its truest form.

An individual's relationship goals is different from his/her relationship expectations in the sense that, relationship expectations are what one hopes to get from their significant other and the relationship while relationship goals are aims and objectives an individual works towards in the course of the relationship.

An individual's relationship expectations are either met or not by his/her partner; the individual has no power over this, while his/her relationship goals are solely up to them.

While building relationships, it is important for partners to know and understand each other's relationship goals in order for them to know each other's aims and objectives and what he/she hopes to achieve in the course of the relationship.

Do We Have Shared Interests and Goals?

It is important for partners to have common goals and interests in a relationship.

When partners share common interest, it reduces the probability of conflicts and disagreements between them and deepens their sense of closeness, intimacy an emotional connection.

It is healthy for partners in a committed exclusive relationship to have some personal interests of their own in the relationship so as not to lose their self-identity (unique characteristic and qualities that makes them who they are) but when partners get carried away with their individual interests and do not share any same interest as a couple, it decreases the amount of time they spend in each other's space and eventually, partners will begin to feel disconnected from the relationship and also from each other.

When partners have shared or similar interests, it widens their conversational areas and creates a more relaxed environment for partners to converse.

With this ease in communication between partners, partners are able to get to know each other better, more willing to share deeply personal details about themselves with each other which leads to an open avenue for the creation of intimacy and a deeper level of emotional connection between them.

Partners with similar goals and interests can understand each other better that partners without similar goals and interests, because they are experiencing the same or similar events, so it becomes easier for them to understand and empathize with each other.

For example, partners with the same career paths will be understand better and be in a position to offer professional advice when one partner is facing work related difficulties.

Shared interests and goals between partners is not a prerequisite or a guarantee for a successful long lasting relationship, however when partners share certain interests, it becomes easier for them to understand each other, communicate better, quickly build intimacy between them and truly enjoy each other's company.

Partners in an effort to build intimacy and emotional closeness and connection might begin to feel obligated to spend time with each other, however if said partners have similar interests, it will cause both partners to be more relaxed and willing to spend time together because they will both be doing what they enjoy.

Some of these interests might include sport preferences, hobbies, similar interests in movies/music etc.

Do We Have Conflicting Personal Interests and Goals?

Conflict of interest arises in relationships when partners have personal goals and interests that work against each other.

These contradicting personal goals may either be in form of major lifestyle choices like whether or not they want children, different views on relationship type, different views on life, etc.

It is healthy for partners to have some different personal interests and goals outside of their relationship to maintain their self-identity; however, when there are no common grounds for them to meet, their relationship may begin to go on a downward spiral.

An individual's life goals set the course for his/her life.

Every major and minor decisions are taken with one's goals in mind, thus when partners personal goals contradict each other, it becomes almost impossible for them to harmoniously coexist in a shared space.

In order for partners to peacefully coexist together, there is a need for a common ground between them where they both share the same perspective on relationships and life in general.

When partners want similar things, meeting the emotional and relationship needs and expectations of each other becomes easy for them; it becomes like a give and take situation (you give your partner exactly what you expect to receive).

Partners who do not have similar or shared interests and goals could develop new interests together in a bid to build intimacy between them by having shared interests and spending more time together, partners could sit and decide on areas of shared interests they could equally enjoy.

This is creating a common ground for both partners to harmoniously coexist on, in an effort for both partners to retain their self-identity (and perhaps expanding it to contain new shared interests with one's partner) and develop shared interests with each other.

Developing shared interests and goals does not mean adopting one's partners own goals and interests.

Developing new shared interests between partners should be a mutually new interests for both partners in order for them to experience these new interests at the same time.

It is normal to want to share your what you are passionate about with your partner and want him/her to feel as strongly about those interests as you do, however this may come across to your partner as you trying to change who they are to fit your own idea of who you think they should be.

Regardless how much partners try to create shared interests and goals by compromising and creating new interests and goals together, there are certain interests and goals that cannot be compromised on.

For example, if partners have different views of their relationship and the roles they each play in it(i.e.; if one partner believes in gender specific roles where the female partner's job is creating a home and the male partner is charged with provision and protection and the other partner is against this idea has career plans of her own), this could cause disparities between partners which can only be solved when one partner gives up his/her views of how he/she thinks the relationship should be.

Also, if partners have different views on whether or not they want children, this will put them on opposing sides and even be a deal breaker for partners.

If one partner wants to focus on his/her career and is of the opinion that children will change the entire dynamics of their relationship and the other partner wants to build a family together with children in the mix, such partners have contradicting goals.

Compromising on such important goals may cause partners to resent each other as time goes on.

In this context, the partner who compromised and opted out of having children because his/her partner was not in agreement with having children, may on time begin to feel like his/her partner is responsible for him/her not having the type of family he/she craves.

Assigning blame on each other for situations which in truth they may or may not have contributed to create an emotional distance between partners, when partners hold each other relationship for unmet goals and aspirations, they may begin to feel like the only way to realize these goals is to break free and terminate the relationship.

It is important for individuals seeking to from an emotional connection and build a long lasting relationship to know that although having shared interests and goals could help foster feelings of affection, closeness and intimacy between partners, it is not a guarantee for a successful relationship.

Partners also need to understand that setting common goals and shared interests in a relationship could help them reconnect by spending more time together.

Also, when there are no common interest between partners in a relationship and partners compromise their own personal goals (which makes up part of their self-identity) to accommodate their partner's own goals and aspirations, it could lead to feelings of resentment and regrets in the future.

Individuals seeking to build long lasting relationship need to ask questions and initiating intimate conversations about each other's goals, aspirations and interests to make sure their personal goals and aspirations even if they are not similar, at least do not contradict each other.

Chapter 13: Secret Strategies for Handling Insecure Partners

1. Ditch Friendships That Genuinely Pose a Threat to Your Relationship

You may want to eliminate certain people from your life if they give your partner enough reason to feel insecure. You may have that one friend who has earned a notorious reputation of being a compulsive philanderer. He/she may dress provocatively, drop hints all the time and generally try to hit on you. This can be enough to have your partner fuming and can be a good enough reason to eliminate the friend from your life.

When there's good enough reason or reasonable enough expectations for you to give up on someone for the betterment of your relationship, do not hesitate to do it. Ensure that this doesn't become a pattern though, and that their demands do not become unreasonable over a period of time. Do it only in cases when you objectively feel that your partner is justified in feeling threatened or insecure.

2. Ditch the Insecurity Triggers

Avoid the jealousy/insecurity triggers whenever you can by trying to be more sensitive to your partner's feelings. When you know something bothers him/her, make a conscious effort to refrain from doing it. Avoid playing relationship games where to feel good about yourself; you purposely make them feel insecure. For instance, if you know they get edgy about overtly flirtatious behavior (however harmless it may seem to you), try and avoid flirting around them and make them the focus on your attention. Lavish generous praises on them, tell everyone about something wonderful they did and keep displaying signs of warmth/affection through your body language.

3. Encourage Accomplishment of Personal and Professional Goals

Since insecure feelings are often deeply rooted in feelings of inadequacy or low self-esteem, helping your partner set and accomplish goals can be a wonderful way to increase their self-confidence. It can be anything from losing weight to working on a challenging new project to signing up for a public speaking class to creating YouTube videos – anything that helps them savor a feeling of personal achievement. When they feel good about themselves, they are less likely to get clingy and keep demanding validation from you.

It helps shift the focus away from "Am I really worthy?" to "Wow, I've done this. I must be wonderful." It gives them a constructive goal to fixate on rather than being obsessed about your whereabouts. As a partner, encourage their personal achievements (however small) with genuine praise. Motivate them to set and accomplish even bigger goals that boost their self-esteem.

4. Let Them Be a Part of Your Buddy Gang

Jealousy or possessiveness often stems from a deep-seated feeling of insecurity of not being "good enough" or "as good as xyz."

Eliminate these feelings by involving your partner more in activities planned with your friend circle or social group. This will assure him/her about your life in general when you he/she is not with you. Rather than keep them guessing or suspicious, make your social life more open and accessible to them. This will increase transparency and trust within the relationship, and gradually diminish pangs of insecurity.

5. Do Not Lie to Avoid Questions

If you constantly find yourself at the receiving end of endless questions and accusations, you may well be tempted to lie to escape these baseless confrontations. However, this can do more damage than good in the long run. If your partner does discover that you've been lying to him/her, they may be even more convinced that you have something to hide rather than believing that it is his/her actions which have caused you to lie.

Take for instance, there's a co-worker your partner just doesn't like for some reason and you have to collaborate with him/her on an important project, which needs you both to stay up after work. The partner questions you about your extended hours, and you avoid mentioning the co-worker to escape the avalanche of questions that will follow. It seems like too much of a hassle to make them understand. Instead, you simply say you have your bosses from the headquarters located in another country visiting, which requires everyone to stay up late for meetings.

6. Speak About the Elephant in the Room

It helps to talk to a jealous partner frankly, openly and compassionately about his/her feelings. You will better understand their fears, apprehensions and anxieties to pin down the underlying emotions that influence their insecure behavior. Listening to them will help you empathize with their behavior and know exactly why they behave the way they do. Do not simply shrug off their behavior as weird or accuse them of being insane. It will only make them more defensive about their insecure or jealous behavior, adding greater fuel to the fire. When people are allowed to share their feelings in a supportive and positive environment, it leads to better problem resolution.

Insecurity is often triggered by fearful thoughts, which ironically cause the very the thing they dread. Discounting your partner's fears makes them feel more misunderstood and frustrated.

7. Seek Professional Help

Getting yourself out of a persistently possessive relationship can be a challenging proposition. However, do not let the fear of being alone get the better of you. Being alone is better than staying in a toxic and controlling relationship.

Counselors or behavior therapists can help you overcome the damage of being at the receiving end of a jealous or insecure relationship. They can tackle your negative feelings, and help you come to terms with ending a bitter relationship. You may also need the help of a support group if you have suffered physical or mental abuse in the hands of an insecure partner. Damaged emotional health can affect your future relationships and overall personality. Acknowledge the issue and move on, without letting go of your self-respect.

Love yourself and be committed to self-development. Toxic relationships can often strip us off our confidence and self-respect. Devote some time to work on your self-esteem. Spend time with close friends, acquire new interests, upgrade your skills or travel to your favorite destination. The idea is to reconnect with your lost self.

8. You Cannot Play Mr. /Ms. Fixit All the Time

While you can help your partner better cope with their insecurity by showing empathy, understanding and compassion, you cannot really fix it for them. There is only so much you can do about it; however eager you are to help. Let your lover know that though you will support their effort to combat jealousy/insecurity, you will not give in all the time just to avoid ugly fights.

Tell them that your role is only to fill the gap of disconnection, if any, between the two of you. Assure him/her that you can work as a positive team to tackle their insecurity, without taking the entire blame on you. While you will do everything in your capacity to show understanding for their issues, it is only him/her who has to ultimately fix the problem by consciously changing their thoughts and behavior patterns.

9. Admit You Screwed Up and Rebuild Things

It is natural for your partner to feel jealous or insecure if you have betrayed them in the past. You cannot expect them to come out of it overnight, and you may have to pay the price of your betrayal by being more patient, reassuring and answerable until they are at ease. Reassure them, spend more time with them, make them your priority, do the little things they cherish, participate in fun adventures together, take some time out to travel, do romantic dinner dates – anything that makes him/her feel appreciated and wanted again. Though it will not be easy for you, reassurances and sincere actions will go a long way in establishing your loyalty.

10. Give it Some Time

They have not spent enough time with you to realize how different you are from an unscrupulous ex-lover. This may lead them to be more sensitive and suspicious of your actions until they get to know you well and begin to trust you. Do not immediately label them paranoid or over-possessive. Give them sufficient time to get over their feelings and start trusting people again. Be there for them. Spend time hearing them out attentively. Involve them more in your social life. Eventually, they may get over their insecure feelings and trust you completely.

11. Avoid Comparisons

How many times have we been tempted to compare our partner with someone who fits the picture of our ideal mate? Or with an ex-lover? Or a parent? It is easy to fall into the trap of comparisons as a means of expressing exactly what you are looking for in him/her. However, even well-meaning comparisons can be downright hurtful for your partner's ego. He/she may feel inadequate and belittled. It may lead to greater damage by inducing a feeling of insecurity or "not being good enough" in them. Do not ever try to measure their worth by comparing your partner with someone else. Try to highlight their unique characteristics that made you fall in love with them, even when they focus on the negative.

12. Demonstrate Your Love and Belongingness in Public

While jealous and insecure people do this all the time, if you do this for your jealous/insecure partner, it may make them feel more assured and confident about the relationship. Insecure folks have a tendency to be highly territorial in nature. If you show them off when you are in public by holding their hand or kissing them to establish that they are yours, it may do your relationship a world of good. It does not take much to show them how proud you are to have them in your life. Your pride in him/her can go a long way in making your partner feel more secure and less fearful in the relationship.

13. Avoid Succumbing to Unreasonable Demands

Do not make the mistake of isolating yourself from friends without any good reason just because your partner does not like them or is unreasonably suspicious of your association with them. Once you start giving in to their demands, it will only encourage them to wield a greater influence about where you go, what you do and whom you talk to. Do not succumb to this pattern of emotional imprisonment.

Take complete responsibility for your actions rather than denying them. Instead of saying you weren't with your friends just to please your partner, say you weren't doing anything wrong and it's normal to go out with friends. Be assertive without being insensitive. If you think there truly is a basis for your partner's suspicion, try and talk to them about it to clear it rather than escape it. Never feel guilty about having a good time with other friends or co-workers without your partner.

14. Manage Retroactive Jealously Diplomatically

Romantic partners of people suffering from retroactive jealously never have it easy. They are constantly questioned and scrutinized based on their past. They are asked for detailed explanations about past relationships, sexual history and other unproductive elements that have no bearing on the current relationship. There seems to be a heightened obsession with their partner's past relationships. Do you find yourself at the receiving end retroactive jealousy or insecurity? Keep in mind that nothing you do or say can "solve it" for your partner. How many ever details you offer or recount the exact events of your past relationships or even your opinion about how you view them – it may never be enough resolving the issue.

Your partner has to resolve the issue for themselves. You will do whatever it takes to help and support them of course, but they will have to overcome their issues with the necessary corrective measures. Try not to encourage conversation related to your past relationships, former lovers or sexual history. Explain to them firmly how tiresome, monotonous and counter-productive it is to re-live your past. Give your partner the time to get over their feelings.

Chapter 14: Communicate to Your Partner

Communication is a necessity for any healthy connection. We are familiar with the fact that contact allows relationships and, in a relationship, it is doomed to fail without proper communication.

It can be difficult to communicate effectively with your partner. It takes time, effort and attention to understand your partner and be understood by them.

People think the only form of communication within a relationship is verbal communication. However, body language, comprehension, level of trust, all lead to successful inter-partner communication.

There are ups and downs in all relationships, but we can make it easier to deal with conflicts by communicating effectively and coming out of them stronger.

Communication lets us explain what we are experiencing and what our needs and expectations are.

Not only does it help you meet your needs, but it also lets you stay connected in your relationship. Communication also keeps us safe from misunderstandings which ultimately result in hurt, frustration, resentment, confusion and conflict.

Good Communication

Remember the following criteria for good communication:

When you are upset by something and you want to speak to your partner about it, try to find the right time for it. Discuss it when you are calm and not worried with your friend.

When addressing a question, avoid using harsh words, using "I" and "We" rather than "you" because it sounds like you're threatening, and potentially making your partner defensive and less open to you and your message.

Be fair and be frank with your partner. Admit when you are wrong and apologize rather than making excuses.

If your partner is sharing something with you, you have to remember your body language. Give full attention as you interact and make eye contact with them, if your friend is attempting to connect with you, stop using the cell phone or watching TV.

Share it with them if your partner does something that hurts you or makes you upset. If you can't, so instead of holding a grudge, try to forgive it.

Importance of Good Communication in Relationships:

Open communication helps create trust and make a healthy and happier relationship. Healthy communication helps to keep relationships smooth.

When both partners are familiar with each other's thoughts and feelings it is a symbol of the relationship's transparency and independence.

Communication is the best way to understand the person you are interested in and smooth the way a healthy relationship can be established.

There are four different types of contact. Which are:

- Assertive
- Aggressive
- Passive-Aggressive
- Submissive

But the healthiest choice is assertive or open contact among those types of contact.

Throughout this style of communication, there is a feeling of respect, comfort, honesty, trust, true love and positivity for both partners.

Additionally, open communication helps create trust in a partnership that eventually makes room for free communication.

Without good contact between the partners no romantic relationship will develop vigorously. Communication is knowledge exchange and communication between the two.

Working together as partners does not work until knowledge sharing is successful back and forth. Effective listening and communication bind partners and heighten intimacy. That helps to reinforce a relationship's bonding.

Good communication

For successful communication in a relationship, follow-up points should be kept in mind: talk more frequently to your partner and listen closely to the partner as well.

The first step is an attraction at the beginning of the relationship, then there is infatuation, then concern and eventually obligation to each other. To enter this stage of accountability, trust is necessary.

Since building trust, there will be no uncertainty in the relationship.

Communication is one form of loving and caring for one another. There should be two-way contact with one another to communicate the feelings.

Communication is the best way of showing your partner love. Be responsive to your friend and make them happy to share their feelings with you as well.

Open dialog brings associates closer to each other. This also makes expressing everything about life simpler whether it's good or bad.

Efficient support network is a partnership. When two people have a relationship, they rely on one another. It is imperative that a partner feel safe and comfortable. And the impression is supported by good contact.

There are certain standards in relationships and for communicating these with your partner, good communication is important.

Arguments and wars are contact which is negative. Alternatively, matters should be addressed easily by improved communication.

We also have to try and save our relationships from uncertainty, misunderstandings, suspicions, disagreements, distrust and skepticism. And, with true love, improve it and better contact.

Signs of Poor Communication in a Relationship

In every relationship we all understand the value of good communication. Lack of contact or mismanagement has destroyed so many relationships.

Many relationships failed, and the poor communication forced many couples to split up. Healthy contact is important for sustaining a marriage or other romantic relationship.

Communication is not only a topic of debate. Good communication requires versatility, consideration, affection, and selflessness to promote successful relationships.

If you find any of the following signs then in terms of communication you have to pay attention to your relationship: The conversation between you two rarely goes deeper than the surface In the early days of a relationship, partners usually talk a lot about each other to know more about each other. Yet this appears to slow down and fade over time. When you feel this in your relationship you have to fix it. How? How?

If you don't ask each other about the day, asking for this demonstrates interest and also gives you a starting point for a discussion. If none of you bother asking for this, then it is a serious matter that needs to be addressed.

You just want to think more about your agenda and not ready to listen to the other person's question.

One or both of you have more often begun to lose control and get frustrated quite quickly.

Now the majority of the interactions were about nagging.

When you are disturbed by something and you presume and leap to conclusions rather than talking it out. It takes the relationship to a breakup. Your relationship needs serious focus here and a big leap in communication.

Thinking you know your partner well, and constantly responding on the basis of past behavior.

If you both stop the personal hot buttons, it is a sign of unresolved problems, and a lack of mutual confidence.

If you share your dilemma with mates, rather than your partner, if sex is absent and your physical connection with your emotional and mental link is starting to wane.

When you encounter one or more of these in your relationships, these are not all but big indicators that will alert you.

Miscommunication or no communication adversely affects a relationship. To get the relationship working again, communication issues need to be addressed.

Here is a list of ideas that can be applied in a relationship to overcome communication problems: Tell your partner "How are you? "And" "how was that day? "Initiating a positive conversational vibe, it shows your love and care to them too.

Seek to spend more time with each other. Go for lunch or dinner or schedule a vacation somewhere and try to get to know each other's thoughts and points of view on different things. Address the difficult moments and remember each other's happy days.

Never take something on yourself about your partner without knowing the truth. Hypotheses and the reading of mind frequently contribute to misunderstandings and hurt feelings.

When your friend is talking to you listen carefully and with relaxed eye contact. If your partner needs you somewhere, react positively to them.

Don't nitpick; tell them if you have any problem. This will corrode your friendship if you don't.

For your partnership, have a daily partnership check-in and talk about your shared decision and also about your relationship.

Believing in life will change things. Display your optimistic attitude about problems and your relationship during contact.

Speak to your friend about things before they happen, any family-related problem that you expect or any difficult job situation.

Tell thank you every time your partner helps you out in something. Appreciate their little movements or behaviors that they are doing to satisfy you.

If you are upset by something, explain yourself and make your partner understand what you mean and how it affects you. When you have to speak to your partner about something you mean they do not like, choose a convenient time to do so. If your partner is distracted or in a rush or in pain, do not discuss something.

Take the time to make things you enjoy about each other complement one another.

Never let those early flirting days die, and always keep those acts alive to spice them up.

Communication is also thought of as being about large and meaningful discussions. Yet in fact it's all about fixing the little problems that happen in everyday life.

Now if you believe like something in your relationship is lacking then go to your partner and speak up. Share your feelings and discuss whatever you want to communicate, this will make your relationship safe and solid.

Keys to Good Marital Communication

This means that there are five times as many positive experiences between happy spouses (i.e. listening, validating the other person, using soft words, voicing gratitude, encouragement, physical affection, praise, etc.) as there are negative ones (i.e. raising one's voice, making a complaint or voicing one's anger).

Tips for enhancing contact efficiency in your relationship:

Be able to spend time communicating together. The typical pair spends about 20 minutes a week talking to each other. Switch off the devices and make it a point for you to spend 20-30 minutes a day catching up.

Using more statements about "I" and fewer statements about "You." It reduces the spouse's chances of feeling as if they need to protect themselves. For example, "I wish you would more often acknowledge how much work I do at home to take care of you and the kids."

Be precise when troubles arise. Wide generalizations like: "You still do it! "It's not helpful.

Avoid mind reading. It is really frustrating when someone else behaves in a way that they know better than you what you really think.

Constructively express negative emotions. There will be moments when you're feeling bitter, resentful, frustrated or disapproved. Such emotions need to be expressed to bring about progress. BUT - It's important how you articulate these feelings. "I'm so sorry that you're working late tonight again," it's very different from, "Apparently one whit doesn't care about me or the kids. If you did, you wouldn't be working late at night. "Hear without being defensive. All partners must be able to hear each other's grievances without being defensive in order for a marriage to succeed. This is much easier than learning how to properly communicate negative emotions.

The good emotions are shared openly. Many people share negative emotions more easily than positive ones. It is important that you declare your partner for the safety of your family. The positive feelings conveyed to your partner, such as gratitude, affection, reverence, admiration, acceptance and comfort, are like making deposits into your love account. For everyone negative you will have five positive deposits.

Communication in Your Marriage

A marriage is important — but tweaking is also a very easy thing. And don't get stressed if you like you don't interact properly. And the thing that you need to know about communication is that it is the little things that make a big difference. Sure, getting into conflict and battling well is very necessary. Actually, being able to fight in a compassionate manner will save a connection. However, if your everyday communication skills are right on the mark, then those big conversations aren't really that intimidating. Since you know that you have the skills to meet each other, and you do so before any question gets out of hand.

Chapter 15: Make a Reflection and Self-Care

Learning to love yourself fully and deeply might well be the most important part of the healing process.

I know changing your feelings on a deep level is a tall order. The challenge is made harder because we are so often besieged with messages of how "unlovable" we are. We believe we're not enough: that no one could truly love us, especially if they knew who we really are.

Though the above statement can feel like the absolute truth at times, I promise that it's absolute bullshit.

Every one of us is fully deserving of love. You are a human being who is not only allowed to love and be loved but who I believe was made to do just those things.

Grasping this is essential because it helps us to have a better sense of our self-worth. This ultimately leads us to stop needing external reassurance (or to need it a lot less), and it helps us learn to choose the right partners and seek relationships with people who will truly value us.

There are many ways to expand these practices, but I'm going to tell you about what worked for me. Hopefully, these ideas can work for you, too, or provide a jumping-off point to discover what does work for you.

Take Time for Yourself: Self-Care

What does "self-care" even mean? It feels like a recently emerged, poorly defined buzzword. When most of us envision "self-care," we probably think of a glass of wine and a steaming bath. Maybe we think of a day at the spa or something similarly relaxing.

These are excellent ways of caring for yourself, but they are far from the only methods of doing so. If you hate baths, rest assured, you can steer clear of the bubbles.

Self-care can take a variety of forms:

- Taking a walk-in nature
- Reading
- Painting your nails
- Watching a comforting TV show
- Singing
- Creating art
- Cooking
- Resting
- Getting a massage

Self-care, to me, simply boils down to taking time for yourself.

Because only when we are truly alone can we dig deep to discover what's really going on inside us, spending time alone lets us get to know ourselves and connect with our innermost nature. Not only is it emotionally and spiritually effective, but it invites us to learn to love ourselves. We learn to delight in our own company.

The Importance of Stillness

We need stillness: the chance to focus on our own thoughts, feelings, sensations, and desires. There's a lot to be said for being still and "sitting with our thoughts."

Stillness. Yikes. Personally, it's something I struggle with a lot, and I'm continually working on embracing it. For me, sitting still is a fight. I feel restless and agitated, and trying to relax seems to have the opposite effect. Nonetheless, I'm actively trying to incorporate more stillness in my life all the time. Learning to practice stillness will be an important step in our journey toward healing from reassurance-seeking.

We can think of self-care as falling into two kinds. The first kind is the more enjoyable one: self-care that emphasizes relaxation and leisure time. The second is the true "turning inward" that I'm talking about. It is often less enjoyable, but it's still necessary.

The two types of self-care can actually co-exist, occurring at the same time and during the same activity. But to practice the second type, you must allow time and space for inward reflection.

It's so easy to block out our thoughts. For many of us, it is quite scary to be alone with them. I get that. Often, the last thing we anxious people feel like doing is focusing on our thoughts, giving them more room in our lives. They are numerous, and they are constantly swirling around, tormenting us, surfacing forcefully and suddenly.

You're likely all too familiar with racing thoughts and constant worries. They're always there, and for reassurance-seekers, they are especially present. They can be loud and invasive. The idea of sitting with your thoughts might seem overwhelming.

At first, it probably will be. Yet, paying attention to our thoughts is how we learn to quiet them.

Instead of hiding from our intrusive (perhaps even obsessive) thoughts, we're going to learn to examine them, to question them, to turn them over in our minds, and to look deeper at what they're trying to tell us.

How does one practice be still?

The most obvious and familiar method is meditation. Meditation is a great tool as it helps you stay grounded and lets you examine what's going on inside you. The goal is clarity and peace. When your mind is clear, there's less room for the scary thoughts to come swirling around, and if they do, you can handle them far better.

Meditation can be simple and straightforward. It can be brief, especially when you're just starting out. Why not shoot for 5 minutes per day? Meditation also doesn't have to involve chanting mantras or anything fancy. In fact, the core of meditation is just sitting still and allowing your body and mind to relax.

I want to emphasize that the goal of meditation is not to clear your head of thoughts completely but rather to let them come and go. I encourage you to keep practicing, and don't get frustrated if you keep getting distracted. Learning to meditate successfully is a journey that requires a lot of practice. There are many great meditation apps that can help you, too.

An addition to traditional meditation, practicing stillness can also take the form of prayer or going for a walk-in nature. The important thing is to allow your mind to be calm, quiet, and open. This is when the real work can begin.

Journal Effectively

Journaling can be a wonderful healing tool, and it's so simple. You may wish to journal while in a meditative state or after embracing stillness, but you can also journal in the midst of high anxiety. There is tremendous value in both approaches.

Journaling was immensely helpful to me on my journey away from constant reassurance-seeking. You may have already picked up on this given how many journal excerpts.

I found journaling to be an all-in-one aid for my anxiety. It can take many forms, which is part of why it's a great tool. You can adapt it to your own purposes and style. Whether you prefer making lists, jotting down bullet points, or writing a stream-of-consciousness record of your thoughts, all approaches are valid. Research has shown time and again that there is really power in writing things down.

Journaling gives us a way to release our thoughts, feelings, and worries. We all need outlets to discharge our anxious energy and let our thoughts flow. Often, letting the thoughts emerge onto paper helps us see them for what they really are: irrational and fueled by anxiety. It's funny how writing things down can help you see the truth of what's going on.

This was very effective for me because it helped me become my own reassure. Instead of looking to Nathan for answers, I provided them for myself as best I could, and this was really important for me. It allowed me to slowly build trust in myself and reduce my need for external assurance.

Grant Yourself Grace

Here's another important part of your healing process: give yourself grace.

The journey we are on is not easy. If it was, it wouldn't require so much from us. But take heart: when things are tough, that often means we are dealing with the things that are most worthwhile.

Have patience with yourself during this time. (And at other times too!) Remind yourself that this is a journey, which means you will make progress and you will also regress. That is okay. The road is choppy at times, and often, things get--or seem--worse before they get better.

When you stumble, don't beat yourself up. If you find yourself reverting to old patterns of anxious thinking and reassurance-seeking, know that this is normal. You're working to alter patterns that may have been established in you over years and years. Give yourself the grace you need. Be patient with yourself as you would a close friend.

And give it time. Don't rush. This stuff is hard. You don't need to be "cured" just yet. You are on the path, and that is the most important thing.

Allow Yourself to Be Loved

For some of us, this will be one of the most difficult parts of the healing process.

For many, relationship insecurity stems from deeply held beliefs about one's own lovability. Are some of your fears based on a disbelief in your worthiness or ability to be loved? If so, it's no wonder that you seek reassurance. You don't have a firm understanding of your own lovability, so of course you're going to feel anxiety surrounding that. Welcome to my life!

It is very, very hard, but we each need to work on opening ourselves up to love by knowing we deserve it. We all deserve love. Again, try viewing yourself as you would a close friend or even a best friend. Would you tell her she wasn't worthy of being loved? Would you let her tell you that she didn't deserve love in her life? Absolutely not! Don't allow yourself to believe those lies, either.

You may be thinking:

But you don't understand. I'm different. There's something wrong with me. I am unlovable because...

Nope. I won't hear it. There is no human who is unlovable. And you, sweet soul, are most definitely worthy and deserving of deep and abiding love.

So, keep reading--and keep practicing!

Did You Know You Were Made for Love?

You may not believe this. You may have a more scientific view of humanity, and that's okay. But I challenge you to take a moment and simply try to see yourself (and the world) from another point of view.

Humans are made to love one another and to love ourselves.

We are amazing, complex, varied creatures. With our abilities to reason, to empathize, to plan, to create, to build, and to dream, I think there is surely something deeper going on here--a deeper purpose than simply to survive as a species.

I think that purpose is to love. Not just romantic love, but all types of love.

While this may be a difficult idea to swallow, isn't it a lovely way of looking at things? Love is natural to us and integral in our lives because it's what we were made for.

If that doesn't point to our own innate lovability, I don't know what does. We all have the capacity within us to love, and to love unreservedly. We also have the ability to accept and welcome love with warmth and appreciation.

Consider meditating on this idea as you go about your day today. It just might begin to revolutionize the way you view yourself and the world.

Opening Up to Love from Others

If love is such an integral part of the human experience, why is it so damn hard? Well, anything worth having is worth fighting for, yes? Some of the best parts of living often wait at the end of a journey.

One of the toughest parts of love is not the loving itself but opening up and allowing us to be loved. As we recognize ourselves as worthy of love, it gradually becomes easier to embrace the love coming our way.

But in the meantime, we continually put up barriers that block us from love. Reassurance-seeking can be one of these blocks, believe it or not. Though it might seem like the opposite is happening--that we are desperately looking for confirmation that we are loved and worthy of love--oftentimes, reassurance-seeking is a form of self-sabotage.

Chapter 16: Creating and Maintaining Relationship

Creating and maintaining relationships comes easy for partners that have a good relationship with each other.

When partners genuinely enjoy being in the same space, conversing, communing with each other and coexisting with each other, their relationship becomes effortless and smooth.

This also gives them a better understanding of each other's behavioral traits and quirks which helps them in predicting each other's behaviors, helps them to understand why one's partner behaves a certain way and guide them in acting accordingly.

Relationships with partners that are existing on the same wavelength and in total sync with each other are more likely to be long lasting and successful than relationships with partners that do not have a strong sense of relation between them.

Being in sync with one's partner aids effective communications as partners who are in sync with each other are able to understand both spoken and unspoken messages being passed across through body language.

When partners do not relate with other people properly, it is easy for partners to be oblivious to each other's sufferings and problems if they are not verbally shared.

This could cause an individual to feel lonely even in the relationship and become emotionally distant from his/her partner.

In order for partners to build emotional intimacy and reconnect their relationship, partners need to examine their level of relation with each other and ask questions and have intimate enlightening conversations on how to deepen their relationship with each other.

How Do We Relate With Each Other?

With the aim of building emotional intimacy and reconnecting relationship, partners have to find a means of relating better with each other. In order to partners to build intimacy there is a need for a sense of closeness and interdependence between them which can only be built when partners relate on a deeper level together.

To reach this level, partners need to ask questions about what drives them, where they feel the most safety, their history and experiences, and other factors that makes him/her uniquely different from every other existing human being.

Every human has different vibes to them, different ways to get comfortable.

Some feel much relaxed and open only when they are outdoors and one with mother nature's gifts.

Some people feel more of themselves when they listen to music and/or other forms of art.

It's just a matter of finding the 'it' for them.

You may find that they talk about that specific thing a lot, they like to be around it a lot, or it brings certain level of peace, enthusiasm whenever they are around it.

Creating better relations with one's partner is a two-way street; both partners have to be willing to deepen the level of connection and communication between them to enhance a deeper level of intimacy and emotional connection between them.

Notwithstanding, there are certain gestures that goes a long way in getting your partner to relate and connect better.

Using Positive and Motivation Words during Conversations

When we use positive words on our partners and ultimately those around us, it tends to bring out their best sides, it makes them feel progressive and valuable.

This can go a long way in ensuring a stable relationship.

Even when faced with challenges from workplace, societal pressure, it is really important that they believe there's someone who would always believe in them despite.

- **Endearing nicknames /pet names**

Adults have found this to be very effective.

Using nicknames for yourselves can help bring out the 'child-like' instincts in all of us.

It makes them feel young again, playful, attractive, less tensed and special.

- **Having shared memories and experiences**

This involves planning and actually doing things together, going on vacations, planning special treats and dates for just you both, doing silly but less dangerous pranks on each other, video blogs, e.t.c. owning something together gets the bonding hormones flowing.

- **Respecting individuals' point of view and opinions**

Whenever arguments arise, be it serious or not, it's always important to try to understand their side of the story.

Trying to prove difficult will only give the impression that you are more apart and will hardly find a common ground.

This is really discouraging for any relationship even if the love started out strong.

Ordinary arguments and disagreements can build up over time.

- **Thoughtful gestures like giving surprising and unnecessary gifts**

The act of gift giving has been the most effective way of showing your loved ones that they matter and that they are special.

It is really important not to underestimate the simple gesture of giving, more so, if it's a thoughtful gift, something they have always dreamt of having, something they love and even surprising those with newer packages can be a way of opening their hearts.

How Do You Keep Connected and In Sync With Each Other?

All relationships require efforts, commitment, and patience to stay alive and work.

It is easy to drift apart and lose the emotional connection between them when partners get too comfortable with each other and stop trying to keep the emotional connection intact.

In order for partners to stay emotional connection even when they are physically apart, there need to be a level of trust and emotional security between partners that allows them to rest easy even when they are thousands of miles away from each other.

When partners have complete sense of closeness, belonging and togetherness, it helps them feel secure in their emotional connection with each other, because then they know that no matter what happens, his/her is on the same team with them.

Different partners have different relationship dynamics. Ie; what works for Mr. A in his relationship might not work for Mr. B in his own relationship.

This is a result of individual and behavioral differences.

Thus, different individuals in different relationships have different ways of staying in sync with his/her partner, based on their behaviors/personalities and the type of relationship they have.

Partners can be informed on how best to stay on sync with each other through asking questions and initiating intimate conversations. However, there are general universal tips that can be used to maintain sync between partners.

Here are some useful tips.

- **Spend quality time with your partner**

Planning and spending some time alone with your partner on a regular basis will help you both stay connected and feel special because quite often, as time goes, by we get entangled by work, raising a family and social duties and so we forget that it's important to keep the spark alive. You need yourselves of all the fun things you both did before all the extracurricular activities came into play.

Sitting face to face and in close proximity to your partner on a regular basis can help bring solace.

• **Keep physical intimacy alive**

Touch comes with a power of affection, closure, trust, sensitivity. Frequent sex, touching, kissing, hugging, holding of hands can be a very effective way of staying connected to your partner.

• **Stay communicated**

Whether short or long distance relationships, all requires adequate communications because communication makes your partner important, it keeps them updated on what you going through at every point in time and it's very difficult to get back on track once the bridge in communication is broken and left unattended to.

This is the most vital part of every relationship.

Make it a habit of telling your partner what you are going through and not making them guess.

• **Give and take**

Relationship is a give and take business.

When you recognize what's important to your partner, it brings wholeness to him/her, it shows a measure of goodwill, thoughtfulness and a sense of devotion.

On the other hand, it is also important for your partner to recognize your wants and for you to state them clearly.

Constantly giving to others at the expense of your own needs will only build resentment and anger

How Deep Is Our Emotional Connection?

In romantic relationships, the level of emotional depth and dependency between both partners determines the strength of that relationship. Communicating with your partner does not guarantee that you do understand what he/she is going through and often, partners may feel like their significant other listens out of sense of duty, not because they genuinely care or feel the way they do which could lead to him/her feeling small and insignificant.

Emotional depth is being able to listen, interpret, and sensitively respond to feelings that arises in your partner, others around you and ultimately yourself.

This is ability to show empathy, to 'feel into' someone else's experiences to know what it feels like to be them.

That level of interdependency gives both partners a sense of reliability, true friendship and a deep intimate connection that is built over time. This, as well as empathy takes time to become insoluble, because there are significant factors that affects the level of transparency and vulnerability needed between partners to achieve desired emotional depth and intimacy.

We often want our partner to be able to talk to us about everything and also to be the first person they think of sharing their emotions with whenever they going through something be it Positive or Negative but we also have to understand that no human being was ready made as certain factors such as early/childhood environmental factors, prominent life changing experience and events, gender and gender roles as dictated by society, and an individual's background and culture can affect and influence an individual's perception and personality which in turn dictates the individual's ability to understand, empathize and form emotional connections with his/her partner.

- **Early/Childhood environmental factors**

Undoubtedly, this forms the base of any character, personality and behavioral traits of all creatures.

During formative years, specific behavioral traits are instilled in individuals depending on the kind of family (on a smaller scale) and society (on a larger scale) an individual is born into.

Families and society at large go on to shape an individual's perception of love and affection amongst many other things.

Individuals while growing up, adopt their families and society stipulated method of showing love and affection.

Therefore, if your partner grew up in an emotionally responsive environment, where feelings are being shared/opened up, ideas are welcomed, personal identities are recognized and welcomed, and chances that you will struggle with emotional connections with your partner are quite low.

However, if their childhood memories were ones filled with condemnations whenever emotions were expressed, traumas, and personal opinions weren't welcomed, felt invincible by those around them, to survive, they tend to generate a responsive character to against such phenomena.

These are often putting up firewalls against everyone in their adult years, self-reliance, hardly feeling the need to need anyone else but themselves, anger, because they grew up fighting to be heard.

It takes a lot to bring all these to awareness, to get them to recognize these behavioral and personality traits and ultimately overcome them.

- **Prominent life changing events and experiences**

It has been said that every individual is a sum of his/her experiences.

Our experiences contribute to our self-identity, perception of the world, our values, views, thoughts, fears, expectations, etc.

However, some experiences and events stand out more than others because of the effect and influence they have on an individual's identity, behavior/personality and his/her life in general.

These experiences are known as defining moments and they are often not recognized when in motion, only after the moments are passed are the impacts of such experiences realized.

An individual's defining experiences can strongly influences his/her ability to form and maintain emotional connections with relationship partners and other members of society.

- **Gender and gender specific roles**

The laws of society dictate that women are nature's caretakers.

They often extend their emotional tables as that's their primal designs. This can cause an upside as they can sometimes not be taken seriously. They appear weak and vulnerable and opportunists can take that and devalue it.

Chapter 17: Reminding Yourself of Your Positive Traits

No matter how much your jealousy and insecurity has led to crazy behavior on your part, or maybe you have pushed your partner into a corner and are deeply ashamed of yourself, there is always going to be something redeeming about you. That is what probably keeps your partner hanging on to your relationship. There is no person who is all bad, everyone has some positive traits that they can expand on to improve their relationship.

What Is Self-Esteem?
Self-esteem stems from an early age where we barely even know our own names. It comes from the need for socialization, attention, love, safety, and belonging from our primary caregivers. When we're denied some of those needs, we develop problems with our self-esteem. Research has proven that even babies are aware of what is happening around them, and they begin to develop ideas and behavior from birth. In fact, self-esteem begins to develop when you are a child, when you have no control of what is happening to you.

In reality, a friend may have rejected you because of their own personal flaws and it had nothing to do with you, but you may not have had the right communication tools to really get to the root of the problem, so you made an assumption. Or they could have been going through their own transition in life and found that you no longer fit into their plans. However, you may have turned to some internal problem you think you may have had, which this choice could stick with you for the rest of your life, especially if you don't figure it out and eradicate those thoughts.

You may notice that some people have been in similar situations and they do not have low self-esteem. So why is that? Well, there's such a thing called a shaming environment. It is where an individual who acts out believes they're not just behaving in a poor manner, but that they are actually a bad person. As an example, a child is sneaking cookies from the cookie jar and their parents continuously tell them they are bad rather than telling them their actions are bad. In that case, that child believes they are truly rotten to the core. Therefore, when they behave badly, they justify their behavior by telling themselves that they are bad anyway, so there is no need for them to change.

If you were that child, and you grew up into an adult with these beliefs, then they will touch different aspects of your relationship. You are more likely to believe that you are bad when you make a mistake, rather than understand that you are not bad but that your behavior is wrong. These mistaken beliefs can lead to you treating your partner poorly because you feel continuous guilt for your behavior. To make up for the guilt, you may try too hard within your relationship, making your partner uncomfortable, while making yourself look desperate and confused. A strong relationship is not filled with a lack of trust or an overabundance of jealousy and anxiety. In order to develop a strong relationship, you must first address those issues. The same thing holds true for a fulfilling relationship, if you want one it cannot be based on guilt.

Children that grow up in that kind of environment tend to believe that the bad things that happen to them in life are deserved; that the good things are just flukes. If this mindset has become a reality, then it would be difficult to truly appreciate positivity in the relationship. One may always believe that their partner has an ulterior motive when they are being kind and building the relationship. So, because they have guilt within them, they project mistrust on to their partners. They have internalized a negative event or string of negative events and it sticks with them. Others are able to see past this and the negative event rolls off their backs like water off a duck's feathers. When you can remind yourself of all your positive traits, you will be in a position to do the same thing.

As an adult, you can look at what happened to you as a child and realize that you were not responsible for your actions. You often did not know any better and were simply reacting to what you had been taught. If a child is able to believe that they are actually a good person that sometimes simply makes mistakes, then they're able to accept their flaws and try to make themselves a better person. People with low self-esteem have a distorted view of themselves and their actions. It is imperative to remember this when you are feeling jealous, anxious, or afraid. You have the control to improve the situation and as a result improve your relationship.

There are some steps that will help you eradicate that poor self-image. They are as follows:

- Make a list of the positives about yourself and focus on those. You'll find that there are many more positives about who you are than there are negatives. As building your self-esteem takes time, you should try and add at least two items to this list on a daily basis.

- Surround yourself with people who are uplifting and positive about whom you are as well as understanding about what you have gone through. This means that they need to have a certain degree of empathy and should not be judgmental. If you're constantly around negative people who take pleasure in pointing out your flaws, you will fail to see the positive in yourself and the world.

- Do some charity work; if you are constantly helping out others or animals by putting their needs above your own, you will find it harder and harder to feel bad about who you are; It is tough to feel guilty about spending time making someone else's life better.

- Try meditation; sometimes reaching into that inner core and looking at yourself for who you are in a relaxing manner will help you understand that you are generally a good person. Meditation will reduce stress and make you feel less wound up when you are around your partner. When you are more relaxed, you can bring positivity into your circumstances much more easily.

- Try exercising to relieve the tension in your everyday life. It will boost the hormones in your body that make you feel good, and this will help you feel better about yourself. In addition to the hormones, exercising will also help build your self-confidence as your body looks and feels better with time.

- Seek out psychological help. If you feel that you're unable to do this on your own, there is no shame in seeking out help from a professional. Therapists and psychologists are well-equipped when it comes to dealing with self-esteem and jealousy issues. You can do it alone or you could bring in your partner for couples counseling so that you can better explain how you are feeling to them.

Adopting a Positive Attitude

The exercises we just mentioned are designed to help you be proactive in building up your self-esteem; they are things that can actually be accomplished each day. While these things can help boost your self-esteem, they are not the only thing that matters. If you really want to see a drastic improvement in your self-esteem you are going to need to work on your attitude. Only you have control over your attitude and your attitude is going to affect every aspect of your life, so you may as well adopt a positive one.

Turning your attitude from a negative one into a positive one is going to take some work. It is not something that is going to happen overnight, but you can start working on it as soon as possible. When changing your attitude, you are going to need to work on how you react to the entire world around you, not just your current relationship.

If you are feeling a bit unsure, which is entirely natural, here are some things that you can do to begin the process today.

- Be aware of the progress that you have already made in your life and the progress that you continue to make each day. Acknowledge yourself; basically, pat yourself on the back, for everything that you have accomplished. For what you haven't accomplished, don't worry or stress over it, you need to simply accept the fact that you haven't mastered it yet and then keep trying.

- Understand that there are going to be plenty of things in life that you can't control, learn what they are, as well as the things in life that you can control. By accepting the fact that you can't control everything you will save yourself from making repeated failed attempts at making the change. And the sooner you quit failing, the sooner you will begin to see an improvement in your attitude.

- Learn what you can from the mistakes that you make. Making mistakes is not always a bad thing, especially when you can learn something from the mistakes that you have made. Constantly dwelling on the mistakes that you have made causes you to live in the past and reinforces those negative feelings. To adopt a positive frame of mind you need to look past the mistakes and focus on improving your life and your relationship.

Boosting Self-Confidence

The more confident you feel about yourself, the less likely you are to be insecure in your current relationship. Many people assume self-confidence and self-esteem are the same thing, they even use the terms interchangeably. They are not the same thing, they are two totally different things, they just happen to be related to each other.

Self-confidence is how much you believe in yourself; how you believe that you can set goals and reach them. When you go about boosting your self-confidence you are enabling yourself to take better care of yourself, but you are also teaching yourself how to be happy and accept yourself for who you truly are. Boosting your self-confidence is vital if you are trying to improve your self-esteem because increased self-confidence provides a solid foundation for improving self-esteem.

Now self-confidence directly affects jealousy because of how you think of yourself. The lower your opinion of yourself, the more likely you are to be jealous of your partner. To ensure you have a healthy relationship, you are going to need to work on boosting your self-confidence. Luckily, there are a few simple, but yet effective exercises you can start doing today.

Smile

This might seem a bit odd, but simply smiling more is a quick and effective way to increase your self-confidence. If you think about when you greet people with a smile, they are more likely to greet you with one back. And, the more people who smile at you, the better you feel about yourself. Plus, the more people you are smiling at, the more people you are helping give a self-confidence boost to.

Dress

How you dress honestly affects how you think about yourself. This might be hard to imagine but take a minute to think about how you feel when wearing certain clothes. When you dress up and look nice, you tend to feel better about yourself. If you are laying around in frumpy clothes, like sweatpants and a holy shirt, you are not usually feeling your best. Everybody feels there best when they feel good about how they look, so pay attention to how you are dressing to ensure you always feel your best.

Mind

Many people underestimate just how powerful the mind is, but mind over matter is a very real thing. When you see or feel yourself thinking negative thoughts, you need to start redirecting your thoughts. When redirecting the thoughts, substitute the negative thoughts for positive ones. You will see immediate improvement about how you are feeling about yourself.

Chapter 18: The Role of Attachment in Relationships with Anxious Individuals

Attachment theory is a model in psychological that seeks to understand how humans form bonds with other humans as a model for their relationships that they will have throughout their lives. Although attachment theory does have its antecedents in the psychoanalytical theories of the 19th century, it is essentially a theory that took shape in the 20th century primarily as the result of observations that were made of infants and toddlers and the relationships that they had with adults.

Attachment theory is primarily a model that focuses on the interpersonal relationships that infants and toddlers form. These attachments are important because they set the stage for how the toddler (and future adult) interacts with others and perceives their environment. It was observed relatively early in the 20tjh century that young children who were deprived of attachment during formative years of their lives seemed to have difficulty interacting with others and forming relationships on in life.

It should be remembered that attachment theory, along with other psychoanalytic and behavioral theories, took shape at a time when the world (particularly the Western world) was rife with various dramatic social changes. Men and women were moving from rural areas into cities; people of all ages were working in factories or other establishments in urban areas, war was common in some areas which left many communities devastated. In short, the fabric of society was changing in ways that were apparent and which could be conveniently observed by anyone who was paying attention.

The purpose of this is to help the reader understand the role that anxiousness can play in a relationship by teaching them about attachment. It has been argued that some anxious individuals behave as if they have suffered trauma. Certainly, some individuals with anxiety disorders may have suffered real trauma and this may have contributed to their condition, but even in cases where individuals have experienced no known trauma there may be the equivalent of trauma in the form of an insecure attachment that they had with their parent long before they were old enough to remember such interactions.

This knowledge of attachment will help the spouse or partner of an anxious person navigate their relationship. They will be able to do this by understanding how they are perceived by their partner in ways that someone unfamiliar with attachment theory will not understand. As in other areas of discussion pertaining to worry in relationships, the goal here is to aid the reader in feeling compassion for their partner, but also to give them real skills that they can use.

Attachment theory is essentially a model that focuses on the relationships that infants and toddlers have with the important adults in their lives, but the theory has been expounded upon to make deductions about adult relationships. This theory is usually referred to as attachment theory for adults. This focuses on how the relationships of childhood and infancy dictate relationships that are had on, essentially forming a type of trauma that is played out in the relationships that anxious people have throughout their lives.

Types of Attachment

One of the earliest individuals to explore the idea of attachment as it is understood today was John Bowlby writing in the mid-20th century. It had been observed earlier in the century that children that were deprived of time with or affection from their mother's experienced problem that seemed to be clearly linked to these deprivations. Bowlby was also influenced by other psychologists and behavioral biologists like Konrad Lorenz who were forming general theories about how animals form attachments.

For those of you unfamiliar with Konrad Lorenz, he was a biologist who explored various aspects of animal behavior. In particular, Lorenz was famous for his studies on imprinting in which he showed that a flock of ducks can be taught to see a human being as their parent and to follow them if they are exposed to this human being at an important formative moment. Lorenz's work was so important that he received a Nobel Prize for it 1973. His work still forms the basis for how animal behavior is understood and researched today.

In terms of attachment theory, the important idea is that young humans form attachment with older adults (usually a parent, called a primary caregiver) in order to enhance their chances of survival and as a model for the relationships that they will have on. As most readers can probably gather, human beings are pretty much useless in the early years of their life: require care and protection from their caregivers. Infant attachment is, therefore, a behavior that evolved to enhance the survival of the human species. By seeking attachment from a caregiver, an infant engages in a bond that is beneficial both to the individual and to the species.

It is easy to focus on attachment solely in infants and take for granted the role that attachment plays in life. Individuals that are insecurely attached to their primary caregivers (which will be explained) will tend to approach their interactions with other individuals from the standpoint of fear and danger. It is interesting to explore the idea that anxiousness on a societal level may be on the rise because of a society-wide problem with attachment during this formative period though this is an idea that has not been actively researched. Studies in the field tend to focus exclusively on the implications of childhood attachment in children and the implications of adulthood attachment in adults.

What is important to understand as a precursor to a study of attachment is what attachment is and how it works. Before Bowlby, many psychologists believed that the behavior of infants and toddlers (essentially children under the age of two in this context) was a result of a complex fantasy world that existed in the minds of children and from which adults were cut off. This fantasy idea has basically been replaced by the attachment model, which recognizes the role that adults play in interacting with children and setting the pattern for behaviors that children see as normal.

Of course, today, this type of thinking may seem obvious to people, but it was not always the case. Psychoanalytic theory perhaps went off the deep end a little bit in the 19th and early 20th centuries as it explored some of the more garish aspects of human personality and attributed to people all sorts of subconscious desires and motivations. Attachment theory essentially goes back to the basics when compared to psychoanalytic theories. Our behaviors as adults and our expectations regarding what is normal and what is not date back to the sort of things that we see when we are children.

Therefore, children who see dysfunction relationships between their parents in their formative years may grow up thinking that it is normal for people to interact this way. This even extends to cases of abuse, where one individual may believe that it is normal to be the target of abuse or to perpetrate abuse on another person. This type of thinking is relatively simplistic compared to attachment theory, but it gives the reader a general idea of how patterns that we are exposed to in our formative years set the stage for our behaviors and expectations as adults.

Anxiousness in adults can, therefore, potentially result from defective forms of attachment that occur in the childhood years. Attachment here is essentially the bond(s) that infants form with the adults around them in the period of about 10 months to 18 months. Although infants may seek attachment from their caregivers prior to this, this is the age range that allows psychologists to assess attachment by placing infants in this age range in certain situations, usually called strange situations.

Research in the area has allowed psychologists to identify four major types of attachment. The goal here is not for the reader to develop an in-depth understanding of the different types of attachment but merely to get an idea of how these forms of attachment play out in the behaviors of adults with anxiousness or other conditions. The four types of attachment described by psychologists include:

- Secure attachment
- Anxious-avoidant attachment
- Disorganized attachment

Secure attachment is the prototypical form of attachment that occurs in infants when everything goes right. Attachment is something that develops in infants, but it results from normal, healthy interactions with their primary caregiver. In the case of secure attachment, children have experienced their emotional and physical needs being met by their caregiver, they have experienced affection from their caregiver, and these two things together allow the infant to feel safe and secure in their environment. The safety that a securely attached child feels allows them to safely explore their environment and will eventually lead to their ability to form healthy relationships with others as an adult.

Anxious-ambivalent attachment occurs when an infant feels excessive worry their caregiver and does not feel reassured when the caregiver returns. In short, the relationship with the caregiver is disturbed in such a way that the infant regards their environment with a degree of fear or uncertainty that a securely attached infant would not typically experience.

Anxious-avoidant attachment and disorganized attachment are two additional forms of attachment that result from problems with how the caregiver interacts with the infant. In anxious-avoidant attachment, the child avoids contact with the caregiver, while in disorganized attachment, the child appears to have no attachment bond with their caregiver at all.

Attachment Problems in Anxious Adults

Several theories have been postulated as to why anxiety seems to have high prevalence in the Western world, including countries like the United States where GAD, specific phobias, and other anxious disorders are common. It was suggested in the individuals in the Western world may be exposed to trauma in the form of information from the news media or social media. It was also suggested that new forms of communication may be heightening and exaggerating a preexisting anxiousness that may exist because of other social factors.

The purpose of this is not to further explore this ideology, but to give the reader a concrete sense of where anxiety may be coming from and how they can manage it. In other words, it may help you to think of the anxious person in your life as experiencing one of the dysfunctional forms of child attachment. The idea here is not for you to perceive your significant other as a child (which they are not), but to gain an understanding of how they perceive their world and where that perception comes from.

Again, it may help to perceive the anxious person as traumatized in some way. The anxious-ambivalent child may become upset when their caregiver departs because they are accustomed to their caregiver not allaying their fears or not minimizing the sense of danger that they perceive in their environment. A child in this category will become upset because they perceive their environment as filled with danger and they want someone to handle the danger that they perceive.

An anxious-avoidant child may avoid their caregiver because they perceive a problem with their caregiver. They may have received mixed signals from their caregiver, which has caused them to distance themselves from them. Perhaps the caregiver displayed anger when they should have displayed compassion or joy. Perhaps the caregiver is perceived as dangerous by the child for whatever reason. This will cause the child to be anxious but essentially to show avoidant behaviors.

Someone with exposure to anxious individuals may start to see some of the similarities here. An anxious person may become upset when their significant others leave and may show jealousy and anger when they return. An anxious person may avoid interacting with their significant other, or they may appear not to care when their significant other goes.

Chapter 19: Benefits of Guided Meditation

You are most likely here right now because you have heard amazing, life-changing aspects meditation can bring to your life. Whether you are looking to improve your mental health, performance, physical health, or better your relationship with yourself or others; meditation could be the perfect practice for you.

Mental Health Benefits

Unfortunately, there are many individuals who suffer from mental health issues. Whether you are dealing with anxiety, depression, or something along those lines; meditation can help place you in a better mindset when practiced on a regular basis.

Decrease Depression

In a study done in Belgium, four-hundred students were placed in an in-class mindfulness program to see if it could reduce their stress, anxiety, and depression. It was found that six months, the students who practiced were less likely to develop depression-like symptoms. It was found that mindfulness meditation could potentially be just as effective as an antidepressant drug!

In another study, women who were going through a high-risk pregnancy were asked to participate in a mindfulness yoga exercise for ten weeks. After the time passed, it was found there was a significant reduction in the symptoms often caused by depression. On top of the benefit of less depression, the mothers also showed signs of having a more intense bond with their child while it was still in the womb.

Reduce Anxiety and Depression

In general, meditation may be best known for the mental health benefits of reducing the symptoms associated with anxiety and depression. It was found that through meditation, individuals who practiced meditation such as Vipassana or "Open Monitoring Meditation," were able to reduce the grey-matter density in their brains. This grey-matter is related to stress and anxiety. When individuals practice meditation, it helps create an environment where they can live moment to moment rather than getting stuck in one situation.

While practicing meditation, the positive mindset may be able to help regulate anxiety and mood disorders that are associated with panic disorders. There was one article published in the American

Journal of Psychiatry based around twenty-two different patients who had panic or anxiety disorders. After three months of relaxation and meditation, twenty of the twenty-two were able to reduce the effects of their panic and anxiety.

Performance Benefits

When you are able to relax, you would be amazed at how much better your brain will be able to function. By letting go of stress, you leave room for positive thoughts in your head and will be able to make better decisions for yourself. It's a win-win situation when you can improve your mood and your performance simply from meditation.

Better Decision Making

A study done at UCLA found that for individuals who practiced meditation for a long time, had a larger amount of reification in the brain. This is the "folding" along the cortex, which is directly related to processing information faster. Compared to individuals who do not practice meditation, it was found that meditators were able to form memories easier, make quicker decisions, and could process information at a higher rate overall.

Improve Focus and Attention

Another study performed at the University of California suggested that through meditation, subjects are able to increase their focus on tasks, especially ones that are boring and repetitive. It was found that even after only twenty minutes of meditation practice, individuals are able to increase their cognitive skills ten times better compared to those who do not practice mindfulness.

Along the same lines, it's believed that meditation may be able to help manage those who have ADHD, or attention deficit hyperactivity disorder. There was a study performed on fifty adults who had ADHD. The group was placed through mindfulness-based cognitive therapy to see how it would affect their ADHD. In the end, it was found that these individuals were able to act with awareness while reducing both their impulsivity and hyperactivity. Overall, they were able to improve their inattention.

Relieve Pain

It has been said that it's possible that meditation could potentially relieve pain better when compared to morphine. This may be possible due to the fact that pain is subjective. There was a study done on thirteen Zen masters compared to thirteen non-practitioners. These individuals were exposed to painful heat whilst having their brain activity watched. The Zen masters reported less pain, and the neurological output reported less pain as well. This goes to show that pain truly is a mental aspect.

Along the same lines, mindfulness training could also help patients who have been diagnosed with Fibromyalgia. In one study, there were eleven patients who went through eight weeks of training for mindfulness. At the end of the study, the overall health of these individuals improved and reported more good days than bad.

Avoid Multitasking Too Often

While multitasking can seem like a good skill to have at some points, it's also an excellent way to become overwhelmed and stressed out. Unfortunately, multitasking can be very dangerous to your productivity. When you ask your brain to switch gears between activities, this often can produce distractions from your work being done. A study was performed on students at the University of Arizona and the University of Washington. These people were placed through eight weeks of mindfulness meditation. During this time, the students had to perform a stressful test demonstrating multitasking before and after the training. It was shown that those who practiced meditation were able to increase their memory and lower their stress while multitasking.

Physical Benefits

While mental improvements are fantastic benefits of meditation, physical benefits can help motivate individuals to begin meditation as well. Unfortunately, the standard of health is to turn to medication. If you are an individual who hates popping pills for every issue you have; meditation may be just what you need to help improve your health.

Reduce Risk of Stroke and Heart Disease

It has been found that heart disease is one of the top killers in the world compared to other illnesses. Through meditation, it's possible you could lower your risk of both heart disease and stroke. There was a study done in 2012 for a group of two hundred high-risk people. These individuals were asked to take a class on health, exercise, or take a class on meditation. Over the five years, it was found that the individuals who chose meditation were able to reduce their risk of death, stroke, and heart attacks by almost half!

Reduce High Blood Pressure

In a clinical study based around meditation, it was also found that certain Zen meditations such as Zazen, has the ability to lower both stress and high blood pressures. It's believed that relaxation response techniques could lower blood pressure levels after three short months of practicing. Through meditation, individuals had less need for medication for their blood pressure! This could potentially be due to the fact that when we relax, it helps open your blood vessels through the formation of nitric oxide.

Live a Longer Life

When you get rid of stress in your life, you may be amazed at how much more energetic and healthier you feel. While the research hasn't been drawn to a conclusion yet, there are some studies that suggest meditation could have an effect on the telomere length in our cells. Telomeres are in charge of how our cells age. When there is less cognitive stress, it helps maintain telomere and other hormonal factors.

Relationship Benefits

There are some people who are looking for a little bit more peace in your life. In the world we live in today, times can be very trying. There are constant deadlines, bills to pay, people to deal with; but now is the time to look at stressors in your life under a different life. Through meditation, you can become a more caring and empathetic individual to create a more peaceful life for yourself.

Improve Positive Relationships and Empathy

When we undergo stressful situations with obnoxious people, it can be very trying to remain empathetic. There is a Buddhist tradition of practicing loving-kindness meditation that may be able to help foster a sense of care toward all living things. Through meditation, you'll be able to boost the way you read facial expressions and gain the ability to empathize with others. When you have a loving attitude toward yourself and others, this helps develop a positive relationship with them and a sense of self-acceptance.

Decrease Feelings of Loneliness

There are many people who are not okay with being alone. Often times, we try to fill our time with activities so that we are never alone with ourselves. The truth is, it can be healthy to spend some time with yourself so that you can self-reflect on your life choices. In a study published in Brain, Behavior, and Immunity, it was proven that after thirty minutes of meditation per day, it was able to reduce individuals' sense of loneliness while reducing the risks of premature death, depression, and perhaps even Alzheimer's.

Along with feeling less lonely, meditation also opens up new doors to feeling a positive connection to yourself. When you love yourself, and you are happy with your own company, you may spend a lot less time on negative thoughts and feelings of self-doubt; both of which can lead to self-caused stress.

Chapter 20: Retraining the Mind

CBT teaches the importance of paying attention to behaviors and increasing the frequency of positive activities through Behavioral Activation. You have learned about the key elements of experience: thoughts, emotions, behaviors, and bodily sensations. You have learned the common Thinking Traps. You have started to learn how the Thought Record is used in CBT to connect automatic thoughts and feelings to particular situations that are arising in day-to-day life, and how CBT defines a number of Thinking Traps that people commonly fall into. The fact that you have learned all this is already an accomplishment.

It is possible, however, to go a step further in your understanding of CBT. What you will now learn is how CBT teaches people actively to dispute automatic thoughts that involve Thinking Traps. But before we get into the details, it will help if you have some background on the cognitive model on which CBT is based. That way, you'll be in a better position to understand what it is a CBT client is trying to do when they are disputing their thoughts. Let's take a quick tour of the cognitive model.

The Cognitive Revolution

It wasn't too long ago that the computer was first invented. It was even more recently that computers became part of our everyday lives. Many of us can remember when the first personal computers first came on the market in the 1980s and 1990s. Since their invention, computers have changed many aspects of life and they have affected the way we think about ourselves.

One very big area of change occurred in psychology. Psychologists began to replace ways of understanding the mind and brain with a computer-based understanding. They started to think of the mind as functioning as a computer. Most importantly, just as computers function to process information, so can the human mind. And just as computers can malfunction in processing information, so can the human mind. To better understand this idea, imagine a user who is using a computer to perform a basic arithmetic operation, like adding 2 + 2. The user inputs "2+2" into the computer, and it processes the input to yield an answer: "4."

Now imagine this same user who is faced with a broken, malfunctioning computer. She inputs "2+2" into the computer, but when it processes the input it outputs something false: "5"

Just as a computer can fail to process information properly, the human mind can also fail properly to process the information it is presented with. The development in psychology of thinking of the mind as a computer is known as the "cognitive revolution." This psychological revolution has allowed for new approaches to treating mental distress like depression and anxiety. Cognitive-behavioral therapy emerged out of this revolutionary new approach. CBT starts from the idea that common mental health disorders can be understood as the mind failing properly to process the information it is taking in.

The Cognitive Model of Anxiety and Depression

According to the cognitive model, anxiety and mood disorders are caused when the mind makes errors in processing information in the environment, resulting in higher levels of distress than is appropriate. Anxious and depressive states are sometimes normal

- they become problems when they are triggered because our automatic thoughts are falsely causing these states to arise.

But it is not useful to you to become anxious in situations in which there is no likely threat. It is the mind that, like a computer, processes information about which situations are threatening to you, and which are not. In anxiety disorders, this information-processing function of your mind malfunctions. It is exaggerating the threat level that you face. For example, if you see a leashed miniature poodle at the other end of the park, and you feel a lot of anxiety, then there is likely a problem with the way that your mind is processing information.

In cases of anxiety disorders, the mind is operating like a smoke detector that is giving "false alarms."

Although it can seem odd to think of it this way, the ability to depressive responses can also sometimes be useful to us. Evolutionary psychologists have suggested that certain depressive responses can be normal reactions if we have invested our energy in a person or project, and then face a loss. A period of low mood and detachment may actually help us to help the person to withdraw our investment in what we have lost so that they may go on to re-invest in new things and move on with our lives. You may be familiar with this idea if you have ever been through the "grieving process" that often happens after a major transition or loss.

But experiencing a depressive state is only useful to you if it is happening as part of a constructive process such as working through a loss. It is not useful to you if you are becoming very depressed and there is no such process unfolding. According to the cognitive model, in depressive disorders, the mind is malfunctioning in the way it is processing information, making situations seem far more negative than they actually are. The minds of people who are depressed are known to produce a stream of negative thoughts that do not provide a full and balanced picture of the situations they are in. These include negative thoughts about themselves, others, the world, and the future. For example, if someone who is depressed fails an exam, their thoughts may interpret the situation through an extremely negative lens as being one of hopelessness. By contrast, the thoughts of someone who is not depressed would provide a more balanced view of the situation.

Questioning Automatic Thoughts

Just as a malfunctioning computer can be reprogrammed, so can a human mind that is malfunctioning to create excessive anxiety or depression. To reprogram the mind, a person will need to deliberately attend to the way it is automatically interpreting situations in his or her life. That way, they can start a process of learning that results in forming new habits of thought - habits that are not as biased towards negative or catastrophic interpretations. There are two keyways to start to correct the automatic thoughts that distort the situation:

- By asking questions that dispute or challenge distorted automatic thoughts

- By carrying out "behavioral experiments" in which the person deliberately enters situations that will provide direct evidence against distorted automatic thoughts

According to CBT, there are some key questions that people can ask about their automatic thoughts in order to reprogram negative or catastrophic biases in their thinking.

- What is the evidence in favor of, and against, my interpretation of the situation?

- What is another way to view the situation?

- Have I overlooked any important information about the situation?

- Is the way I'm thinking helpful to me?

- How might someone else (who is not already depressed or anxious) view the situation?

In a CBT program, the therapist asks the client questions like these to help them to challenge their automatic thoughts. This type of questioning is known as "Socratic" questioning, after the Ancient Greek philosopher Socrates. Socrates would ask people challenging questions in the course of philosophical discussions that would lead them fundamentally to rethink some of their basic beliefs. When someone is continuing with CBT on their own after they have finished working with a therapist, they are encouraged to continue to ask themselves challenging questions such as these. In this way, one goal of a CBT program is to eventually help people to become their own therapists.

Let's illustrate this process by considering how Sam begins to ask herself questions that challenge some of the automatic thoughts connected with her anxiety and depression.

Recall that, last week, when Sam woke up one morning and checked her email, she discovered an email from her manager. Right away, she started to panic and feel bad. Her automatic thought was "I must be in trouble." When she found the courage to read the email, it turned out that her manager was asking about her return-to-work plan. Sam identified her Thinking Trap as Fortune Telling since she was anticipating a bad event (getting in trouble) but did not have direct evidence that this was going to happen.

We have already seen how Sam completed the first four columns of her Thought Record. Now we can focus on the last two columns. In these columns, she will dispute the automatic thought, "I must be in trouble," in order to arrive at a more balanced thought.

5. Disputation - Evidence for and against

For: My manager has been critical in the past

Against: She has Not criticized me in all of our interactions, and I know that I have not done anything wrong

6. New balanced, realistic thought

"Although there is a chance that my manager will be upset with me, there is no good reason for her to be upset with me now"

Notice the question Sam asks herself in disputing her automatic thought about being in trouble. She asks the first question listed above: What is the evidence in favor of and against my interpretation of the situation? Many people find it helpful to start with this question.

But the choice of which question or questions to ask is a matter of preference. Sam might have chosen instead to focus on the question "How might someone else (who is not already depressed or anxious) view the situation?" In that case, she might have brought to mind a friend or family member who is doing well emotionally, and who would have brushed off the email from the manager without taking seriously the possibility that they were in trouble.

To further illustrate the disputation of thoughts, let's consider a second example.

Sam was planning to go to the gym to work out after lunch, since she has found that this has been helping her to feel better. But while she was eating lunch, she started thinking about work and had the thought, "I will never be any good at my job." This made her feel depressed and caused her to lose the motivation to go to the gym. That day, she realized that this thought had derailed her plans to take care of herself. She completed an entry in her Thought Record.

This is what Sam's entry in her Thought Record looks like:

1. Activating Event

Wednesday PM: Eating lunch, started to think about work

2. Belief / Thought

"I will never be any good at my job"

3. Consequences - Emotions, behaviors, bodily sensations

Sadness, low energy, lying down on the couch (instead of going to the gym)

4. Thinking Trap

All-or-nothing thinking

5. Disputation - Evidence for and against

For: my new manager has criticized me for mistakes I've made at my job

Against: I have produced a lot of good work and my other colleagues come to me when they have questions

6. New balanced, realistic thought

"Although I have not been perfect at my job, there are many things I do well, and many people do believe that I'm good at my job"

In this Thought Record entry, Sam decided to focus on the Thinking Trap of All-or-Nothing thinking. There might be other Thinking Traps, too (such as Fortune Telling or Mental Filter). But it is often helpful to focus on the one that stands out most prominently in the situation. In this case, Sam was struck by the way her automatic thoughts had made it seem to her that she was either all-good or all-bad at her job. In fact, the reality lies somewhere in-between.

Chapter 21: Solutions for Anxiety in Relationships

Tension can be challenging to oversee. However, there are solutions, and when you are seeing someone, those solutions can be worked through altogether. Although some anxiety in a relationship is ordinary, having it rule your relationship can turn it harmful, regularly harming the individual you love most. For some people who suffer from anxiety, bouncing from relationship to relationship helps to ease their anxiety only for a short period, when insecurity creeps in again. They are regularly left inquiring as to why their connections consistently come up short, never entirely understanding that it is their anxiety that is pushing individuals away.

Studies have indicated that individuals with low confidence have far more elevated levels of insecurity, especially in their relationship. It keeps them from making a profound and significant association with their accomplices. Individuals with low confidence not just need their partner to see them in a superior light than they see themselves. Still, in moments of self-doubt, they experience difficulty, in any event, perceiving their accomplice's confirmations. Acting out their insecurities pushes their partner further away, creating a self-fulfilling prophecy, and because this struggle is internal and goes on most of the time, the anxiety compounds. It is essential to manage your weaknesses without involving your partner in them. You can do this by taking two steps:

- Uncover the real roots of our insecurity.

- Challenge your inner critic that sabotages our relationship.

You should set up where your uncertainty originates from regardless. Nothing stirs inaccessible damages like a cozy relationship and being open to somebody. Our connections work up old sentiments from our past more than all else. Our brains are even flooded with the same neurochemicals in both situations. Our first example can shape our grown-up connections. Your style of connection impacts which kind of accomplices we pick and the elements that happen in our relationships. A safe connection design encourages an individual to be progressively sure and aloof. At the point when somebody has an on edge or engrossed connection style, they might be bound to feel shaky toward their partner.

There is a mystery to overseeing and conquering the obstructions that reason you to experience the ill effects of your uneasiness. The secret is recognizing that the hindrances that scare you and make your negative musings are the way to carrying on with a reliable and secure life. When you grasp these impediments and choose to work through them, you will have the option to begin to build up more profound attention to where and when your frailties are originating from. The minute you start using your anxiety as a mindful reminder that your insecurities and mistrust are rearing their ugly head; you are better able to manage the consequences positively. Furthermore, here is the uplifting news; all frailties are an opportunity to benefit some work in bettering yourself. When you begin to focus, and you are never again determined by your uneasiness and your uncertainties, you will have the option to take a shot at some incredible strides to reinforce your relationship. These steps are.

They Forgive Your Past

Since the more significant part of your insecurities has been formed by a family member or authority figure reprimanding you, recognize this and try to identify who they are. At that point, begin to excuse them gradually. Defend and comprehend that they were driven by their frailties, battling, and were in all likeliness battling with their very own evil spirits. People are not great, and given that they carry on incompletely, we as a whole do. This doesn't mean they were directly in what they did, but instead that you can comprehend, they also were battling through their very own fights. To forgive them for their bad behavior will be healing for you because holding on to resentment isn't helping you. When you go of the past, you can start to mend, slowly and carefully.

Acknowledge Yourself, the Great and the Awful

Pause for a minute to respite and take a self-evaluation of your life and how you are living it. Notice the pieces of yourself, both your body and your internal identity that you don't care for or might want to change. Presently, investigate these pieces of you, and attempt to imagine the love for yourself. Consider yourself to be a whole individual made up of large and flawed parts. Recognize that you are meriting love as an accomplice since everybody, paying little respect to their flaws, has the right to be adored. On the off chance that you are doing combating, attempt to imagine why you love your companions, in any event, realizing they are flawed. In the same manner, you love your companions; you should show love toward yourself.

Start to Rehearse Self-Approval

Insecurity drives an individual to look for others' endorsements. If you see yourself needing another person's applause and consideration, attempt to stop for a minute and supplant that requirement for support with self-approval. When you remove the intensity of others' approval and begin to give your endorsement, you move the power of certainty working to yourself. Having another person's consent is decent to have; however, having your very own support is ground-breaking. Try not to misunderstand us; this doesn't mean you are dismissing or don't need association with others, or love from your partner. You can, in any case, be adored by your accomplice while additionally rehearsing self-approval.

Stop Comparing Yourself

Comparing yourself and what others look like, what they're doing, how fruitful they are, or the amount they have is never a significant correlation. This conduct effectively hurts you, so as opposed to getting desirous or contrasting yourself and another person, change your point of view. Understand that you are unique and comparing yourself with someone else is like trying to compare an apple with an orange. Attempt to be cheerful for them and happy in their prosperity, understanding that they are on an alternate way to you and that they also have their very own issues. When you wish everyone well and embrace the path you are on, you take away your anxiety's power over you and can be joyful for yourself and others. In all honesty, there is somebody who might be listening who is most likely contrasting themselves with you as well.

Figure Out How to Be Trustful at the Time

By using the devices this and rehearsing them, when nervousness raises its head as well as consistently, you will confide in yourself. At the point when you can create trust at the time that you can support, you can appreciate the minute without nervousness dominating. Figuring out how to be trustful at the time sets aside some effort to create. Recollect that figuring out how to believe yourself is indistinguishable to figuring out how to confide in another person. In any case, when you can tell in yourself and trust that you will know the distinction among tension and genuine indications of threat, you and your partner will have the option to start to appreciate each other's conversation again.

While strolling your way to mending and joy, you will consistently discover things that will incite your nervousness, yet the more mindful you become, and the more you practice the methods in this, the simpler it will be to haul yourself out of full tension. Before long, you will end up getting all the more tolerating of yourself and your accomplice's love. Together you will have the option to fabricate your relationship to a reliable spot that both of you can appreciate without dread or hatred.

After perusing the parts above on connection type, you should realize your connection style. This is useful because it can assist you with achieving ways you might be reproducing a dynamic from quite a while ago. It can help you with choosing better accomplices and structure more advantageous connections, which can change your connection style. It can make you increasingly mindful of how your sentiments of frailty might be lost because of something old rather than our present relationship. By changing your connection type, you can battle tension with actual conduct and a caring, steady accomplice to you.

Your weaknesses can likewise originate from the essential inward voice that you've disguised dependent on negative programming from quite a while ago. This inward pundit will, in general, be exceptionally vocal about the things that truly matter to you, similar to your connections. Connections challenge the center emotions you have about yourself and drive you out of your customary range of familiarity. They drive up the volume of your inner voice and reopen unresolved wounds from our past. If you are already negative or have a tendency to be self-critical, relationships will amplify your anxiety, often forcing negativity to the surface.

Here is a recap of how to deal with your tension in your relationship through every situation and help you in recuperating and pushing ahead.

•**Think about what is causing your jealousy** – You can think about what sentiments, individuals, and sensations cause you to get desirous and flood your brain with envious musings. Is what you are feeling connected to a past occasion? Perhaps it a family relationship or an existing negative perception from your childhood. When you can associate your feelings and eruptions to the things that occurred in your past, you will have a more precise way on the most proficient method to work through those feelings in the present.

- **Remain vulnerable and stay calm in the present–** It doesn't make a difference how envious you are, there is continuously an approach to discover your way back to your actual self and to mollify your viewpoint. This should be possible by tolerating that you are human and by managing your sentiments mercifully. Recall that desire and tension travel every which way in waves; they will step by step construct and die down after some time. You can acknowledge your envy and recognize your sentiments without responding to it. Learning devices that assist you with working through your jealousy without overcompensating. Alleviating breaths and long strolls are only a portion of the strategies that will help you with calming yourself. Recall that it is simpler to quiet down when you do not endure or tune in to the negative words and thoughts that originate from your inward critic. Getting the hang of quieting procedures can be troublesome; however, it is a theoretical apparatus to assist you with facing your essential musings.

- **Stop acting out –** The internal voice that makes you blow up and guide you to lash out at your accomplice and companions cause long haul harm in your connections. If you allow it to spiral out of control and you are stuck in a look of jealousy, it may even wreck your relationship. This is a form of self-sabotage because jealousy causes you to lash out or punish someone you care for without it being their fault. This is particularly valid for individuals in a relationship. At the point when you do this, you are making the very situation you are generally scared of. You may wind up harming and undermining your accomplice, which disregards their adoration for you. This thus will intensify your sentiments of doubt and the dread that they will leave you. You may accidentally urge them to follow up on your conduct, making them become deterred from you, concealing their emotions or their activities to dodge your doubt and jealousy.

•**Find security in yourself** – Focusing on yourself and finding your very own feeling of self-security is the best thing you can accomplish for sentiments of jealousy that trigger nervousness. It may not be simple yet by taking every necessary step to quiet the pundit inside you and persuade yourself that you will be alright, regardless of whether that implies being without anyone else is fundamental. The acknowledgment that you needn't bother with one explicit individual to adore you to entire and glad is enabling.

Chapter 22: The Purpose of Relationship

Did you realize that relationships are unceasing and eternal? They show karma and the energetic ties to be played out an incredible manifestation, as we pass on them along on our profound adventure.

In truth, we've been meeting essentially similar souls, again and again, attempting to mend our wounds and figuring out how to relate with love and empathy for each other, or possibly enough separation to break any toxic or difficult bonds.

Now and then we meet them for one minute and some of the time we maintain relationships that last years, contingent upon what we've decided to take a shot at.

This is the reason you may feel a moment connection or fascination in certain individuals, just as an aversion toward specific people and these may incorporate relatives that you are supposed to love. To be sure, close relatives are the ones we normally share the most negative karma with. However, we have to encounter those difficult relationships to determine old enthusiastic patterns and inclinations, to develop and advance.

Relationships are multi-layered and mind-boggling. On one level, they associate us to the world, invigorate the physical faculties, and carry differentiation to our experience of the real world. On another level, they trigger the sense of self-personality and actuate the oblivious passionate texture that is an amazing establishment.

So, despite the fact that we may think we know who we are going into a relationship with, we may not really observe the hidden vibrational patterns that connect us to that person-since they come from the past.

A portion of those examples make positive purposes of connection (shared interests, dreams, convictions, aspirations, standards, and so forth.) while others show as struggle since they touch the injuries that we make a decent attempt to maintain a strategic distance from and disengage from. The personality acknowledges that relationship is generally self-fulfilling: they give support, sex, friendship, and so on. Conflicts arise when our mental self-view needs aren't met.

From a significant perspective, however, close relationships are planned to be a learning stage for self-development and self-advancement.

They serve as mirrors that show our conviction framework, particularly what we accept about ourselves and reactivate past emotional injuries that should be resolved and dealt with.

Find the Purpose of Your Relationships

We pick relationships to place all our stuff in our face, in a manner of speaking, since it's simpler that way for us to deal with what needs consideration. Obviously, it's by all account not the only method to determine our issues, however since we get exceptionally attached to the individual we are in relationship with, we have an inclination that we need to manage them so as to stop the torment and push ahead either in light of the fact that we need to proceed or cut off the relationship.

Obviously, we can likewise decide not to manage any of it and jump from one relationship, basically repeating and re-experiencing a similar kind of issues with various individuals, while our ego attempts to camouflage them as something totally new. No big surprise why it takes lifetimes to determine our issues and find a sense of contentment with certain individuals!

That is until we come to comprehend our reason of been in a relationship and shift our perspective and approach.

You may imagine that you need a partner for friendship or to encounter love (truly, life is extreme and it can get forlorn), however at a soul level each relationship is a chance to find out about yourself and recuperate the wrong perceptions, wrong perceptions, implicit understandings, and negative propensities that you've been conveying for quite a while. As it were, they are intended to make you mindful of how much or how little you really love yourself. So, what are your relationship reflecting back at you about yourself?

In the event that you imagine that a close relationship ought to satisfy every one of your needs, well, I have news for you: no single relationship can ever do that.

You can utilize every chance to move in the direction of self-awareness and emotional freedom, rather than allowing your life to rotate around others. It might sound nonsensical, but if you truly need to make adoring relationships, you first need to figure out how to be separated from everyone else and build up a profound, cherishing, and meaningful relationship with the most notable individual in your life: which is

You!

This one turns into an example of every single other relationship in your life.

Figure out how To Be in Love with Love

Love is definitely not a wistful, self-satisfying game. Love is your actual nature. Also, in the event that you need to truly encounter love in a relationship, you need to nurture your self-love and choose a partner that does the same-someone who's not growing cannot allow you to grow.

In other words, you both need to set up more cherishing and loving relationships with yourselves first and furthermore be open and ready to give the other individual a chance to be who they really are. Something else, the propensity will be to associate from an oblivious wounded place, just attempting to recuperate your injuries through the other, while your partner tries to do likewise.

If asked, "Can you loan $500 out to me?

You'd presumably look in your wallet or your pocket to check how a lot of cash you have. On the off chance that you don't have any, you'd state, "Sorry, I don't have any cash." If you have precisely $500, you wouldn't have any desire to give me all your cash, isn't that so?

In any case, on the off chance that you were conveying $10,000 in your pocket, you could go after the $500 and hand them to me decisively.

Thus, how might you love transparently without feeling that something is being detracted from you, or without anticipating something consequently, in the event that you don't develop and renew your self-esteem all the time? Without that catch to keep you engaged and strong, it's definitely not hard to get stirred up in the relationship.

It's not on the grounds that you love excessively, this is a direct result of an absence of focal point of a solid inward connection to yourself. Desire, enthusiasm or shared interests are insufficient to hold a relationship for long; they inevitably blur away and change. Love and development are a lot of more grounded columns for durable relationships.

So, I'd suggest that you focus on the first:

Cultivate love inside yourself and let your cup run over toward others.

Tackle your intense subject matters to associate at a heart level, not from the injured sense of self-personality.

Remain free and support exercises that keep you focused and associated with yourself.

Be in love for the good of love and pick a partner with whom to share the quest for self-development.

Be Independent and Connect from the Heart

In the dysfunctional world that we are today, love has become a product and an exchange: you see people saying that if you give me what I need, I give you love or consideration consequently. In the event that you don't act in the manner in which I expect, at that point, I retain my love. We as a whole gain proficiency with these enthusiastic examples in early adolescence, and they shape convictions that nullify the point of building relationships that ooze of love. Rather than nurturing and enabling love to develop, we expect and request more. And if we are unable to get our way, we become dissatisfied and resentful. We become self-centered rather than self-loving.

In any case, as the Feminine energies of the planet keep on reclaiming their place, we are tested to audit, return to and reconsider our relationships, and to build up adoring relationships in creative participation, with each other and in our communities.

This is necessary to support the rebalancing of the Masculine and Feminine standards on Earth. It clearly appears to be more difficult than one might expect, on the grounds that for a large number of years we've contributed a tremendous measure of energy setting the power-based relationships that we are so acquainted with, however we can start upsetting that now. The time has come, and you are completely upheld if you are happy to make another worldview in relationships.

To get there, it is important to assume full liability for your enthusiastic prosperity and break the karmic cycle of intensity battle kind of relationships that emerge from an injured individual blame dynamic.

Else, you'll be squandering extraordinary chances to find what love genuinely is and reconnect with your heavenly nature and with other people who might be looking for precisely the same thing you seek, your true self.

Chapter 23: Setting a Goal for a Healthy Relationship

In relationships to succeed, like in every area of life, you need to know what you want. While out of dumb luck you can come upon a successful relationship, it helps to be clear about your target. This clarification can be used to point you in the generally correct direction and guide you along the way.

Broadly speaking, what makes for a stable bond in childhood always makes for a safe adult relationship. So, you should think of relationships as having the following three basic characteristics: emotional availability: Children need to be physically and emotionally close to their parents to make them feel safe, but adult relationships are more dependent on emotionally close partners. Although separations and romantic long-distance relationships can trigger a strain, they are not necessarily deal-breakers. Partners must accept each other's needs and be responsive to them. When your partner remains emotionally distant or aggressive, you are likely to feel isolated, ignored or discarded, and you may doubt your worth as an individual.

Secure haven: Just as a child runs back to his mother when threatened or upset, partners in a stable relationship turn to each other in times of tough times when they need reassurance or support. Since life often requires at least some pain and fatiguing challenges, it is vital to have a partner who is willing to provide support, aid and relief from those problems. The problems of life are less overcome by people who know they have this trustworthy "bridge in a storm." Unfortunately, if your partner dismisses or criticizes him, then you will not turn to him; or if you turn to him, you will eventually feel insulted.

Secure basis: To feel fulfilled in life and truly loved in a relationship, it is important for people to be able to pursue the desires of their hearts — or even just to be able to explore what those desires might be. Healthy partnerships are ships where partners are promoting and supporting these activities.

When you think about these attributes of a healthy partnership, note that in order to build them, all partners will work together. Partners must be able to agree and agree that is necessary for emotional availability; security and relaxation, providing a safe refuge in times of trouble; and supportive and supportive, making the relationship a stable base from which to explore the world. While you are probably more worried about a partner being able to give you these "gifts," it is equally vital for him to be able to accept them, as an open reciprocal giving-and-take nurtures relationship. In the same way, it is important for you to be able to give and receive these items.

What to Look for in a Partner

The person best qualified to be there for you in this way technically speaking has the attributes mentioned below. I offer this with the qualification that someone whose characteristics do not match parts of this list could satisfy your needs. That's perfect. This is intended only as a rough guideline — as something to consider (though seriously considered) while you are looking for a new partner or evaluating how well the person beside you is meeting your needs. This being the case, you want a partner who is:

Securely attached and mature: Since these people are confident with themselves and their relationships, they are able to be emotionally intimate, as well as continuing to pursue independent, personal interests with themselves and with their partners. We are also able to talk about themselves and their lives in a way that is accessible, reflective and emotionally linked. This allows them to recognize their limitations and to admit to their mistakes in a non-defensive manner — all without sacrificing their positive sense of self. Understanding that other people are similarly flawed they will quickly forgive their spouses.

A successful communicator: These partners are excellent at listening and communicating, which allows them to nurture and maintain close relations. We are also able to work together through disputes. They have these skills in part because they are inherently excellent at detecting and controlling their emotions — a definite bonus when you attempt to communicate and work through the challenges that naturally occur in an emotionally intimate relationship.

Appreciative of you: Falling in love is not enough. Since relationships are co-created, they will only make you happy in the long run if your partner loves you and supports you — and works in a way to express this. You need to give your partner an interest in getting to know you. And, while it is at first a steep learning curve, the journey to know you better should never be completely plateau. You would always be happier with guidance and motivation to pursue your personal interests and achieve your full potential.

A good fit: Enjoying the time together is crucial. Generally speaking, this means having at least some shared interests. Yet it also means doing things together, even if this actually includes participating in conversations. Sharing values of each other, or at least honoring them, is very important for a long-term relationship. And the more that influences those ideals in everyday life, the more important it is to share them. For example, when one partner is willing to have children and the other partner is completely against it, catastrophe awaits.

Ready for a partnership: The partner must be able to pursue the partnership. This means devoting time and paying attention to it, both when you are together physically and when you are apart.

Again, it's important to note that you don't have to find Mr. or Ms. Perfect — which is fine, because there are none of those men. And you don't even need to consider Perfect-For-My or Mr. That can prove to be an endless search, hoping to find a better person just around the corner. What you need is to consider Mr. or Ms. Good-For-Me, instead. I'm not suggesting you settle for someone you're not really happy with, but make sure you've got your priorities straight. For that stable base, you're going to be able to tolerate a little mess, or little interest in scaling a corporate ladder, or any other "fault" much easier — and might even come to understand that. For example, less-than-ambitious career ambitions that represent the importance of relationships and other non-material aspects of life that your partner places upon.

One final caution: Don't be too quick to push past a date "nice-but-boring."

Nurturing a Relationship, You Feel Secure In

It can be completely fun to watch couples dance together. Watching two people flow up in perfectly timed motions is fascinating. Those that are most successful are apparently connected by some magnetic force. Seeing them dancing offers the vicarious feeling of sharing a wonderful relation to another. What could be more seductive than this?

You'll want to nurture a relationship after finding a romantic partner, which can feel like that perfectly coordinated dance at its best. The two of you would work well together in such a relationship, communicate effectively and trust each other, all while being in tune with each other as well as with each other. You would still want that to be a coordinated effort, even at its worst. You would find ways to accept and work with differences among yourselves, instead of trying to force each other to change.

Part of the beauty of enjoying such a supportive relationship is that it helps you feel more secure within yourself and your relationship as well.

Self-Disclosure

Your initial experiences with a potential partner set the stage for how your relationship story will unfold. It will go most smoothly at the very start if the two of you open up in synchrony to each other. One of you shares something personal and the other one responds with empathy, sympathy, and a dis-closure of a similar nature. You both feel stronger and you are motivated to share more, to deepen the level of openness. You also develop a sense of security and faith in each other's company as you enjoy those intimate moments. The love and fondness that naturally emerges from these relationships is necessary to sustain a healthy long-term relationship.

If you have an insecure attachment style, getting to know each other with this kind of give-and-take probably won't go smoothly. For example, you may hope that expressing a lot of your problems at once would gain your partner's attention, comfort, and reassurance. On the other hand, the need for closeness may make you feel too vulnerable to share; so then, you may stay away and near. You risk shutting your partner off in both situations. This often interferes with getting to know her and feeling empathy for her, as your attention is on whether your partner can support or hurt you.

If your relationships have been disrupted by the way you choose to communicate, perhaps it is time you approach it differently. Start by thinking about your disclosure motives-or not disclosure. So, keep an eye on when and how you share when you go forward.

You will want to share your personal experiences with your wife at the right time, as a way of getting closer and helping her understand you. But, as tempting as it may be to "unpack all your luggage" and share everything in detail, be mindful about what you are sharing. In general, share enough to understand your partner, so she can be empathetic and supportive. The rest will come out with time, if you so choose.

Of example, you might confess, "I'm worried about letting my guard down because my last girlfriend has been critical of me all the time." By deciding not to say anything about it for the moment, you may keep your focus on your current relationship. You give this prospective girlfriend an opportunity to talk about herself or inquire about you more. She might say, "I know how you feel ...." Or she might ask you, "What do you mean?" "This way, you can direct your discoveries and growing sense of connection to happen synchronously with your partner — leading to a sense of warmth and love that will ideally tide you over the years.

Conclusion Part 1

Anxiousness does not have to derail your life or the life of your partner. If you are in a relationship where anxiety is an issue, you should take comfort in knowing that anxious symptoms can be managed effectively in various ways, relieving the hold that anxious thoughts have on your relationship. Part of what makes anxiousness so difficult to manage in relationships is that many people do not have an accurate understanding of what anxiety is rendering the simple act of recognizing it a difficult one.

Anxiety can be defined as an emotion characterized by excessive worries or fears. It is this anxious emotion that allows a class of disorders referred to as anxiety disorders to be described.

Perhaps the most well-known anxiety disorder is what psychologists refer to as generalized anxiety disorder. This is the disorder that some people are referring to when they talk about anxiety, although it is estimated to account for slightly less than fifty percent of all cases of anxiousness. A common category of disorders characterized by anxiety is the specific phobias. Specific phobias are associated with excessive fear around a specific object or trigger, like crowds, spiders, or speaking publicly.

The first step to successfully dealing with anxiousness in the relationship setting is to educate yourself enough on the subject so that you can understand the condition and all the ways that it may surface in a relationship. The goal of the first was to give you a thorough understanding of what anxiety is and why anxiety may be more common in certain parts of the world and certain groups. This allows you not only to approach the anxiety in your relationship from the standpoint of knowledge, but it also permits you to show sympathy for your partner's anxiety because you understand it better and have an idea of where it may be coming from.

Being fully educated about worry requires that you have a basic understanding of anxiety disorders. Although many relationships may be characterized by the general anxiety that is associated with generalized anxiety disorder, other conditions like panic disorder, specific phobias, obsessive-compulsive disorder, or post-traumatic stress disorder have unique symptoms which makes dealing with them a unique ordeal. The goal is not necessarily that the reader should know how each disorder should be managed, but at least to be able to recognize what type of anxiety their partner suffers from and to be aware that different types of anxiousness should be managed differently.

The question of where anxiety comes from is a loaded one. Although it has been observed that this condition does frequently run in families, it has also been found that anxiety appears to be more common in Western countries than developing countries (in addition to other notable demographic trends). A potentially important cause of anxiety is the dysfunctional relationships that some men and women may experience in their youth. This is the idea behind attachment theory: the model that shows how children learn how to interact with other people and their environment based on the relationship they have with their primary caregiver.

Anxiety can be treated successfully, providing relief for the millions of men and women in relationships and out of them that deal with anxiousness. Anxious symptoms can be treated with medication, but it can also be treated successfully with therapy, dietary changes, and natural remedies. These natural remedies include things like herbs found in the environment, inositol, and transcendental meditation. Although more research has to be done to show how effective these treatments are, they represent another option for people looking for alternatives to the more common medication and therapeutic options.

This would not be an effective about dealing with anxiousness in relationships if it did not provide the reader with tips, they can follow to help them maintain their relationship in the face of worry. It is not easy dealing with anxiousness either as the individual suffering from it or as the partner of the anxious individual, and this is a concept that this recognizes.

An important fact to know about anxiety is that it usually does not go away on its own. If anxiety is left untreated, it will persist, potentially derailing the anxious individual's familial and romantic relationships and preventing them from forming new, enduring ones.

Love is enjoyable when you let go of the anxiety that comes between you and your partner. When you give anxiety a chance to run free in your love life, it may be difficult to know when and how to react to some sensitive situations. This may lead you to feel indifferent or unconcerned to some vital relationship issues or put on a show of being uninvolved and forceful when speaking with your partner. While it's certainly not your fault, it's beneficial to understand how anxiety may be affecting the manner in which you see things.

When it feels like anxiety is genuinely keeping you down, you will need to overcome it both for your well-being and for the health of your relationship.

Anxiety is love's most noteworthy executioner. It makes others feel as if you are suffocating them. It's not easy to overcome this, but it's possible.

Anxiety makes it hard to realize what's important and what's not. It can blow things out of proportion, distract us, and cripple us. But it doesn't have to control us.

You deserve to be in a happy, loving relationship that isn't marred by anxiety's vicious grip. All it takes is conscious effort and a new perspective to realize that anxiety's weakness is a loving connection. By strengthening your relationship, you weaken anxiety's grasp. What's a better example of a win-win than that?

PART 2

ANXIETY IN RELATIONSHIP

Introduction Part 2

A good relationship can be one of the most interesting and pleasurable things in life. It is something that most of us look forward to experiencing and building. However, thinking about the complexities involved in a relationship can be a fertile breeding ground for feelings and thoughts that lead to anxiety. Anxiety in a relationship can arise at any stage of the courtship or even marriage. Many young people can get feelings of anxiety and stress just from the thoughts of being in a relationship. In the early stages of a relationship, people may get feelings of insecurity leading to more anxiety. One can experience worrying thoughts such as "Does this person really like me?" "How serious is this relationship?" "Will it work out?"

One might think that the feelings of anxiety in the early stages of a relationship will subside once the person realizes that the relationship will last, for instance through getting married or even knowing that the partner will not hurt them. Well, this is not always the case. For some couples, the feelings of anxiety get more intense as the two people get closer. Destabilizing thoughts such as "do I really like this person?" "Do I want to spend the rest of my life with him/her?" "Will he/she loose interest in me?" "I'm I good enough?" come flooding in like a storm.

All these worries can make a person feel lonely even when in a relationship. In fact, these anxiety triggering thoughts can make a person to distance him/herself from his/her partner. Worse still, anxiety in relationships can make us give up on love completely. It is therefore important to understand anxiety and its triggers and the consequences. Understanding anxiety in relationships can help us to detect the negative thoughts and actions that sabotage our love lives. How can one keep the feelings of anxiety in check and overcome the relationship wreaking feelings?

This encompasses the wealth of my experience and lessons with jealousy and the knowledge of many other renowned relationship experts who continue to help people gain firm control of jealousy. It will open up your understanding of what jealousy is and why you may be experiencing this feeling. You will understand why jealousy is not considered abnormal and why underlying factors can materialize into jealous feelings. You will learn practical, real-life examples to effectively gain control and eventually overcome your jealousy while keeping your relationship intact. You will also learn to battle insecurities and low confidence so you can feel great and secure about yourself and your relationship again. So why wait?

Whether you have obvious issues with jealousy, are currently dealing with a jealous partner, or are looking to protect yourself or a friend from jealousy issues, this is the one for you. It is short, engaging, and promises to give you the confidence boost that you need to keep your relationship flying high and devoid of jealous feelings.

Unfortunately, jealousy has its roots deep-seated in the evolution of humankind and is ever-present in our daily lives. Therefore, we must learn to deal with this emotion that is ingrained in us. So, how can we truly enjoy a beautiful relationship without being consumed or manipulated by jealousy? Can we have a long-lasting relationship devoid of jealous feelings?

This has saved hundreds of relationships, sprouted thousands more that are healthy and sustainable, and helped some to leave unhealthy and unsalvageable relationships with dignity and hope for the future.

Dive in right now to start you on your journey to long-lasting love and healthy relating and leave the misery and stress and anxiety behind forever!

244

Chapter 24: Understanding Your Anxiety

Falling and being in love challenges us in various and numerous ways. A number of these challenges are unexpected and when we face them the first time, our human nature makes us defensive. For instance, if you love someone very much, and he/she breaks your heart, chances are, you will avoid being vulnerable. On a certain level, we all fear being hurt, consciously or unconsciously. Ironically, this fear tends to increase when we are getting what we want. If a relationship is good, one starts to think about fear the 'impact of a breakup.' Consequently, he/she starts to take the defense, creating distance and eventually ending the relationship. If we are experiencing love and being treated in an unusually good way, we become tense.

That defensive tension becomes a barrier. It is important to note that anxiety in a relationship does not only arise because of the things going between the two parties involved. This feeling may also arise because of our perception. The things you tell yourself about a relationship, love, attraction, desire, et cetera will affect our lives. This means that you might be having the best partner in the world but still, your thoughts hinder you from realizing it and enjoying the moment. The proverbial 'Inner voice' is very dangerous if it is negative. This mental couch can tell us things that fuel our fear of intimacy. The critical inner voice can feed us bad advice such as "You are too ugly for him/her" "Even the other people have left you before" "You cannot trust such a man/woman."

What do such thoughts do? They make us turn against the people we love and most importantly, ourselves. The critical inner voice can make us hostile, paranoid, and unnecessarily suspicious. It can also drive our feelings of defensiveness, distrust, anxiety and jealousy to unhealthy levels. Basically, this tiny negative voice feeds us an undying stream of unhealthy thoughts that make us worried about relationships and undermine our happiness. It literally prevents us from enjoying life wholesomely.

The main challenge comes in once we focus on these thoughts. We get into our heads and focus on whatever that minute thought is saying. Then we process it and ponder over it and roast and re-roast it until it appears like an unmovable mountain. At that moment, one is distracted from his/her partner thus no real relation and interaction. After brewing over the thoughts, one might start to act out, either immaturely or in destructive ways. For instance, one might start to boss the partner around, monitoring all his/her moves, making unnecessary nasty comments, ignoring, or mistreating the other.

Supposing your partner stays late at work or passes by the local bar for a drink before coming home. The critical inner thought will trigger thoughts such as "where is he/she? What is he doing?" with who and why? Does she/he [prefer to be away from home? Maybe he/she doesn't love me anymore." These thoughts can run through your mind so much that by the time your partner gets home, you are feeling completely insecure, paranoid, furious, and defensive. In this state, it becomes hard to have a constructive conversation about his/her whereabouts. Consequently, this partner will feel misunderstood and frustrated. Furthermore, he/she will also take a defensive stance. Soon, the dynamic of the relationship shifts from pleasure and comfort to irrational and unfair treatments, instead of enjoying the rest of the evening, it becomes wasted as everyone feels withdrawn and upset.

Do you realize that in such a case, you have effectively created the distance you initially feared? O you also realize that your partner might have had no negative intentions. The fact is, the distance you have created was not caused by the situation itself or circumstances, No. It was triggered by that critical inner voice which might have been wrong. That voice colored your thinking with negativity, distorted your perception and in the end, led you to self-destruction.

The biggest challenge that leads us to self-destruction in relationships is self-doubt. If we assess most of the things we worry about in a relationship, we realize that we can handle the consequences. Majority of us are resilient enough to experience heartbreaks and heal. It probably has happened before, and you did not die from it. However, our inner voice tends to blow things out of proportion, especially the negative ones. That voice terrorizes and catastrophizes everything making it hard to stay rational. In fact, it can trigger serious spells of anxiety over some non-existent relationship dynamics that do not even exist and strange, intangible threats.

Probably, breakups would not be so painful if we did not have that critical voice. It is the thing that analyses things and tears us apart by pointing out all our flaws and things we failed to do. The distorted reality makes us think that we are not strong and resilient enough to survive. That critical voice is the negative friend who is always giving bad advice "You cannot survive a heartbreak, just stay guarded and do not become vulnerable."

We form our defenses depending on unique life experiences and adaptations. The inner voice also borrows from those unique experiences. if a former partner said that he/she will leave you because you are overweight or underweight, the inner voice will use that line to distort reality. It will make you think that another partner is noticing the same flaws and that he/she will leave because of them. When feeling insecure or anxious, some of us tend to become desperate or clingy in our actions. Others become control freaks, wanting to possess the partner. A large number of people start to feel crowded, like there is no breathing space in the relationship, thus choosing to distance themselves from their loved ones.

In extreme cases, we detach from the feelings of desire in their relationship. We can start to be aloof, guarded or completely withdrawn. Such patterns of attachment and relating can come from our early life experiences. In childhood years, we develop attachment patterns, unconsciously, depending on our environment. The patterns become the model for our adult life. They influence how we assess our needs and how we get them fulfilled. These attachment patterns and styles are the main determinants of the amount of anxiety one feels in a relationship.

Understanding the difference between normal sensations of anxiety and an anxiety disorder calling for clinical attention can assist an individual in identifying and treating the problem.

Everybody feels distressed now and then. It's a normal emotion. As an example, you may contact worried when faced with trouble at the office, before taking a test, or before making a vital choice.

Stress and anxiety conditions are different, though. They are a group of mental diseases, as well as the distress they trigger can maintain you from carrying on with your life regularly. For individuals who have one, worry and anxiety are constant as well as frustrating and can be disabling. However, with therapy, many individuals can take care of those sensations and get back to a satisfying life. When an individual encounters possibly harmful or distressing triggers, feelings of stress and anxiety are not just typical but necessary for survival.

Since the earliest days of humankind, the method of predators and also incoming threat triggers alarms in the body and also permits incredibly elusive activity. These alarm systems become noticeable in the form of an elevated heartbeat, sweating, as well as boosted level of sensitivity to environments. The risk causes a rush of adrenalin, a hormone, and chemical messenger in mind, which consequently triggers these anxious responses in a procedure called the "fight-or-flight' reaction. This prepares people to physically confront or leave any type of potential hazards to safety and security.

For many individuals, ranging from bigger pets as well as an impending threat is a much less important issue than it would have been for very early human beings. Stress and anxieties currently revolve around the job, cash, domesticity, wellness, and also other important issues that demand a person's focus without always calling for the 'fight-or-flight' response.

The anxious sensation before an important life occasion or throughout a difficult situation is an all-natural echo of the initial 'fight-or-flight' reaction. It can still be essential to survival-- anxiety about being struck by a car when crossing the street, as an example, means that an individual will naturally look at both methods to avoid the threat.

Stress and anxiety are your body's all-natural action to stress and anxiety. It's a sensation of concern or worry concerning what's ahead. The first day of the institution, going to a job interview, or providing a speech might trigger many people to feel scared and worried. Yet if your feelings of stress and anxiety are severe, last for longer than six months, as well as are hindering your life, you might have an anxiety condition.

The period or extent of a distressed feeling can, in some cases, be out of proportion to the original trigger, or stress factor. Physical signs and symptoms, such as raised blood pressure as well as queasiness, may also develop. These responses move beyond stress and anxiety into a stress and anxiety condition. The APA defines a person with an anxiety disorder as "having persisting invasive thoughts or problems." As soon as stress and anxiety get to the stage of a disease, it can hinder daily function.

It's typical to feel distressed about transferring to a brand-new area, beginning a brand-new job, or taking a test. This type of anxiousness is unpleasant, but it may inspire you to function more difficult and to do a much better job. Ordinary anxiety is a sensation that reoccurs; however, it does not interfere with your everyday life. When it comes to an anxiousness condition, the feeling of fear may be with you at all times. It is intense and also often crippling.

This kind of anxiety may trigger you to stop doing things you appreciate. In extreme cases, it might prevent you from going into an elevator, going across the street, or even leaving your home. If left neglected, the anxiety will undoubtedly keep getting worse. Anxiousness problems are one of the most usual types of mental illness as well as can influence any person at any kind of age. According to the American Psychiatric Organization, females are more likely than men to be identified with an anxiousness problem.

Chapter 25: The Various Types of Anxiety

Generalized Anxiety Disorder

Imagine a person called John, he is the owner of a start-up company. As a newly established entrepreneur, he feels that he is always stressed out, even over the most trivial things. Thoughts such as Will the business manage to generate enough profit to stay afloat. Will he and his partner, Jane, manage to earn enough to afford college for their children? Is he feeling constantly tired simply because of work, or is he sick? What if his taxes will be audited and something goes wrong? How will he and Jane manage if something goes wrong and the house requires a serious repair? At this point, John understands that most of his fears are unfounded and unlikely to ever turn into reality. Despite this fact, he still can't manage to calm down and clear his mind. His partner, Jane, tries to help by assuring him that everything will be fine, but she is unable to comfort him.

John is a classic case of generalized anxiety disorder. Those who are suffering from this psychological ailment often live out their lives always worried about something, even when there is no real basis for that worry. People like John always expect some disaster to occur. Whether it involves finances, health, or relationships, however, it never manifests itself outside of their thoughts. Generalized anxiety causes people to struggle with letting go of excessive worries, even if they are aware are mostly a figment of their imagination. Other disorder such as an eating disorder, depression, or excessive drug use can characterize it.

Obsessive-Compulsive Disorder

Now imagine Joan, a 38-year-old mother who has two children. She always seems to find herself with the uncontrollable urge to wash her hands multiple times after performing activities. If Joan takes a walk in the park or exposes her hands to something considered dirty, she needs to scrub them precisely 12 times to feel clean. The repetition is a comfort until she touches something else, and she will need to start over. The constant washing leads to physical problems such as irritated skin and bleeding hands. Even with all of the pain, she cannot stop. Her significant other is starting to worry about Joan as she doesn't want to stop and listen to her concerns.

This example is a perfect case of obsessive-compulsive disorder, as Joan is incapable of controlling her desire to wash her hands after touching something or someone. As the name suggests, people like Joan have obsessions, in the form of thoughts or beliefs, they feel forced to perform as a particular ritual to alleviate the source of stress. These compulsive rites are supposed to offer relief, even if they don't invoke pleasure. People suffering from OCD do this as if there's no other option to reduce their levels of anxiety induced by the obsession

This extreme hand sanitizing example, as well as any other germ fear, is just one form of obsessive-compulsive disorder. Some people may be obsessed with their home security, for instance, and therefore invest a great deal into locks and then perform a safety check on all of the doors and windows. Other people may find relief for their anxiety by merely touching certain objects in a special pattern, or by counting up to a certain number. Another common form of OCD is experiencing the irresistible need for achieving perfect symmetry. Establishing the "perfect" order can become a lifetime challenge that will prevent some people from being able to function regularly inside an office environment or even at home.

OCD can sometimes accompany other anxiety disorders, depression, as well as eating disorders. Often people dive into heavy drug use as well because they find that the substances reduce the amount of anxiety they experience.

Post-Traumatic Stress Disorder

Imagine Mark, a young 23-year-old man who has served the military for five years and has completed two tours of active duty in war zones. Now that he has completed his last deployment, he decided to leave the military and settle down together with his fiancé, Lisa. However, he's been experiencing severe difficulties trying to readapt to civilian life and building a new home. He has trouble sleeping and when he does finally fall asleep, he has nightmares about screaming and dying people. When he's awake and going on with his day, he's often startled by loud, unexpected sounds. Whenever Lisa tries to surprise him from behind, Mark freaks out. He also experiences flashbacks on occasion, which forces him to relive the combat anxiety as he starts to remember the smell and taste of it all. All of these events are beginning to tear the relationship apart as Mark starts losing his grip on reality. Lisa becomes afraid of him as he often goes into outbursts of rage or has overreactions towards safety as if he still fighting a war.

This entire scenario is a typical example of post-traumatic stress disorder or PTSD. You may know from the media has been covering it extensively due to a large number of combat veterans experiencing it. However, this disorder doesn't just develop because of traumatic combat experience. The root of it can stem from any traumatic experience, such as the victim of robbery, assault, or even early childhood bullying. The trigger for this anxiety disorder can be related to a traumatic event that happened to you directly, or that you witnessed happening to someone you care deeply about.

Some of the symptoms can occur over a brief period, as not everyone develops PTSD directly after a tragedy. To be diagnosed, the symptoms would be present for around four weeks, and even the duration of the disorder varies from person to person. It's not always a permanent form of anxiety. Some people manage to overcome the trauma after a short amount of time, while others need to learn how to live with it. Self-destructive behavior such as drug or alcohol abuse is also common among people living with PTSD as they try to use anything to dull the traumatic memories.

Panic Disorder

Thomas is a college student about to graduate, and he's getting ready to take his final exams. Just like any other student, he's feeling anxious as these exams are important and will determine his future. However, during one seemingly ordinary day, while studying a challenging subject, he starts to feel strange. He is having difficulty breathing, experiencing chest pains and he's sweating profusely. The pain only lasted a few minutes but was sharp, and with no health problems, it made him nervous. Thomas didn't seek help at first, but his overly concerned girlfriend convinces him to go to the emergency room for tests. He reluctantly yields to her requests and heads to urgent care to get tested. The tests came out negative however, and this only increased both of their concerns that something more serious might be happening. What if this happens again while Thomas is driving, and he ends up causing an accident and taking someone's life?

This situation is scary for anyone as it can have dire secondary effects, on innocent bystanders in the wrong place at the wrong time. What Thomas experienced was a panic attack, and it occurred when he was sitting at his desk, studying for finals. A panic attack can happen at any time without warning before. It manifests suddenly, accompanied by an extreme sensation of fear and dread, together with intense sweating, dizziness, chest pain, and nausea. Because of the sheer number of physical symptoms, some people go into a deeper state of panic once the episode is over. They think they're about to pass out or have a fatal heart attack. While panic attacks may indeed resemble heart attacks due to the common symptoms, you will usually survive, however if one were to occur while driving or working with power tools it can endanger your life. Suffering from a panic attack while driving or working with dangerous tools can endanger your life Keep in mind that panic attacks are so unpredictable that they can occur even during sleep. This is why they are mistaken for heart attacks as they can wake a person out of a calm sleep with painful symptoms.

While a panic attack usually doesn't last for more than a few minutes, it can lead to long-lasting or even permanent symptoms. Why? Because those who undergo such a frightening experience end up living with the fear of it happening again. This is enough for most people to develop other anxiety disorders and even have new panic attacks as a result of this fear.

Social Anxiety Disorder

Imagine Emma, a lead software developer working at a large tech company. She's been growing her career in that business for over ten years but lives under the constant fear that she might be fired. Despite the fact that her peer is positive, she turns in excellent work, and she is a massive asset to her team, Emma will tense up whenever someone comments on her work or offers criticism. Even if the comment is coming from her teammate and it isn't critical, she struggles, thinking her work isn't good enough. Even if the comment is coming from her teammate and it isn't critical, she struggles, thinking her work isn't good enough. On top of this reaction, Emma avoids banter with her colleagues, preferring to work through the day without interaction. Emma regularly declines invitations to social events because she's afraid that her colleagues won't like her. She firmly believes that if she quits, or is fired, she will never find another job because her skills aren't good enough.

In many similar cases, people are rarely successful in school or work because of the difficulty they find in building relationships, as well as the constant self-doubt. If you think you are not good enough to be employed, you could end up in a position you hate, wasting life because of your socially overwhelmed brain. Social anxiety is powerful and can control many aspects of your life. A small amount of fear when giving a speech is normal, but the anxiety is overwhelming and causes you to quit, then it's a problem that needs attention.

Keep in mind that social anxiety disorder can manifest itself either in a very specific and sometimes limited fashion, such as encounters with your boss or participating in a group activity. For instance, some people will stop performing a task if someone is looking over their shoulder out of fear of their work being judged and criticized. With this in mind, here are several situations that cause paralyzing fear in people suffering from this disorder:

1. Performing any activity in front of others. For example, writing while someone is overlooking.

2. Holding a casual conversation with a coworker or a stranger.

3. Joining any group activity, debate, or discussion. This includes asking a question in front of the group.

4. Most social gatherings and events.

5. Coming into contact with new people.

6. Interacting with anyone who has authoritative power. A student may experience social anxiety when faced with asking the teacher a question. The same thing can happen when facing a supervisor or manager at work.

7. Using public facilities.

8. Making unplanned phone calls, especially to a stranger.

Phobias

Imagine Sam, a hard-working sales executive at a financial firm. His duties require him to work over twelve hours a day, making a large number of phone calls and regularly traveling to discuss deals with clients. Despite long hours and exhaustion, he convinces himself, as well as others, that he loves the active pace and the challenges that come with his position. However, he sometimes has to take long flights to reach certain clients, and during these flights, he experiences a rapid heart rate, excessive sweating and troubling thoughts. To control this situation, Sam stops taking long-distance clients so he can avoid flying.

Chapter 26: Anxiety in Different Types of Relationships

Each and every relationship is a little schizophrenic. Every relationship is somewhat schizophrenic. There is a natural tendency to be closer to the person you have some relation with, a desire to come closer by sharing your thoughts, pleasures, dreams, and desires.

At the same time, there is a natural tendency to want to distance himself from him. The desire for independence, vulnerability avoidance, remains free and unburdened.

Both these inclinations are natural and create a healthy twilight and flow when they are finished mature, which helps relationships to mature gradually.

Both powers push and pull build a type of interpersonal dance. No, not a Congo or Macarena side

Although they remain connected at the opposite ends of the rink to music guided by the same choreographed routine, anxiety can easily spill into our relationships and create the same kind of problem. Some of us are plagued by the fear of being similar to others. These anxieties also centered on feelings of weakness, inadequacy, or the fear of assuming responsibility. The solution to these feelings is very often to find ways to gain emotional distance.

These connections often do not gain momentum. They stumble, lose direction, and ultimately die of a lack of deep respect.

A different kind of anxiety around relationships is the reverse. This insecurity will contribute to one's attachment to others. Your partner, friend, or even your child's freedom can sound frightening.

Such fears often lead one to demand intense attention, affection, and time from a partner. There is a reliance on constant reassurance. The person who receives these requests will quickly be drained. Each attempt to show genuine love and commitment is never enough. It is never enough.

Such relationships break up under pressure.

Anxiety has crush-related capabilities. However, even if a relationship survives this stress, you cannot depend on it to be as complete and fulfilling as anxiety would be out of the picture.

Bear in mind that the kind of anxiety we concentrate on has a specific connection with concerns of commitment and emotional intimacy. This differs from social anxiety, panic, phobia, and other anxiety disorders.

Each of these worries can have a major impact on relations, but none of them are specifically concerned about emotional intimacy. The distinction differentiates how fear is surmounted.

Signs That Anxiety Is in Your Life

You may wonder if relational anxiety causes trouble in your life. It can be hard to know. After all, everyone is nervous to some degree, so how you can tell if your relationships with family and friends have been affected.

The following questions can clarify if this is a problem:

1. Often do you worry that your partner will leave you for another person.

2. If he or she is out with friends, do you trust your partner?

3. Do you often require the reassurance of the love and devotion of your partner?

4. Should you worry about how your partner is going to respond to a mistake you made?

5. Are there any talks that you avoid with your partner because you're worried, he or she'll get angry?

6. Are you still afraid that your partner is unfaithful?

7. Are you someone who's getting jealous easily?

8. Do you have to control the time of your partner, known in detail where he or she was, and with whom?

9. Do you not depend on your partner?

10. Would you feel uncomfortable if your partner depends on you emotionally?

11. Have a number of people said you're hard to get to know?

If you replied' yes' to five or more of the questions, it would be nice to have a very honest talk with your partner, talk frankly about your anxieties. Try to understand how you can influence your relationship in trying to cope with these fears. Then, work as a team to see how changes can be made, how you connect and improve relationships.

Getting Rid of Relationship Anxiety

I don't think any human being who is attracted to other people can say that they never felt concerned about a relationship, but relationship fear takes things to another degree.

It is the direct result of your relationship feeling insecure. You are worried about all sorts of things that might have a negative effect or ruin your relationship.

If you have had bad experiences in the past, your brain will have learned to respond in a way and expect trends to happen again.

You could live with constant rates of underlying anxiety about your relationship, or it could cause waves of tiny, seemingly insignificant things. You doubt yourself and doubt the feelings of your partner towards you.

When you think what you are feeling might be anxiety about relationships, these telling signs will help you identify whether it really is a concern for you.

1. You Believe the End is near

No matter how well your relationship is doing, you cannot overcome the nagging feeling that you're going to go a little' Titanic' and hit an iceberg before you sink on board.

Even the least significant discrepancy between yourself and your partner has the fear that your odds have well and truly bite the dust.

2. You're Jealous

Jealousy is a pretty common emotion, but if it gets out of hand, no relationship can survive.

You will not necessarily show signs of jealousy that your partner will change their behavior, and it may well push them away. But if one thing is certain, it will certainly make you miserable.

It's no wonder that you get jealous if you were deceived in the past, but it definitely makes you nervous.

3. You are controlling

You control your anxiety, which means that you desperately control your relationship so that you don't get hurt. You feel that if you have a handle on exactly what is happening, then it will be all right.

4. You are too relaxed

This may sound counter-intuitive, but one way to control things is always to go the extra distance to satisfy your partner and be the person you think they want you to be.

They can somewhat have no good reasons to bail out the relationship in this way. After all, every time they get what they want, so what's to talk about?

5. You're reluctant to commit

This is all about self-preservation. Although it may not seem so logical, you may be reluctant to lower your protective walls and move towards a more serious relationship.

This may be because you are afraid that the relationship ends and that you do not want to be exposed to hurt.

Maybe you were burnt when in the past, you committed yourself to someone, and this now fosters your anxieties.

6. Questioning Your Compatibility

You ask questions about your relationship with your marriage phobia, and you try to find excuses why you and your partner simply are not compatible.

Often you find things so insignificant that they can easily be solved, but that's not how you see them. You see them as mines waiting to be seized.

(Truly, your anxiety may also be focused on real differences which may prove to be too broad to overcome convictions such as the way you believe about marriage or children, or where you would like to live in the long run.

7. You get angry

You're always on the brink, so it's easy to lose your patience if something happens that causes your agony. You do expect something to go wrong, so it's hard not to burst.

But, because you're insecure in your relationship, you probably worry that your explosion will change your feelings.

8. You ask many questions

You are never glad to accept an explanation. You ask questions and interpret the responses, bringing their words into your head and trying to find a hidden meaning.

9. You do not enjoy sex

This might be n, as a result of your uncertainty about the relationship makes relaxing in the bedroom difficult for you.

10. Come Across as Cold

Your relationship anxiety may mean that your partner thinks you're cold, stand-off, or remote. You are defensive, and if they enter and then damage you, they don't like to expose any holes in your armor.

11. You are too clingy

And, on the reverse side, your relationship anxiety may mean that you go completely the other way. You may need constant physical and verbal affections and assurances that you still love yourself and that you have not changed your mind since they were last saying it 5 minutes ago.

Overcoming Your Relationship Anxiety

1. Always remember that it's all going to be all right

If you are in the middle of a disintegrating relationship, it can easily feel like the end of the world. It can be extremely difficult to keep things in focus and see the light at the end of the tunnel when all those emotions rush.

It's as easy as to note that whatever happens, it's all alright. Think back. Think back. You have had heartbreak before, and you just got through it okay.

When you met your friend, you were perfectly fine, and life would go on after them if things ever go south.

Your life won't end if your relationship does and being in a relationship isn't everything and not everything. A friendship can be fantastic, but it never determines you.

If somebody doesn't want to be with you, you can't do anything about it. You deserve to be with someone who moves heaven and earth.

However, the less you fear the end of the relationship, the more you can relax and enjoy it at the moment.

2. Discuss how you feel with your partner

A lack of communication or miscommunications also causes anxiety about relationships, so it's best to talk with your partner proactively.

If you plan to see each other, be the one to look for concrete details, like when and where. And this does not mean that you always have to decide (though you want to share this responsibility), it does mean that you are the organizer in your relationship.

You could say that it's just an extension of being too controlled, but it's not. You don't drive any small thing by yourself, but you are talking about flying.

If your relationship is more established but still anxious, talk from a place of honesty and openness to your partner, explain how you feel and remind them it's not they, but your past experiences. Try to provide examples of situations that are difficult for you and how they can alleviate your fears.

3. Build your independence

If you're in love, you may feel that you're happy to live in your partner's pocket if you can but losing yourself in your relationship is sure to boost your anxiety about your relationship.

If you just start defining yourself in terms of your relationship, you put too much pressure on it to be successful in the long term. Who would you be, after all, if you'd break up?

Make sure you do things consciously for yourself and keep a life apart from your partner. Try to retain the things that make you special, perhaps because your partner was first drawn to you.

Your companion is not your' other half,' and they are not finished you.

4. Stop analyzing your every move consciously

People comment throwaway. You don't ponder every word you say or evaluate how your nervous mind can view every text message you send. You should, therefore, not allow the little stuff to influence your state of mind.

5. Note that you control your mind, and it doesn't control you

You're not at your mind's mercy. You have the power to guide, shape, and train it. You may still experience fear once you've realized this, but you can recognize it for what it is and allow it, rather than allow it to consume you and guide your behavior.

Chapter 27: Principal Frequently Worries

If you have ever been diagnosed with any anxiety disorder, there are chances that you know what it's like to live with constant worries. It is worth noting that feeling of being unease and being focused on your current difficulties in life as well as potential problems may cause issues that affect an individual's life. Many worrying conditions can be exhausting and might increase when stroked with more anxiety and fear about the future. The art if worrying is dangerous in the sense that it makes one worried about their safety and one might have difficulties to unwind or even relax. Also, the art may contribute to sleep disturbances as well as extreme conditions of insomnia.

It is worth noting that worry has a direct link with anxiety. In other words, people who are associated with this condition have been in one way or another been diagnosed with panic disorder.

If you keep worrying from time to time, you need to prepare for future events in advance and avoid any confusion that might set in. For instance, you might have to exercise or engage in physical activities that will help you release the tension you have over the upcoming events. You need to organize your home as well as the office and watch a funny movie that will help you recover from the feeling of being unease. You may also engage in an activity such as drawing or writing and try to get support from your colleagues. For instance, you may need to hear a perspective of another person that might help you change your minds.

The other aspect that is worth doing is sharing. For instance, you may spend some time sharing your worries with someone. A good friend will help you overcome the situation and help you mind off the concerns that might be affecting you. Also, you might have to network with other individuals who will help you take some time and relate with others. In other words, the art of sharing becomes more effective and efficient when shared between individuals why have ever had such experiences.

Practice Relaxation and Self-Care Techniques

It is worth noting that most of these signs of worry are linked to one`s mindset. Thus, if you need to release the worrying tension that you might be having effectively, you may need to practice some of the effective relaxation techniques. For instance, relaxation techniques tend to serve the purpose of improving one`s art of thinking, and it helps lower the tension that one might be having. Some of the relaxation techniques that have proved to be effective include yoga, meditation, as well as progressive muscle relaxation. Some of these techniques don't require a company or rather, a lot of individuals for them to be effective. Some like Yoga can be practiced at the comfort of your living room and achieve excellent results. However, it is good to determine some of the activities you need to do in life. The aspect is essential in the sense that it allows one to for the future and be effective in attending all the events without any tension.

Panic Attack

It is worth noting that the pain reaches a peak within a few minutes and involves several symptoms. Such symptoms include palpitation, pudding heart or rather an accelerated heartbeat rate as well as profuse sweating. There are cases where an individual may shake or trembles. In other situations, one may feel dizzy as well as unsteady or even light-headed or faint. Abdominal distress or nausea may be part of the signs and symptoms of this condition.

Scholars, as well as a psychiatrist, have identified that many people have developed one or two panic attacks in their entire lifetime. It is worth noting the problems go away when the stressful situation or the cause of the distress disappears. However, if an unexpected panic attack faces one, the problem seems to persist and might stay for long before one resumes to their normal state. Although the condition isn't life-threatening, there are cases where frightening tend to affect the quality of life significantly. In such a situation, treatment tends to be effective.

Some of the worst situations about this panic attack are that there is intense fear that tends to develop and affect the way a person lives. There are cases where people fear developing some of these attacks and end up improving the symptoms of the condition. One of the alarming signs that are common in such situations includes dizziness, extreme headaches as well as the feeling of unreality or somewhat detached from the rest of the society.

Causes

There are no known causes of a panic attack. However, there are a few factors that are associated with this condition. Such factors include genetics, significant stress, a temperament that is more sensitive to pressure or somewhat prone to some of the negative emotions that one may develop. It is worth noting that the condition may develop suddenly without any warnings at first.

However, most of these sighs are triggered by a particular situation.

In most cases, when the situation fast attacks one, the rate of breathing rises sweet, and the heartbeat rate also increases. However, some risk factors may expose one to frequent panic attacks. Such factors include family history, significant life stress, a traumatic event such as a sexual assault as well as substantial changes in one's life, such as divorce or an addition baby in life. Smoking, as well as excessive caffeine intake, might be a significant cause of this condition.

Chapter 28: Signs that Anxiety is Affecting Your Relationship

What Causes Anxiety in Relationships?

We are experiencing passionate feelings for challenges us from various perspectives that we don't anticipate. The more we love another, the more we lose. We fear being harmed from numerous points of view, both cognizant and oblivious. Somewhat, we as a whole have a dread of closeness. Curiously, this nervousness consistently comes when we get what we need when we experience love as at no other time or taking care of newly.

At the point when we get into a relationship, we are not only anxious about the things occurring among ourselves and our accomplice; they are simply the things we tell about what's going on. The "touchy inner voice" is a term used to portray our mean mentor who scrutinizes us, offers us terrible guidance, and powers our dread of closeness. It says to us:

• "You are excessively monstrous/fat/exhausting to hold an intrigue."

• "You're never going to meet anybody, so why even attempt?

• "You can't trust him. He is searching for somebody way better."

• "She doesn't adore you. He's searching for somebody better." Get out before you get injured.

We betray ourselves and the individuals close to us through that essential internal voice. It can encourage forceful, negative, and suspicious reasoning, diminishing confidence, and expanding unfortunate degrees of doubt, forswearing jealousy, and dread.

Fundamentally, it takes care of us on a steady stream of considerations, which undermines our joy and stresses over our relationship rather than only getting a charge out of it.

If we harp on those concerning emotions, we redirected from genuine associations with our accomplice. We can begin to act in damaging manners, remark severely, or become infantile or parental towards others.

Think about your accomplice remaining at work late one night, for example. Sitting alone at home, the internal pundit starts to state, "Where right? Okay, trust her? Maybe she needs to be away from you.

She attempts to keep away from you, and she doesn't adore you any longer. Such emotions will snowball in your brain until you feel uncertain, baffled, or suspicious when your accomplice returns home. You can be angry or cold, which at that point, disappoints and ensures your companion. You changed the dynamic between you too soon.

Rather than hanging out, you may squander an entire evening feeling pulled back and upset. You constrained the hole you were at first terrified of. The deficiency behind this hypothesis isn't merely the circumstance. This crucial inward voice affected your idea, slanted your convictions guided you in a damaging way.

At the point when all the issues that we stress overseeing someone included, we are more durable than we might suspect. In truth, we can manage the damages and refusals that we dread to such an extent.

We can feel the torment and progressively recuperate. The compelling internal voice, in any case, will, in general, threaten and debacle reality. It can cause intense nervousness about non-existent elements and dangers that aren't even substantial.

In any event, when things occur, somebody breaks with us or has an enthusiasm for another person, and our fundamental internal voice will destroy us in manners that we don't merit. It twists reality and demolishes our capacity and assurance. This negative flat mate likewise offers horrible exhortation. "You can't live.

You can't endure this. Continuously put your watchman up and never be defenseless against any other person. "We have our own novel experience and adjustments in the insurances we make and essential voices we hear.

If we are anxious or shaky, a few of us will, in general, stick to our activities and be edgy. We may feel had or controlled in light of our accomplice. On the opposite side, a few of us will rapidly feel meddled in our ties.

The example of connection is framed in youth connections and stays a working model for grown-up relationships. It influences how all of us react to our necessities and how we satisfy them. Different connection types can add to numerous degrees of nervousness about connections.

What Thoughts Perpetuate Anxiety in Relationships?

Sexual suspicions and perspectives towards oneself, as well as other people that are compelling overseers, had will attack our present recognitions.

While the internal analysis of everything is extraordinary, a portion of the commonplace essential, inward voices are:

Essential Inner Voices about Relationship

- Relationships never work out
- People wind up getting injured
- Voice about your accomplice
- Men are so untrustworthy, childish and uncaring
- Women are so defenseless, penniless and aberrant
- He couldn't care less about you, and he just thinks about his companions
- You can't confide in her
- What is so extraordinary about her? Why so energized
- He can't get anything directly in his life
- He's likely undermining you
- Voices about yourself
- It isn't your flaw if he gets furious
- You will never discover somebody who gets you.
- Don't stall out on it. Try not to get excessively snared on her

- He couldn't care less about you
- She is likewise ideal for you
- You can just get him intrigued
- You are in an ideal situation without her
- She will dismiss you when she becomes more acquainted with you.
- You must be in charge.
- Don't be too frail or simply get injured.

How Does Anxiety in Relationship Affect Us?

At the point when we spark a light on our history, we rapidly understand that our connection design, mental guards, and compelling internal voices have had numerous early impacts.

Every one of these components adds to our pain and can, from multiple points of view, ruin our lives of joy.

Hearing our internal analysis and adding to this distress will prompt the accompanying measures:

- Cling: If we are concerned, our tendency might be to act towards our accomplice forcefully. We may stop to feel like the autonomous, stable individuals we were the point at which we got included. Therefore, we can without much of a stretch break separated, act enviously or dangerous or no longer take an interest in free exercises.

- Control: We can attempt to control or control our accomplice when we feel compromised. We can and can't make govern just to facilitate our sentiments of instability or uneasiness. It can distance our accomplice and create outrage.

- Reject: on the off chance that we are stressed over our relationship, and we may go to detachedness for one guard. We may get cold or decline to secure ourselves or assault our accomplice. Inconspicuous or straightforward, these demonstrations are quite often an exact method for constraining separation or creating vulnerability in our accomplice.

- Withhold: We regularly want to retain from our accomplice, in contrast to clear forswearing, when we are anxious or apprehensive. Maybe things drew near, and we grope blended, so we're going to getaway. We have little love or abandon some piece of our relationship. Retaining may resemble a latent demonstration, yet seeing someone, is probably the calmest enemy of energy and fascination.

- Threaten: Our response to our pain is, in some cases, progressively vicious, and we rebuff our accomplice. We can yell and yell or treat with complete disdain to our accomplice. It is fundamental to be cautious about how our activities react to our accomplices and how they react to our essential inward voice.

- Retreat: When we are frightened in a relationship, we can surrender certified demonstrations of adoration and closeness and retreat into a "dream relationship." In this dream state, we focus on shape over substance. We remain in association with have a sense of security; however, we surrender the fundamental pieces of the relationship. Frequently in a dream bond, we take part in a large number of the above damaging practices as methods for removing ourselves and safeguarding ourselves from the uneasiness that is, obviously, free and cherishing.

Signs That Anxiety Is for Your Life

You may think about whether social uneasiness raises a ruckus in your life. It tends to be challenging to know. Everybody is apprehensive somewhat, how you can tell if your associations with loved ones have influenced.

The Accompanying Inquiries Can Explain If This Is an Issue:

1. Often do you stress that your accomplice will leave you for someone else.

2. If the person is out with companions, do you confide in your accomplice?

3. Do you frequently require the consolation of the affection and dedication of your accomplice?

4. Should you stress over how your accomplice will react to a misstep you made?

5. Are there any discussions that you keep away from with your accomplice since you're stressed, he or she'll blow up?

6. Are you still apprehensive that your accomplice is unfaithful?

7. Are you somebody who's getting envious rapidly?

8. Do you not rely upon your accomplice?

9. Would you feel awkward if your accomplice relies upon you inwardly?

10. Have a few people said you're challenging to become more acquainted with?

If you answered 'yes' to at least five of the inquiries, it is pleasant to have a real to life talk with your accomplice—discussion honestly about your tensions. Attempt to see how you can impact your relationship in attempting to adapt to these feelings of dread. At that point, fill in as a group to perceive how changes can be made, how you associate, and improve connections.

Chapter 29: The Management of Anxiety

Strategies for Anxiety Relief

When you are suffering from anxiety, it can become easy to get so caught up in the negative that you feel as though there is no hope for survival or freedom from the negativity. You get so stuck in that negative mindset that you fear that you will be there forever. However, that could not be further from the truth. You can, in fact, achieve anxiety relief.

Realistic Thinking

This is one more method of controlling your emotions and thinking in a reasonable manner when you engage in realistic thinking, you are identifying which thoughts are realistic, and if you find unrealistic thoughts, you are making them become reasonable in some way. When you do this, you are essentially ensuring that you can correct thoughts on the go.

The first step to this process is knowing what you are thinking about in the first place. This is where your mindfulness tools come in when you utilize those skills, you can identify where your mind goes, and that can help you locate all sorts of loose ends and thoughts that are unrealistic. Identify which of those thoughts make you feel bad somehow, and target those. For example, if you feel devastated that your date night that you get weekly fell through, you have an unrealistic thought. Pay attention to how that makes you feel and identify the thought behind it. Why do you care about why you were unable to attend your date? Yes, this is similar to identifying negative automatic thoughts. In fact, that is exactly what you are doing here you want to identify that negative thought so you can simply correct it with one short sentence.

Your answer to being upset about the date night maybe that you do not want your partner to feel like you no longer love him because your partner always leaves you and you really want to make sure this one is the one. When you stop and look at that thought, you may recognize that the thought is quite the overreaction for missing a single date night, and you remind yourself of that: You tell yourself that if a relationship were destroyed over a single date, then it was not a worthwhile relationship in the first place. By correcting that thought and making it more positive, you essentially fix the problem in your mind. You are able to calm yourself down a bit because you see the truth.

Seeking out a Therapist

Sometimes, the best thing you can do for persistent anxiety is seeking out a therapist. This is far easier said than done, but even if you feel like you do not need one, it may be worthwhile to consider. Therapists are not evil or a waste of money they are actually quite useful. They can help you navigate through all sorts of negative thoughts and ensure that you are able to better handle yourself no matter what the situation at hand. Through these processes, you will get customized content that cannot provide for you. You will get real-time feedback, telling you how you are doing and whether you are making a mistake in the execution of something that you are doing.

If you think that actively seeking out a therapist may be useful to you, you should make an appointment with your primary care provider to get advice or a referral. Sometimes, insurance will not cover any therapy without a referral, so this is one way to skip that step. As a bonus, your doctor will also be able to ensure that there are no physical causes to the symptoms you are having, particularly surrounding your heart. You only have one of those, after all.

When you have gotten a referral for therapy, you can then begin to consider what kind of therapy would work best for you. Would you want a cognitive behavioral therapist? Traditional talk therapy? Some other kind? There are several different forms of therapy for anxiety, and ultimately, the one you pursue will be your own choice. When you have made your decision, you should then check out any in your area that accepts your insurance, or if they do not, that is affordable to you.

When you do eventually meet your therapist, keep an open mind, but also keep in mind that you need to click with the individual. You want to make sure you feel comfortable with the person that you are talking to. However, it is hard to judge that after a single session in many instances. Try to meet with a therapist at least twice before deciding that he or she is not right for you. Finding the right match for you is essential if you want to make sure that your therapeutic process is actually effective.

Worst Case Scenario Roleplay

Another technique some people find useful in managing anxiety is to engage in what is known as a worst-case scenario roleplay. In this case, you are challenged to imagine the worst possible ending to whatever you are anxious about. For example, if you are anxious over getting a divorce, you may then stop and consider what the worst-case scenario would look like you plan out exactly what would happen. Perhaps you fear that your soon-to-be-ex will get full custody of the kids and get to keep possession of the house, leaving you with a massive child support bill for children you never see, and your children are quickly alienated against you so they no longer want to interact with you at all. Maybe this goes a step further and you lose all contact with your children, and all you become is a wallet for all of the activities, medical insurance, and everything else the children need while your ex marries someone else who gets to be the parent to your child that you wish you could be.

Stop and play out that situation. Then, you need to consider how realistic that is. How often do parents lose all contact with their children unless they are doing something that is bad for the children? How often do you hear about people who do drugs retaining custody of their children, or people who abuse their children retaining custody? How likely is your ex to stop, take the kids, and run? Why would your ex want to do something that is so bad for your children, who would benefit from having both parents present, barring any abuse or neglect?

As you dismantle the situation, you start to realize that the chances of your worst-case scenario actually happening are exceedingly slim, and that gives you some of the comforts you need to move on without further anxiety over the subject.

Play out a Situation to the End

The last of the methods to cope with anxiety that you will learn is to play out a situation until the end. In this case, you will be thinking about considering your fear and allowing yourself to think through what will really happen in that particular situation. For example, perhaps your fear is that you will lose your job when you go to work tomorrow because you were sick for a week and missed a lot of work. Your anxiety is keeping you up and you know you need to sleep, but you just cannot manage to do so.

In this case, what you should do is stop, think about that fear, and then play out how you think the situation will go. If you are afraid that you will be fired when you show up, imagine what you think will realistically happen. Perhaps you imagine that you will arrive, and your boss will come over. Rather than telling you that you need to talk in private, however, your boss asks you if you are doing better and says that you were missed. He does not say a word about you being sick because he is a good boss and he understands that people get sick sometimes.

Because you play out the realistic ending, you are able to contrast it with the worst-case scenario that you may have also developed for that particular situation. You are able to look at the two and realize that you will be okay. You know that being fired is a possibility, but it is always a possibility. There is always a chance of being fired at any job for any reason. You are then able to relax a bit and tell yourself that things will be fine, which enables you to finally fall asleep and get the rest that you need.

Strategies for Improving Quality of Life

Now, you are going to be walked through several steps to improve the quality of life you have. These are other ways that can benefit you that are not necessarily directly designed for anxiety in particular but can help you find more enjoyment and value in the life that you have. As you go through this process and read through these four different activities, imagine how you could apply any of these possibilities to your own life to develop the life you want to lead. You may realize that there are several different ways you could implement more positivity into your life that may have a pleasant side-effect of lessening your anxiety.

Understanding Body Language

In learning to better read other people's body language, you do two things you teach yourself how to read others, so you know what they are thinking at any given moment in time. You also ensure that you are able to develop the skills to get yourself acting in ways that are directly related to the mood that you would like to be in. Remember fake it until you make it when you engage in learning to read other people's body language, you are able to better engage in the body language that you, yourself would need to get your mind thinking in certain mindsets. Further, you also develop the idea to recognize your own body language, learning what your own body language means, and in doing so, you are able to better understand your own moods when you are struggling to read them.

Studying Emotional Intelligence

The last piece of advice you will receive to learn how to become a more emotionally intelligent individual. In doing so, you are making yourself more capable in social settings. You are ensuring that you know how to control yourself and your own behaviors. You are ensuring that you can always behave properly because you know how best to regulate yourself. You also are developing the self-confidence that you need to get the skills desired to keep your own anxiety at bay. By learning to be emotionally intelligent, you are saying that you want to better yourself, recognizing that you can always improve and that you can always find a light in a dark situation, no matter how small that light may be. That light can guide you to a learning experience that you may find is incredibly beneficial to you.

Chapter 30: Steps to Overcome Anxiety in Relationships

The key to dealing with anxiety and finding the love you deserve is truly inside of you! What happened in the past is in the past, and you can rewire your brain to concentrate on your positive attributes and to silence that negative script constantly running in your head.

You may want to consider getting help from a trusted friend, partner or therapist, to help you look at these thoughts as objectively as possible, figure out what triggers you and how to stop for a second and reevaluate before responding, how to calm yourself and learn a new positive secure attachment style.

There are many habits you can adopt to help you achieve this.

Slay Those Dragons and Find Love and Contentment

You do not have to be a victim of your past.

Think about this sentence, savor it, let it sink in, and then tell yourself that you no longer want to be a victim – of your childhood, of your past experiences and relationships, hurts and mistrusts.

In business, when planning for the future, you would carefully evaluate the path the business has followed up to here, what went well, and what went wrong. You would understand that decisions were made based on the information available at the time, and with the best intentions.

You would understand that in some instances catastrophic changes left the business overwhelmed and floundering and that better decisions could have been made; however, it is now sunk costs and it is time to write it off and move on. You would be objective and keep emotion to a minimum.

The same applies to your life – if you are less fortunate than some and have not yet developed a secure style of attachment to help you navigate adult relationships and interactions, you have the chance to develop a secure style with 'earned security.'

Building up security in relationships by developing a secure relationship with a friend or psychotherapist, or working with your securely attached romantic partner, is the best way to light that fire inside of you and nurture it until it can flourish on its own, in a secure and emotionally mature adult romantic relationship.

The most important part of this journey is to reconcile with your childhood experiences, understand how unconscious decisions to help you survive impacted your behaviors and understand how your past relationships impact your present relationships and will continue to do so in the future unless changes are made.

Effects of Earned Security

Developing a secure attachment style can lead to:

Basic trust – that your needs will be met, to expect that help will be available, therefore enabling you to reach out for it.

Positive self-image and high self-esteem – accepting positive inputs helps build the way you see and treat yourself.

Positive belief sets and outlook on life – seeing the world as non-threatening and people as well-meaning.

Autonomy, goal orientation, determination, and good problem-solving skills – it creates a sense of mastery and accomplishment.

Good emotional control and behavior flexibility – mastering your emotions and building 'ego resiliency' helps you control impulses and adapting to new situations.

Strong relationships – intimacy, trust, and positive expectations become second nature and foster the ability to build and maintain strong, healthy, long-term friendships, and romantic relationships.

What to Aim For

You want a meaningful relationship – in secure attachment relationships, there are appropriate boundaries, and it is based on empathy, honest and true communication and trust. You want to feel secure, enjoy each other's company, and feel comfortable sharing intimate thoughts and feelings. You want certain aspects of your day where you do things together, also have your own space for doing things separately.

You need flexibility and distance to create intimacy. Think of a new rubber band, it can stretch without snapping and will bounce back once released. If it is not stretched regularly, it becomes brittle and crumbles, and if stretched too far for too long, it snaps.

Self-Awareness

It can be challenging to address insecure attachment as it is deeply rooted in our psyche, but self-awareness is the best first step you can take.

Becoming aware of what shaped you and your object relations can help you identify what belongs in the past and what to pay attention to now. It is all about developing self-awareness and being able to contextualize your emotional responses (Leo, 2018).

Insight can give you the opportunity to look at your behavior and see whether it is helping you and how it is getting you closer to what you want. It is always a lot easier to identify self-sabotaging behavior in others; you need to really dig down deep to look at your own as objectively as possible.

Recognize Your Triggers

Think about the case studies below, and go back to your Emotions Journal, looking for the triggers and patterns in the exercises you have completed so far. Keep up the exercises every time you are triggered.

They are typically not in a constant state of anxiety, being clingy, demanding, and engaging in dysfunctional conflict resolution, but revert there when triggered.

Their responses are evoked by stressful situations that threaten the quality or stability of the relationship:

- negative external events - dangerous or threatening situations

- negative relational events - relationship conflict, separation, abandonment and

- cognitive/emotional stressors – ruminating about negative events

Whilst these events elicit distress in virtually all people, it is magnified in those with insecure, anxious attachment.

Once triggered, you are keenly aware you are upset and want immediate assistance from their partners. You try to reduce stress by getting as close to your partner as possible, by intense and obsessive proximity, support, or reassurance-seeking from their partners, which may often fail.

Using your typical emotion-focused or hyper activating coping strategies leads you to ruminate over "worst-case" outcomes and prevents you from finding a solution rationally.

During stress, you often underestimate the care and support your partner does provide, and perceive their intentions as less benevolent, and will see any frustration with your constant need for reassurance as a rejection.

If the secure partner buffers (i.e., modulate emotional and behavioral regulation) the response appropriately, the reaction is lessened. This helps the anxious partner to experience less negative affect and behave more constructively.

Once you are triggered, your working model of attachment will affect your behavior, your perception of your partner and his behavior and ultimately your quality of life and wellbeing.

Make a list of things that trigger you, based on the three categories above. Keep adding to this list in your Emotions Journal.

Try to work through each of them, using self-awareness and self-compassion, and find a solution for each – a positive thought you can tell yourself when the trigger happens.

Chapter 31: Tips to Help Reduce Anxiety Levels Using Exercise

Do you ever wonder how all these couples stay in love and go through everything together? Do you wonder what their secret is? The answer is certainly not good fortune or luck. It all boils down to commitment and effort. They have a happy relationship because they have figured out certain dos and don'ts of a relationship. It is not something only a few have, but even you can have a happy relationship if you know what you must and must not do. I don't think of these dos and don'ts as secrets. They are certain truths most people seem to overlook.

Realistic Perspective

Be it romantic movies or the fairytales from your childhood, the one thing they all have in common is a happy ending. This notion of a happy ending often brings with its unrealistic views about what a committed relationship is about. Well, these movies and fairytales, and the reality of life are quite different things, as you may have found out. If you want a happy relationship, you must have a realistic view of what a relationship must be. While the romance is new and love is blossoming, there exists a degree of crazy infatuation. This infatuation fades away, and, in most relationships, so does the romance. As the relationship grows, you must hold onto this romance while developing a stronger bond. Every relationship has its ups and downs, but you must find the strength and resilience not to give up. To do this, you need a realistic outlook toward a commitment and the relationship. It is not always sunshine and rainbows, so it is time to let go of any unrealistic expectations you have. Instead, work on developing a positive and realistic perspective. Learn to manage your expectations.

Hard Work

There is little you can achieve in life without hard work. A happy relationship takes plenty of hard work. What will happen to a garden if you don't tend it regularly? Weeds will start to grow, and even the healthiest of plants will die. Likewise, you must tend to your relationship as well. Start addressing any misunderstandings or problems you have immediately. I often come across couples that believe that a good relationship just happens. If you seem to think a relationship will work without any effort, then you are sadly mistaken. If you want to be successful in life, you must put in the necessary effort. Likewise, you must work on improving your relationship. If you keep neglecting it, you can forget about all the dreams you had for a happy relationship.

Quality Time

We live in a world that's full of distractions, be it in the form of work, gadgets, or even social media. Keep in mind that there is nothing in this world that can substitute quality time. You must spend time together. If you want to establish and maintain a strong bond, spending quality time together is quintessential. Make it a point to be together without others around you. It is okay to go out, spend time with your loved ones, and socialize. However, it is not the key to ignore the importance of quality time spent with each other while doing all this. I'm not suggesting that you need to sit at home and watch TV because this doesn't count as quality time. Instead, be with each other. Find some common activities you can do together and indulge in them.

Alone Time

I know I did say spending quality time together is important, but it is also important to have some alone time for yourself. It might seem like contradictory advice, but it is quite important to have some room for a little separateness. When in a relationship, it is obvious you want to do a lot of things together. However, during this process, you must not forget about yourself and above all else, your needs. You must tend to yourself and take care of yourself to ensure that you retain your individuality. There are couples that lose their individuality once they are together. If you do this, it might be fine initially, but eventually, you will get frustrated with the relationship. Therefore, ensure that you have certain interests or activities that are different from those of your partner. This might make you miss your partner a little, and it will certainly remind you how important that person is to you.

Differences Are Good

Take a moment and answer this question, "What attracted you to your partner in the beginning?" I am almost certain that the one trait you were undeniably attracted to initially be also the one thing that is making you mad today. Well, it is time to take a step back and get some fresh perspective. A change in perspective will help you appreciate your partner's unique traits. No human being is perfect, and everyone has certain negative qualities. Start focusing on their positive traits and show appreciation for all those things that make you different from each other. I believe that these differences tend to balance each other out and make you good together. Differences don't mean disagreements. They merely mean a difference in opinions, and that's healthy for two individuals.

Trying to Change

A common mistake a lot of couples make is that they try to change each other. If not, one partner tries to change himself or herself for the other. Neither of these things will work in the long run. If you try to change your partner, they will eventually lose their individuality. For a relationship to work, you must both retain your individuality. It is okay to make certain changes that are helpful for the health of the relationship. However, trying to change yourself completely or your partner is a recipe for disaster. Don't think that you can eliminate the source of all the disagreements by changing your partner. That being said, you must focus on giving each other more of what you know the other person wants, even if it doesn't come naturally to you. For instance, don't complain about how your partner never unloads the washing machine, try doing it by yourself without any complaints. Your partner will certainly take note of the effort you're making and will try themselves to play a more active role at home. If you do this, you will not only avoid unpleasant confrontations but will have a healthier relationship too!

Acceptance

At times, the best solution is to agree to disagree. It is not possible for two human beings to agree on everything. A difference of opinions is quite natural, and if not on one thing, there will be something or other you both never seem to agree upon. In such instances, don't try to change the other person and do not convince yourself to make any unreasonable changes. Instead, merely accept the fact that you cannot agree, and some problems cannot be resolved. A simple solution is to come up with a compromise to work around the issue. The real test of a relationship is how you deal with such unresolvable issues. It is about coming to a compromise or understanding the fact that some things are just not worth fighting over. For instance, if your partner keeps complaining that you never make the bed in the morning, then why not just start making the bed in the morning? It certainly is a reasonable request and doesn't take much effort.

Learn to Communicate

One of the most common reasons why several relationships fail is due to the lack of proper communication. Human beings are not minded readers and expecting your partner to understand you without communicating is a major pitfall you must avoid. If you want something, you must communicate the same. To do this, you must become an effective and active listener. Start by listening to whatever your partner is saying without interrupting them. Just listen, and once they are done, you can quickly summarize the issue. If possible, don't disagree with them immediately and instead try to empathize. It is okay if you don't agree with whatever your partner feels. However, by following this advice, you are effectively taking your partner off the defensive. Once you both are calm, you can talk about the issue and express your disagreement politely. There is always a way to talk about things without it becoming a full-blown fight or argument. By doing this, you can easily come up with a mutually agreeable solution instead of an argument that leaves you both spewing anger at each other.

Be Honest

There might be certain things you want to share with your partner that you know they will not agree to or might not want to hear about. It is always better to share such things instead of not talking about it. It is better, to be honest than to allow your partner to start doubting your honesty. Being honest ensures that there exists trust in the relationship. One of the major relationship deal breakers is mistrust. Once trust is lost, earning it back is almost impossible. Think of trust as a mirror; once the mirror shatters, you cannot put it back together, and the cracks will always stay. So, start being honest. I'm not saying you must be brutally honest, but you can always express your honesty in an easily understandable and nonthreatening way. Don't hurt your partner and be mindful of their feelings as well.

Respect Matters

You might both start taking each other for granted. Never do this. I mean, never ever must you stop respecting your partner or take them for granted. A casual reminder about how much they mean to you will certainly strengthen the relationship. Once again, this is a two-way street. You must respect your partner, and your partner must reciprocate this. A relationship where one partner doesn't respect the other is not a healthy relationship. And it will almost always end in heartbreak. Saying something as simple as, "I love you," or "I cannot believe how lucky I am to have you," will certainly make your partner feel happy and put a smile on their face. It doesn't take much to say this, does it? So, why not just say it? Be respectful, be appreciative, and never take them for granted. Honestly, a lot of people don't realize the worth of their relationships until they no longer have them. Don't let this happen to you. Don't withhold yourself and be genuine whenever you express yourself.

Well, these obvious suggestions are often overlooked by a lot of couples! It might take a little effort initially but think of it as an investment that keeps giving. If you keep up your effort, your investment will pay off in leaps and bounds.

Chapter 32: Cultivating New and Healthy Relationships

Allow Vulnerability

One of the first signs of being in love is when you become suddenly very vulnerable. This vulnerability is present in your feelings, longings, and fear. When you begin to fall in love, your heart will open to your partner. You begin to entrust your heart to your partner and show yourself to them, as you do only with very close people.

You may be worried about being vulnerable, especially if you've had bad experiences in relationships. When you are open and vulnerable, those issues that were otherwise suppressed by you can come into your consciousness in new relationships. Therein lies the fear that is often justified - but don't allow it to scare you away. New relationships are just that - new. Judging them based on past experience isn't fair to you or them.

True Beauty Comes from Within

Another sure sign of falling in love is the ability to see the inner beauty of a person. At the beginning of a romantic relationship, much attention is paid to the exterior.

Over time, as the feelings of love blossom, you will see the true personality of your counterpart - their true inner beauty. At this thought, the saying "love makes you blind" is confirmed.

The Family

If you are in a relationship with someone who one day asks you if they can meet your family, you can be sure that the person is falling in love with you or even deeply in love with you. The family is very important and getting to know the family of your partner makes the seriousness of the relationship clear. If you have been introduced to both the family and the circle of friends, you can be sure that the feelings of your partner are genuine.

Selflessness

The last and clearest sign of falling in love is pure selflessness. This happens when you or your partner put the needs of both of you in the foreground and subordinate your own needs.

A one-sided relationship does not help you. Even if you feel that you cannot live without your partner and love them beyond measure, if the both of you aren't on the same page, the relationship will go nowhere. Here are some ways to cultivate meaningful and healthy relationships in the early stages:

1. **Be clear about what you need**

On your first date, before your entrées have even touched the table, the both of you should examine what you truly want for from a relationship. Be clear about what you are looking for. This way, you will both be on the same page from the get-go. The idea of this can be alarming, but in any case, learn to expect the unexpected. They just might disclose similar wishes.

2. **Talk about your dreams and wants**

Would you like to build a small home and live off the grid? Take a year off to travel the far reaches of the planet? Share these dreams with a potential partner. Discover whether your objectives compliment another person's and if you have overlapping interests. It's far more fun to find out about someone when discussing dreams rather than general hobbies.

3. **Have wide open communication**

If something is troubling you, do not hold it inside because of a paranoid fear of what may occur if you bring it up. Address the issues and have quiet, caring discussions to see the two points of view. It's such a much-needed refresher to know you both want to cooperate to discuss anything before something turns into a major issue. It's not about being right or wrong — it's about the two individuals working together.

4. **Accept each aspect of yourself**

If you don't accept yourself for who you are, why should someone else? There may be aspects of yourself that you don't like or would change if you could, but they aren't important. The sooner you can look at yourself and be happy with everything you see, the better of you'll be in life and in love.

5. Manage stress together

Stress will never leave — it's the means with which we handle it that matters. When your partner is disturbed or stressed, be there for them to vent to. Don't attempt to fix it all; rather, allow them to work through the problem as they wish to. All they need is to know that you're there.

6. Offer thanks regularly

Having a mutual appreciation for each other is massively beneficial. It's also important to give thanks for other aspects of your life. Grateful people are happy people, and a couple that is grateful for each other is better able to build a healthy relationship.

7. Talk about the big things

Talk about everything, from moving in together to building a home, from children to funds and family travels. Don't wait until these events are here - get a head start and begin discussing your expectations early. Many couples dread this sort of talk for fear that their partner will not agree with them. But the sooner you uncover differences, the sooner you can begin working to come to a compromise.

8. Have dinner together

People bond over shared food, so make the most of it! Put on some romantic music, dress nicely, and connect. The meal almost doesn't matter as much as the full, undivided attention of the both of you.

9. Be available

When you need your partner, do you want them to be available, or will you be able to deal with them prioritizing something else over you? If you wish to be put first, start by putting them first. Be ready to come to their aid if they need you. You don't have to drop everything on a whim, but ensure you know what you're going to do if they ever let you know that they're going through a crisis and could use your support. Your actions in their time of need set the tone for the future.

10. Work toward being a better partner

If you're like most people, there are things you wish to change about yourself. Some of these desired changes can positively affect your relationship. By striving to be the best person you can be for the one you love, you're also becoming better for yourself.

A solid relationship is two people cooperating to build a life together. A solid relationship is somewhat similar to a trinity, two people make something more profound and superior to themselves, yet they are still themselves. For a relationship to develop, you should likewise develop as an individual and not lose yourself.

Enjoy Being in Love

Are you newly in love? Then you are probably feeling great right now! I have a few good tips for you to help you get the most out of your love and keep it strong for a long time.

Additionally, talks should not be neglected despite the romance. Celebrate your shared romance, because it gives strength for less good times and creates a great common ground. Conversations are just as important as experiences, though. Share your feelings with your partner and give them the opportunity to get to know you as well.

Tips for a Long and Happy Relationship

The following tips will help keep your relationship healthy for a long time.

Avoid nagging

Any kind of criticism of your partner's idiosyncrasies either leads to quarrels or makes you feel annoyed. Psychologists are of the opinion that criticizing your partner in many cases is a projection of your own shortcomings.

Rather than frustrating your partner with complaints, you might think about what makes you uncomfortable about their traits, and work on reframing your viewpoint.

Understand that your partner is their own personality

You must accept the fact that your partner is an individual with a unique personality. Nevertheless, we subconsciously and sometimes consciously treat our partner as if they are an extension of ourselves. Accept that your partner is a being with a character of their own with appropriate feelings and perceptions, opinions, and experiences.

Accept your partner's mistakes

To err is human. Your partner is not an angel, so they are bound to make mistakes. When that happens, learn to forgive and do not capitalize on the mistakes of your partner.

Above all, there are lots of things we cannot change about our partner, so rather than grumbling or nagging, why not learn to live with them? Small mistakes are not a matter of life and death. If you find it difficult to cope with your partner's idiosyncrasies, call their attention to it, and explain yourself in a polite manner. Don't blame or accuse, simply discuss.

Do Not Tolerate Destructive Behavior

Learn to tolerate your partner as long as their behavior is not destructive or life threatening. If you discover that your spouse or partner is very aggressive, don't paint over the situation and learn to "cope." Your safety is important. If you ever feel threatened, don't stick around to try to keep the peace. Get out.

Take Emotional Time Out

Our skin needs sunlight for the production of vitamin D. However, prolonged and frequent sunbathing can cause life-threatening skin cancer.

So, the right dosage is important. This applies to relationships, as well.

Of course, we need each other to fill our lives with happiness. But we also need emotional time-outs in which one does not think of the other person or is involved in the planning of joint activities.

Meet alone with friends or join a club alone to develop yourself as a person. If both partners experience something different from each other, there is also something to talk about at the dinner table.

Do Not Tie Conditions to Gifts

A gift is a gift. And a favor is a favor. In a marriage or intimate relationship, you should never attach any condition to a gift or favor. If you want to do something good for your partner, then go ahead without any ulterior motive.

Do not make a game like "I'll give you a massage if you give me one." The same applies to the prices of gifts. Just because you have given your partner a computer, that does not mean they have to express their affection with something equally expensive.

Accept favors and gifts for what they are: gestures and symbols of love. Incidentally, this also applies to compliments.

We often tend not to take the compliments and praise from our partners seriously. But just because your partner loves you, that do not make their opinion worthless. If your partner tells you that you're pretty, then accept the compliment and do not disappoint them by dismissing it with an "Oh, that's just what you say."

Be Faithful and Sincere

Unless you have made other arrangements, share a duvet exclusively with your romantic partner and no one else. To be deceived and cheated on by a close person is one of the cruelest experiences that can happen to anyone.

If you really love your partner, you will spare them that experience. Ultimately, faithfulness builds such deep trust that you can't replace or fix it once broken.

Address Problems

No partnership is in complete harmony. You are two different personalities with thoughts and feelings. A relationship, no matter how much love and dedication you feel for each other, is always the result of many compromises.

Therefore, face critical matters head on rather than waiting for the other to address the problem. Couples therapists unanimously agree that communication is the key to a long, healthy, and fulfilling relationship.

Appreciate What You See in Your Partner

The first infatuation does not disappear forever, most of the time it gives way only to another feeling, that of deep attachment and love.

You have found that you can rely on your partner, that they think of you, and in so many ways suit you perfectly. That you as a couple harmonize and like to be with one another.

Chapter 33: Build a Healthy, Long-Lasting and Loving Relationship

You also learned where they come from and how to communicate about them. But there is more to the relationship, especially if you want to build a strong one.

All relationships need nurturing. You and your partner need to be able to walk together through life. This can be achieved only if you trust each other and you know how to communicate effectively. Even when your relationship is at its worst, to be able to survive, you both need to invest in it. But relationships also need you to understand that you and your partner are separate individuals that have their own differences. Never try to change your partner. Relationship means compromise.

Change Naturally

We all do change through our lives due to new experiences, and we can't be the same person we were before this relationship. But that kind of change is natural, and people don't even notice it. But don't force the change, don't insist on it and don't expect it in your partner. Observe the ones that happen to you, they are important lessons and they need to make us better person. For example, before you met your partner you never really gave a thought about exercising. Your partner loves to hike and to spend more time with him you decide to join him. This new activity you share with your partner made you realize how your body is changing for the better, you come to conclusion that your health improved due to hiking, and you decide to give even more to it. You start going to the gym every now and then and you take care of yourself more. This is influencing you; you changed something about yourself in a positive way, and it is making both you and your partner happy. This is an example of good change that happened naturally, and it came from an experience. The forced change would be your partner making you go hike with him even if you don't want to. He forces you to go to the gym by conditioning you with various things. You don't like it, but you feel obligated to do it for your partner. Given enough time, your insecurities will trigger, and you will start arguing about it. After all, you are doing something you don't want to. It will build anxiety between you and the relationship will suffer.

Keep the Connection Alive

Partners drift away from each other sometimes due to everyday stresses. It can be related to work, family, or friends. Our attachment styles, the same ones that cause insecurities, may give us an early warning and we have the advantage of having the time to react and work on reconnecting with our partner. Keeping the connection, you and your partner built requires work. There are things you can do so you don't allow your relationship to suffer from loss of connection:

Set a daily ritual. At the end of the day, spend some time with your partner talking about the experiences you had that day. Listen how your partner spent his day and get involved by asking questions. Be an active listener and ask how he felt. If they were bad, show compassion and affection. Tell him about your day, what you did or who you met. Talk about your family and shared friends. If you don't feel like doing this, consider making plans with your partners for the future. Spend time just the two of you and share ideas about the future. It can be individual things you want to do or something you want to share with your partner. Conversations at the end of the day often provide support and a feeling of coming back to something secure, your relationship. It will help you to share through difficult times or share your happy times. There is no need to spend specific time talking, do it as long as you feel comfortable but do it every day. The routine of these conversations will leave you with the feeling that there is something to be happy about at the end of the day, and there is security at home.

Spend quality time together. This is about experiencing the same thing together. Without this part, the relationship might not exist. Couples do get caught up in their personal lives and they do forget that they need to spend more quality time with their partner to be happy. We live in an age when we have to work most of our time, and we work when we are home. Instead of spending our free time for ourselves and our partner, we often use it to catch up with work or school. It is important to spend quality time with your partner. It can be going to a concert, dinner date, enjoying a sport together, or having a movie night. That is not quality time. It's just being in the same room. Remember how exciting it was at the beginning of your relationship to spend each moment of the day together? You can relive those times if you give yourself a bit of time to share activities with your partner.

Share a project. Many couples say that the best spent quality time with their partner is when they shared a task. From repainting the house and playing together with your children, volunteering together for the same cause, couples find it helpful to reconnect if they have a common goal. Working together on a project will reveal the true meaning of the word "partners" and it will shed light on how to plan your life together, how to communicate better and how to focus on each other. It is a great way of combining obligations and quality time.

Show Love through Actions

In a relationship, both you and your partner do nice things for each other. When this happens, they feel disconnected, lonely and even rejected.

When there is a lack of affectionate actions in the beginning of the relationship, you might need to ask yourself if he or she is really the one for you. Is the attraction going both ways or are you the only one who is interested? Maybe it's just your insecurities of rejection or failure that make you want to continue seeing this person or maybe he is triggering your insecurities and your attachment style keeps you feeling affection for your partner.

Some people expect from their partners to know what will make them happy and believe that if there is a need to say out loud what you want. It invalidates the action their partner took to please them. But is it really fair to expect your partner to read your mind? Nobody can know you that well to be able to predict things about you. You have to ask yourself is the action really more important than your partners intention to make you happy? After all, if you are obsessing about the action itself, or the gift itself, you are completely missing the point of relationship. Show off your newly learned communication skills in situations like these. Be mindful and tell your partner openly what would make you happy. You can even ask for it, just be smart about it. Instead of saying, "I want you to buy me this painting for my birthday," say something like, "You know, my birthday is getting close and I saw this really amazing painting…" It's a hint nobody can miss. It is obvious what you want, yet you are leaving space for your partner to think about it and maybe come with his own idea that will surprise you.

Be Honest

Trust and honesty are very important key ingredients for successful relationship. They are also probably the most difficult to maintain. It takes hard work from both you and your partner to be able to maintain them and keep your relationship from falling apart. There are guides on how to keep the honesty in relationship to a satisfying level, and both you and your partner need to follow so you can make each other happy.

Promote honesty. It is essential in building a healthy relationship. Attraction and love were just the components that made the relationship happen, what will keep it going and make it last is honesty. Forget about little white lies you've been practicing with your partners or friends and family. If you want this relationship to really work, be completely honest. We use white lies mainly to make our partner feel better or happy, but if he or she finds out the truth, it may crush them, trigger their own insecurities and make them not believe you in future.

Detect dishonesty. Use your intuition to detect if someone is lying to you. Intuition is a great weapon and it works in our favor.

Observe body language, facial expressions and intonation of a person if you suspect he is lying to you. If you catch your partner in lie, don't be dramatic about it. Maybe he's just not aware how much truth means to you. Don't start quarrels and arguments, use your communication skills to let them know you are aware of the lie, and how much it would mean to you to know the truth. Let them know you understand why they might think lying is the right option, but also make clear that you value the truth even if it hurts you. Our loved ones lie to us with good intentions, they want us to avoid feeling pain or they think it is acceptable to tell a small lie to make us feel happy. Let them know this is wrong and show them by example how much you value truth.

Don't keep secrets. Unless they are birthday surprises, Christmas presents, or just surprise affection acts. Those are safe to keep. Anything else can lead to your partner not trusting you anymore. It is same as with white lies; keeping secret might hurt your partner and start the downfall of your relationship. Most people find out if the partner kept a secret so what's the point? Avoid any uncomfortable situations and see that it's only beneficial for your relationship if you don't keep secrets from your partner.

Once the trust is broken, it takes building up the relationship from the beginning to gain it back. It is a very difficult and long process, but it can be done. Communicate with your partner what went wrong and why was the trust broken. Only through understanding can you move on. Don't just shrug it off because it will return and bite you. Broken trust is the number one reason for a breakup. The key to rebuilding trust is to live in the present. If you made peace with the fact that your partner lied to you, don't think he will always lie. Don't evaluate all of his actions to see if he is being truthful. That means you are not able to let go. Observe his actions in present and don't associate them with past lies. Trust yourself to be able to detect if he is being untruthful, don't go above and beyond searching for lies. If you lie, there is no action that will prove your honesty to your partner.

Chapter 34: Build Connection

Connection

As we've learned, the journey of healing from reassurance-seeking is a very personal, individual process. The problems are not with our partner but, rather, are internal and must be dealt with by us.

Yet your partner can be an integral part of the solution. They can be an amazing resource to draw on for support, love, and patience (but not reassurance!) as you go through the process. But first, they have to understand what's going on with you.

Let Them Know What You're Going Through

I count myself lucky in that I have a partner who also has dealt extensively with anxiety. This meant that he was very understanding and sympathetic with my own anxieties, even if they showed up in different ways than his own.

Make sure you sit down with your partner and talk about this with them. Choose a moment when you're feeling less anxious so that you can approach the topic with clarity. Explain the emotions that surround your anxieties and fears. Share how reassurance has come to offer you a temporary fix.

It can definitely be difficult to have this kind of conversation. The issues are extremely sensitive and personal, and talking about them demands tremendous vulnerability. That can be super scary.

But it's also amazing. When you're in a healthy, productive relationship, you must be able to experience that vulnerability with one another. It's the key to growing together in love and trust.

For those who don't have anxious attachment issues or reassurance-seeking tendencies, this type of anxiety can be mysterious.

It may be tough at first for them to understand what you're going through but opening up the conversation is a great first step.

Set Boundaries: Outline Your Expectations

Now that you've told your partner what you're dealing with, how can they help? While this process is mostly up to you, your partner can do a few things to help you out.

The most essential of these is to set some reasonable expectations together about how you communicate and how you show love and affection on a regular basis. But to set them properly, you must first examine the expectations through the lens of your reassurance-seeking behaviors. What I mean is this:

What (realistic) expectations do you have regarding how your partner will show you love on a daily basis?

What expectations do you have when you are reassurance-seeking?

Examine both of these to delve into what needs to change.

For instance, when in a normal, non-anxious state, I like to be told I'm loved each day and I depend on/expect a small to medium amount of physical intimacy with my partner. This is sufficient to meet my needs to feel loved and cherished.

But when I was in a needy, anxious state, my expectation was that Nathan would go above and beyond to show how much he loved me. In my fear-based state, a basic "I love you" or some simple cuddling wasn't enough. I told myself that I needed to hear highly emotional words from Nathan: strong assertions that he loved me, would go to the ends of the earth for me, etc.

Clearly, my anxiety was elevating my expectations to a downright excessive level. I was testing Nathan (unbeknownst to him) and "grading" him on his response. If his answers matched my expectations, I would find the reassurance I sought; Nathan would "pass" the test.

This is no way to approach a romantic relationship, and when you're not in an anxious state, you can probably see that, too.

First of all, if you have highly specific and exacting expectations of your partner, you're nearly always going to be disappointed. Your partner is not a mind-reader, and they don't know the imaginary script you've written in your head. No matter how kind and caring their response, it will not seem good enough. For me, this was at the crux of my reassurance-seeking behaviors.

Second, it is unrealistic to think that relationships will always involve heightened emotion. This expectation is built on false ideas (perhaps partly based on watching too many romcoms), and it leads to dissatisfaction in relationships. Together with your partner, you can have an ongoing conversation about what expectations are appropriate and healthy.

Learn Your Love Languages

In relationships, each individual best experience love in certain ways. The means by which we like to receive love and give love are a major driving force in the expectations we set for our partners. These means are called the Love Languages, a concept coined by Gary Chapman in his bestselling the 5 Love Languages.

The five love languages are as follows:

- Words of Affirmation

People who identify with this love language feel most loved when they receive love verbally. These people enjoy words, whether spoken or written. Compliments, affectionate phrases, and those three important words--"I love you" --are like music to their ears. These people will never get sick of hearing how special they are to you. They are also likely to find verbal communication easy and prefer showing love to others verbally.

- Acts of Service

To those who speak this love language, being generously served means the world to them. It's all about action. They feel treasured and adored when their partner takes the time to handle a chore for them, prepare them a meal, or otherwise give of their time and energy for their partner's good.

- Quality Time

Action is important to these folks, too, but what matters most is quality. These individuals want your undivided, genuine attention. They want to feel that they are the most important person to you. They deeply value meaningful time spent together.

- Physical Touch

Physical touch is the most easily understood of the love languages. Those who primarily speak this language are wild about physical interaction. This can be sexual or intimate in nature, but it can also mean that they cherish cuddling or simply sitting side-by-side. If you speak this language, you love being close to your partner, and nothing feels so good as a hug or kiss.

- Receiving Gifts

People who speak the fifth love language experience love through the gifts they receive from their partner. This doesn't just mean that they like "stuff"; what matters is the thoughtfulness that goes into the gift-giving process. These individuals feel adored when they know that you've spent time selecting the perfect gift just for them.

While each person tends to enjoy all of the love languages on some level, there are usually one or two that speak to you the most. Which one is yours? Which is your partner's?

Once you learn your love languages, it can become a lot easier to set relationship expectations that are meaningful to both of you.

Build Trust

Trust can be difficult to achieve in a relationship, especially if you've been hurt in the past. In adult relationships, trust issues abound. Nearly all of us have been through painful breakups or had our hearts broken in some way. We may have been betrayed by an unfaithful or dishonest partner. We may have internalized messages that people cannot be trusted, and that vulnerability is dangerous.

While building trust in a relationship can be a major challenge, it is vital to a long-lasting, loving partnership.

Keep in mind that creating this trust might take a lot of time, and it will likely be an ongoing process throughout your relationship. But it is absolutely a worthwhile endeavor. When you are with a partner whom you trust fully, it opens your relationship to amazing growth (and opens you to personal growth).

So how do you build trust?

Trust takes time. We need time to see that, over and over again, our partner is there for us. That their actions match their words, and that their words are truthful.

We need to be patient with this process and with ourselves. If we have issues with trust, we must be extra patient and remind ourselves that what we're doing is not easy and that trust won't be built overnight. We need patience with the faults and foibles of our partner. We need to know that no one is perfect and that even a trustworthy person can mess up sometimes.

And we need to remain open. The best way to build trust is simply to do just that: trust

Be Direct

Directness is a hallmark of great communication. Being direct in the things you say--straightforward in intention and without game-playing or beating around the bush--saves time and frustration.

For a person who tends to seek reassurance, being direct is vital. Through direct communication, you can get your point across and have your needs fulfilled.

Think Long Term

When interacting with a partner, especially during a conflict, keep your end goal in mind. Hopefully, you both share the same goal: a happy, fulfilling, and respect-filled relationship that will last for many years.

By keeping this overarching goal in mind, you can more effectively steer your conversations. Remembering that you and your partner are on the same team goes a long way during a tense situation, helping you to keep your words aligned with your goal and allowing you to listen better to what your partner is saying. In this way, unnecessary hurts can often be prevented, and extraneous, irrelevant points can be kept out of the conversation. (For instance, you might forgo bringing up last week's fight, knowing it would be counterproductive.)

Stay Focused

Speaking of counterproductive, staying focused on the issue at hand plays a major role in effective communication. It is very easy to bring "extras" into the conversation: dredging up past slights and arguments, comparing an issue to something else your partner does wrong, or making broad generalizations about your partner's behavior are all ways that you can derail a conversation. While you might want to get that hurtful barb in during the argument, you know it is not relevant to the current subject, and you know it will likely cause hurt and misunderstanding (and therefore goes against the "think long term" component of good communication). Keep your focus and keep that communication working.

Truly Listen

The fourth key to effective communication involves listening. For us reassurance-seekers, this may be the most important of all. We must learn to truly listen to what our partner is telling us.

If the two of you are practicing these communication principles, you can feel confident that your partner is attempting to convey what they mean to you. Do your part by really and truly listening. Note the words they are saying and consider the speaker's intention (hint: they care for you and have good intentions). In this way, you can fully absorb their message and respond authentically and truthfully.

Remember That Your Needs are Valid

I want to make this important point: don't forget that your needs are totally, 100% valid. Yes, even as a person who seeks frequent reassurance, your needs are valid.

Listen, friends. For whatever reason, you and I have emotional needs that require extra sensitivity and care. We need strong, specific reassurance about our fears and anxieties. We need to be shown with clarity that we are loved and treasured and cared for. And you know what? That is okay.

Sure, we're working on finding more balance in our love lives because we want to feel more secure and independent, but those needs are real, and we have them met. So even as you strive toward healing, know that your needs are valid.

Chapter 35: Dating, Relationships, and Finding Love

"There is somebody out there for everyone." I know. I want to rabbit-punch someone every time I hear that one, too. But like every other eye-roller cliché, it is irritatingly accurate. In our monogamous framework for love and marriage, love is a numbers game: there is a relatively endless pool of possibilities, and all you need is one successful outcome.

We reinforced your worth and confirmed that you have inherent value that you can offer to someone else. Now that you're not so fragile, we're going to test you a bit.

. Our objective is to help you understand that love, the endgame for dating and romantic relationships, is binary. I can help you get to the top of the mountain, but only you can decide whether you're willing to jump.

A Culture of Patience

Based on recent evidence, we're collectively a lot more careful about selecting a partner. In the United States, people are generally waiting longer to get married. According to the Pew Research Center, the number of Americans 18 and older who were married had remained stable for years, but in 2017, the figure was down eight percent (to about half) as compared to 1990. The median age for marriage in 2018 was 28 for women and 30 for men, up from 20 and 23, respectively, in 1960. People are staying single longer, which means that the eligible pool of prospective partners will stay larger for longer. In the "numbers game" that is the dating pool, this is encouraging news.

The Fear of Rejection: Practicing Failure

Now that we have the encouraging news, I'm going to give you some not-so-encouraging news. Whether you like it or not, communication must occur. Luckily, you have options, but be warned: face-to-face interaction is the most effective.

This isn't a bad thing. Finding a partner is not just about you and your needs. It's about someone else, too. Like anything else in life that is rewarding, it's not free. No matter how comfortable modern technology makes things for us, we will ultimately have to do things that test the limits of our comfort zones, make sacrifices, be vulnerable, and more importantly, fail. A lot. Because guess what? Anyone that we want to connect with on a deeper level will have to do the same thing. The "spark" will be predicated on not only shared joy, but also shared pain. It's the commonality of struggle and bend that makes love so powerful, and without understanding those feelings, you won't be able to forge and sustain a loving relationship. Your partner will be your support system throughout your life, and you will need to prepare yourself for a reciprocal role.

As introverts, we're constantly fighting a losing battle with the fear of rejection. It's largely why we're hesitant to take the first step in a conversation. We see someone we find attractive...and then that person exits our lives forever. Another missed opportunity. But this anxiety is not unique to introverts, as extraverts struggle with this as well. Moreover, the fear of rejection not only appears in other personality types, but also appears in other facets of our lives, including our business, job interviews, and friendships.

Modern research suggests that the fear of rejection is largely due to a survival mechanism that causes one to focus only on the pain arising from the worst-case scenario. This is the same survival mechanism that governs our "fight or flight" reaction. Our fear response starts in a region of our brain called the amygdala. Located in the temporal lobe part of the brain, the job of the amygdala is to detect things that are unusual or that stand out. When the amygdala detects a threat, such as a predator, it processes the possible physical harm that could arise from an encounter with the predator. This ultimately triggers a response of fear in the amygdala, which, in turn, activates areas in the body responsible for the motor functions involved in fight or flight. It also triggers a release of stress hormones in our sympathetic nervous system.

Interestingly enough, the human brain doesn't distinguish physical pain from emotional pain. According to one study, as far as the brain is concerned, a heart attack feels just as painful as a broken heart. Some would argue that this explains why taking Tylenol can relieve or reduce social anxiety in a fashion similar to how it relieves physical pain.

The most effective way to overcome your fear of rejection is to get used to it. By familiarizing yourself with the risk of the worst-case scenario, you'll soon realize that which you have feared with so much intensity was not worth your anxiety. If you're looking to start small, try something with lower stakes. Clean a messy house by starting with the nastiest room first. Apply for a job that's way out of your league. When you're at work, do the toughest, most boring project at the bottom of your pile first thing in the morning. Practicing diving into the most daunting tasks first and hitting them head-on.

Day 1 of Jiang's 100-day rejection plan began with a request to borrow $100 from a stranger. Surprisingly, the stranger agreed. Most of his other endeavors were hilariously unsuccessful, including:

- asking a diner for a burger refill
- playing soccer in a stranger's backyard
- asking a police officer to drive his car

Jiang was told no. Lots and lots and lots of times. But from all of these rejection experiences, he began to notice a pattern: every "no" had the possibility of being rehabilitated into a "yes." In the early phases of the experiment, he would respond to rejection by walking away, head down and tail between legs. Toward the end, he found himself persisting, remaining engaged, and believing he could change the mind of his counterpart. The lesson here: handling and combating rejection from a stranger is a skill that can be learned, practiced, and developed.

Being social is not your thing. I get it. It's not mine, either. And that's exactly why you have to do what I'm going to ask you to do, even though it's going to sound like medieval Spanish torture. Or whatever kind of torture sounds worse than the Spanish kind.

Managing Expectations

Your initial reaction may be "What!? Hit on a total stranger? Have you lost your damn mind?" This is a perfectly understandable and reasonable reaction, and it's also completely unfounded and misses the point entirely. The exercise above is not hitting on someone, which necessarily connotes an ulterior objective. While Catch and Release may have the unintended collateral benefit of starting a mutually beneficial conversation with a stranger, that is not its aim. Also, yes. I have lost my damn mind. If you want results in your social life that are different from what you're presently experiencing, you'd be well-advised to break free from the conventional constraints of your own mind as well.

So, what's the purpose of Catch and Release? To practice taking initiative. That's certainly one of its benefits, but not the goal. To desensitize yourself to rejection. Not quite. While the feeling of rejection is merely one of multiple possible outcomes from Catch and Release, as opposed to a fatal judgment about one's self-worth, rejection itself cannot be a possible outcome of this exercise because you are not proposing anything that is subject to rejection. What about eliminating fear? Closer, but that's not the full picture.

The purpose of this goal is train yourself how to love yourself and others. Most of us, including myself at one time, are under the misguided impression that love is intuitive, simple, and a serendipitous occurrence that "just happens" to us. That's a beautiful thought. It really is. Unfortunately, it's also pure and unadulterated bullshit. While fortune may manipulate time and location to become a factor in bringing two people together in the same place at the same time, to suggest that one can find and maintain love solely through hope and inertia is naïve. In order to truly love someone, and be worthy of someone else's love, you have to make sacrifices, take risks, navigate outside your comfort zone, and shift your focus from your own happiness to someone else's.

This is not unlike any other worthwhile pursuit in life. The rich entrepreneur didn't get rich chasing money and the famous musician didn't get famous chasing fame. Being rich and famous is a consequence of working hard to create something that other people value and that makes the world a better place. Catch and Release teaches you to shift your focus from your own needs and wants to the needs and wants of others. It allows you to practice observing the good in someone else, to make yourself uncomfortable in order to make someone feel beautiful, and to give without asking for or expecting anything in return.

Now, you can only control so much, and someone else's reaction is not one of those things. Sadly, our society has taught us to be selfish, superficial, and insecure. Not coincidentally, and perhaps somewhat understandably, we often regard any random act of kindness from another person with suspicion. What does this person really want? Why is she being so nice to me? Is he trying to sell me something or get into my pants?

The worst-case scenario arising from the Catch and Release Exercise is that someone reacts unfavorably and that such a reaction hurts your feelings. What you need to remember is that if that worst-case scenario happens, it is not a reflection on your worth. In fact, it has nothing to do with you and everything to do with the other person. The other person is reacting based on a survival instinct that has taught him or her that any kind stranger is a wolf in sheep's clothing. Don't feel angry, guilty, or hurt. All you have done is offer a token of kindness to a stranger in hopes that it might make that person feel beautiful, loved, admired, or appreciated. It's unconditional charity, and that remains true irrespective of how the other person reacts. You have nothing to be ashamed of. More importantly, your simple actions in this exercise constitute a simple act of kindness that makes our world a more loving and kinder place.

Improving Communication in Social Situations

The most common cause of a break-up, divorce, or termination of any relationship, inside or outside of the romantic setting, is a breakdown in communication. Preston Ni, a professor, communications coach, former executive at Microsoft and other Fortune 500 companies, and author of numerous publications on communication, including articles in The Oprah Magazine, and Psychology Today, identified communication as one of the top reasons a relationship fails. Whether it is trust issues, different expectations and priorities, or boredom, maintaining communication is vital to the health and success of a relationship. Something as simple as a small fight can lead to a bigger domino effect due to a lack of communication.

The S-Words

Before I proceed down this road, I want to make something indubitably clear so my detractors can sit quiet for a few minutes: introversion is not coterminous with shyness, which is a sub-facet of the related, and much broader, clinical condition of social anxiety and which we will refer to for our purposes as Social Anxiety Shyness, or "SAS." There. I said it. Now, with that out of the way, I also want to make equally clear that a significant stratum of the introversion population does, in fact, struggle with some element of SAS. Yes, that's right. In the Venn diagram between the universe of introverts and the universe of SAS-affected individuals, guess what? There is an intersection. If you're the kind of reader that wants to learn more about introversion on a broader level, I encourage you to stick around for a few paragraphs.

Chapter 36: Disagreements and Arguments

It is easy for partners to fall into a recurring pattern of conflicts and disagreements when they do not fully understand each other's behavior and personality. This does not mean their relationship is flawed, it simply shows that in order for partners to reduce the rate of arguments, disagreements and conflict between, partners have to try to understand and empathize with each other

Why Do We Disagree?

There are an infinite number of causes for disagreements in relationships ranging from major reasons like incompatibility in partner's behavior, parenting methods, communication methods, finances, etc.

But there are generally specific reasons why partners engage in conflicts and disagreements with each other.

Understanding these reasons helps both partners to understand why his/her partner behaves a certain way or react to certain behaviors and why it results in conflict and disagreements.

Some of these issues are:

• **Unrealistic expectations and demands.**

When partner's relationship expectations and needs are not met, they tend to become grumpy, frustrated, angry, dissatisfaction, unhappy and may even develop feelings of resentment towards his/her partner.

These negative feelings may affect the individual's relation with his partner, making him/her sarcastic and offhand towards their partner.

It is expected that partners in relationships have certain expectations from each other, but in order for this expectation to be met, partners have to clearly state them. It is unreasonable to keep mute about one's expectations and needs from the relationship expect such needs to be addressed.

Although partners with deep connection between them could communicate through body languages, relationships expectations ought to be voiced out. If there is no clear communication of these needs and expectations, it is impossible for them to be met.

Expression of one's needs and expectations of each other and their relationship ought to be done in a friendly conversational manner; demanding one's expectations be met will only put his/her partner in a defensive state and lead to another argument between partners.

Irrespective of the level of connection between partners, they cannot completely agree on every issue. They are two different individuals; therefore, it is expected that they will have different opinions and views on the same issue

In relationships, couples have a partnership in place that stipulates that they be emotionally and physically available for each other in times of need.

However, the idea that one's partner will be readily available every time is a bit unrealistic.

Individuals have their own sense of self outside their relationships, they have their own personal interests, friends, extended family, career, etc. Although partners should try to be available for each other as often as possible, it is ludicrous for an individual to expect to be his/her partner's sole focus.

- **Constant criticism**

In the same way an individual has expectations from his/her relationship, there can also be grievances and shortcomings.

Humans are genetically flawed so a perfect behavior cannot and should not be expected from one's partner. However, the method used to relay shortcoming to one's partner is very important.

When partners begin to accuse and assign blame to each other (who did what, who didn't do what, who said what, who didn't say what) the point they are trying to pass across becomes lost in translation as emotions begin to run high, feelings gets hurt, and partners begin a screaming match.

However, this could be avoided if partners share their grievances in a simple conversational manner without complaint and assigning blame.

- **Negative comparison, projection and stereotyping**

An individual's past relationships can affect and influence his/her behavior and attitudes towards new relationships and formation of emotional bonds.

Conflicts can arise when partners allow past experiences to regulate their attitudes and perception of their current relationship.

Comparing one's partner to other individuals reduces their self-worth and gives them the illusion that their partners do not appreciate them.

For example, a man who always compares his significant other to other more slender women will have his partner the idea that he does not find her attractive and wants to change her which may cause her to develop feelings of insecurity and resentment towards him.

In order to prevent conflicts and disagreements, Individuals with toxic past relationships have to take care not to project negative feelings from relationships into current relationship. This could lead to disagreement and conflict between current partners.

New relationships should be entered into with a fresh start and partners with emotionally hurtful pasts should let go of negative feelings, give their new partner a chance to build intimacy and trust, without portraying feelings of insecurity and resentment from past relationships into the current one.

What Issues Do We Disagree On?

Understanding the specific issues causing disagreements in relationships can be a first step towards reconciliation of conflicts and disagreements. Partners in a committed relationship have an equal partnership and have to make every decision affecting their lived together.

Because they are two entirely different individuals, the have different opinions and views about issues and if partners do not know how to effectively communicate his/her opinion and listen to and respect his/her partners opinion too even when they don't completely agree with them, there will be constant argument and conflict between them.

There are a million and one issues that can cause conflict and disagreements between partners and the solutions to these issues are equally that many.

Partners can have disagreements on a number of issues ranging from what to have for dinner and to where to buy a house.

Disagreements are a normal part of relationships; partners are encouraged to have different opinions about certain issues which helps them retain their self-identity separate from the relationship, however this difference of opinion could lead to conflict between partners when both of them are unrelenting on said issue.

The most effective way to resolve conflict between partners is through a system of compromise.

Compromise involves a system of settlement of differences by consent reached through mutual concession.

Compromise involves both partners agreeing on a midpoint between their differences where the decision reached equally serves both of them and serves none.

Compromise entails settling differences in a win-win manner where both partner's needs are met.

For example, a couple jointly buys a car, and can't agree on who gets to take the car to work since they work at opposite ends of the city.

The obvious compromise choice in this case is that they get to take the car to work on a weekly shift basis.

This way, both partners can be satisfied.

It is ideal to settle differences in a relationship using compromise because when partners compromise on issues and successfully arrive at a mid-point that meets if not all but parts of an individual's needs, there is no aftermath feeling of resentment.

During disagreements, the partner that always "loses" might begin to generate feelings of resentment towards his/her significant other. Regardless of the cause of argument or who is at fault and who is not, partners will always want to win the fight.

There are no medals that one hopes to gain from winning fights or an argument with his/her partner but for the satisfaction and bragging rights of being right (I told you so).

Not all arguments between partners are hostile. Some people like to argue to hear their partner's perspective on an issue and may not want to ask directly, thus he/she would incite an argument.

Partners bond on different levels. Some partners bond over shared interests, others bond over intellect, and others bond as a result of physical attraction while some bond over the arguments they have.

It is important to note that these types of arguments are without malice and are more of argumentative conversations than disagreements.

There are also disagreements between partners that could be deal breakers for the both of them.

In this case, there are no compromises between partners; it's either all or nothing. In cases like this, both partners are unrelenting on their stands and the inability for partners to resolve these differences between themselves could lead to termination of the relationship.

The issues that could lead to partners having an uncompromising argument where both partners are unwilling to back down from their stands even at the risk of terminating their relationship are usually on life changing decisions.

Some of such decisions may include deciding whether or not to fully commit and get married (In this cases, one partner feels the need to move the relationship to the level and fully commit while the other partner is not quite there yet.

The partner arguing for full commitment might give the other partner arguing against it an ultimatum to either get married or end the relationship.), whether or not to have children (in this case, one of the partners may not want to have children either due to financial reasons or underlying health issues or for fear of responsibility that children bring or because he/she is of the belief that having children would interfere with his/her career plan, while the other partner wants to focus on building a family and wants a child /children.

To resolve this difference between them, one partner has to be willing to let go of his/her goal for the success of the relationship.

Adoption cannot be seen as a point of compromise in this case because the individual that wants a child still wins even if he/she is not the birth parent.), whether or not to have a career (in this case, partners might have different opinions about gender specific roles, where the man thinks a woman's place is at home building the family, while the man provides and protects.

The woman in the case might strongly object to that and want to build her own career and have her own source of income.

In this case, the probability for compromise is considerably low and partners; if they do not find a common ground for compromise may terminate the relationship.

Some even argue that in cases like this, the reasonable thing to do is to terminate the relationship.

This is because for partners to resolve the conflict and arrive at some sort of solution, one partner may have to give up on their core values which may lead to loss of self-identity.

How Do We Reconnect and Maintain Intimacy After Resolving Conflict?

Maintaining intimacy is crucial for the success of every long-term relationship.

Existing intimacy between partners helps both partners to understand each other, identify unspoken feelings of hurt faster and to better empathize with each other. It is relatively easier to identify partners with a strong sense of intimacy between them, there is usually a sync of communication between them, understanding without explanation, constant show of affection like touching as often as possible, holding hands, and a sense of togetherness between them.

Creating and maintaining emotional intimacy requires genuine interest, transparency, vulnerability and reciprocity.

The degree of intimacy in a relationship is determined by the ability to listen to and understand one's partner.

Couples in an intimate relationship must develop genuine interest to create intimacy and be willing to lower their emotional barriers and be vulnerable with each other.

It is important for partners to be intimate with each other and to have intimate knowledge of one another to smoothly coexist together.

This is not to say that partners with emotional intimacy between them do not experience the occasional emotional disconnection, disagreement on issues and conflict.

Both emotional bond and connection and physical bond and connections suffer when there is a conflict between partners.

There is an elasticity on the emotional connections between partners which is determined by the level of emotional intimacy between them. The deeper the level of emotional intimacy between partners, the stronger elasticity of their emotional connection.

The emotional connection elasticity is the degree to which intimate partner's relationship could withstand wear and tear.

The band of elasticity of partners emotional connection, eventually contracts and bring drifting partners back together in harmony and intimacy.

Chapter 37: Rebuilding Trust Once It's Broken

All throughout this we have talked about jealousy, anxiety, and insecurity and how the three of these things often lead to trust issues. As you are already aware trust is a big part of any kind of relationship, if you don't have trust you won't have a relationship for very long. As we have talked sometimes the trust issues are not the fault of your partner, they are based on your relationships. However, sometimes it is the fault of your partner; they do or say something that shatters the trust you have given them.

Once your trust in your partner has been shattered your relationship often starts to go downhill. You are literally second guessing everything that your partner says and does, and the reason for that is the lack of trust. Once the trust goes, so does the sense of security and safety you had in your relationship. Once trust is broken the feelings of love, respect, and friendship are often replaced by anger and fear.

Trust issues can stem from all sorts of scenarios, whether its lies or infidelity, the reason doesn't matter, just the end results do. Once that trust has been broken, it might seem like all hope is lost. I mean after all; how can you reasonably expect to trust that person again when you have never felt so violated in your life? Now even if your life currently right now is filled with nothing but arguments and everything seems hopeless, there are some things that can be done to help rebuild the trust that you two once had.

Step One: Come Clean

The first step that you will need to take when trying to rebuild the trust in your relationship is to come clean with what you have done. Nobody can move beyond the hurt and the anger, if you continually deny that it happened. You have to step up and take responsibility for what you did, which includes admitting what you have done. Taking responsibility doesn't necessarily mean including all of those minute details, sometimes sharing the details only causes more pain and anger, so be honest but don't over share.

Step Two: Be Aware of How you Act

You need to pay close attention to how you are acting. Being on the defensive or even acting casually about the problem at hand can have disastrous results. If you act like what you did doesn't really matter, your partner is not going to be very willing to work things out. You need to put forth a very sincere effort to show your partner that you do feel bad for what happened. This comes down to the way that you communicate. There is verbal communication of course, where your apologies for the mistake that has been made and try to make up for it. Then there is also your nonverbal communication which reveals much more than the words that you say. With your non-verbal communication, you can express your remorse over having broken trust, or you could reveal an attitude that shows you do not really care. It just needs you to be sensitive to what you are doing.

Step Three: Talk about It

After you have come clean about what you have done, you will want to find the time to talk to your partner about what made you do it. I don't recommend doing it right away, wait a few days for things to calm down a little bit. Talking about why you did it, how you might need help, as well as how you plan to fix things so it doesn't happen again is a great way to show your partner that you are serious about working things out, and just might convince them that you can be trusted again.

Before you decide to do this, take the time to carry out an intense self-analysis, so that you can determine what happened that you broke trust. Unless there is something wrong with your personality, such that you have a personality disorder, it is unlikely that you purposely went out to break the trust of someone. There will be something that is lacking for you, a gap that you needed to fill, or something deep down inside that drove you to do the wrong thing.

When you sit down to talk with your partner about everything that has happened it is important to do it correctly. When talking you want to sit so that you are facing each other, and as we learned from trust building exercises, as close as possible, to help reestablish that trust. Proceed to tell your partner the entire truth, do not go into hurtful details, but be honest about exactly how you feel. If you make things seem better than they are, you are not doing yourself or your relationship any favors. Honesty really is the key to rebuilding trust.

Step Four: Be Gentle

Communicating is vital to rebuilding trust, as long as it is done correctly. While you want to be perfectly honest and open with your partner, you don't want to be harsh. Coming right out and confessing might make you feel better, but it isn't how your partner deserves to be treated. Talking openly and honestly doesn't mean you have to forget about tact, you can still get your point across about how you are feeling while being tactful. And, no matter what happens or who confesses what, the worst thing either one of you can do is attack the other.

Also ensure that you do not put your partner in the wrong, or in any way blame them for the mistakes that you have made in the relationship to break trust. This will be the easiest way to ensure that they clamp up. It is so important to take responsibility for the role that you have in breaking the trust, and that is why this is a point that is raised over and over again.

Step Five: Let your Partner Talk

Part of communicating freely involves letting your partner speak. This can be especially hard if your partner has recently hurt your feelings, but you won't be able to resolve anything if you don't listen to what they have to say. By listening to what they have to say, even if it's not something you necessarily want to hear, it is something that they need to do. It can also help you decide if it's worth trying to rebuild the trust, just don't make that harsh decision while you are still feeling angry.

There is a difference between hearing what they have to say and listening to what they have to say. Hearing what they have to say is easy, as this means that you do not really take it in and consider the implications of what is being said. When you are listening to what your partner has to say, it is more the words that you are taking in. You are also absorbing the emotions that surround these words, the anger and sadness that they may be feeling, the defiance that may come through and everything else. It may not be what you want to experience, but your relationship will be much better off if you choose to put yourself in the shoes of your partner by truly listening.

When letting your partner talk that means they are going to also have questions. The worst thing you can do is avoid answering your partner's questions. No matter what question they have you need to respond to the questions, avoiding them makes you seem guilty of something. And, remember, when answering their questions, you need to remain honest, yet tactful. Belittling them or attacking them is only going to work against you.

The way that you ask these questions is also important, as is the way that you respond. At the back of your mind, you need to remember that you should be coming from a place of love all the time.

Step Six: Be Transparent

In order to prove that you are doing everything that you can to be trusted again you are going to need to make yourself entirely transparent to your partner. Making yourself transparent to your partner includes giving them access to everything, emails, voicemail, etc. While this might sound easy, it really is not because you are simply giving up your privacy and that can make a person edgy. Being edgy often means you end up getting defensive with your partner, which can cause even more problems. Just remind yourself it's either your privacy or your relationship, only you can decide what one is more important.

In addition to being transparent with your partner, you also need to willingly share information. If you feel like you have to withhold information from your partner, you are setting yourself up for trust problems on down the road. If it is something that you have to hide, either you shouldn't be doing it, or you shouldn't be in the relationship. Being open and honest with your partner means they have less reason to doubt you when you tell them something.

Step Seven: Renewing the Vows

Most people think that in order to renew their vows they have to be married, but that is far from the truth. If you are simply in a relationship you and your partner need to sit down and talk about what you first felt when you entered into the relationship. Talk about the values that both of you considered sacred. You need to have a serious discussion as to what you want and how you want things to be in the future. Each partner can write up their own vows and you can even perform a ceremony in front of your friends to help make it even more official.

The one thing that you need to remember when it comes to rebuilding the trust in your relationship is that it is not something that is going to happen overnight. Even though the trust was lost overnight, the actions that lead up to the loss of trust probably took place over an extended period of time. If you really want to rebuild your trust in your partner or you want to start believing in your partner again, you are going to need to put forth the effort required. You can't give up just because it's not easy.

Is It Safe to Trust Again?

Once your trust has been broken, it can be very hard to trust that person ever again. We will be perfectly honest here, there is no way to guarantee that your partner won't break your trust again, but at the same time there isn't anything saying they will ever do anything to break your trust again either. This kind of puts you into a catch 22, and only you can decide if you are willing to take the chance and trust in them again.

Once you do decide to trust your partner again you are going to be overrun with various emotions. You are going to wonder if they are going to be betrayed by them again. Don't worry, these fears are 100% normal, but being aware of them is a good thing. These fears if left to fester in your head can be the downfall to your relationship, as they can get in the way of rebuilding trust and getting things back on track.

You end up being cautious because you are afraid to be hurt again but being cautious can work against you and your goal of saving your relationship. Trying to move forward past the anxiety and insecurities can be very hard; it would be easier if you had a sure-fire way of knowing that nothing like this would happen again in the future. If only there was some way to know for sure that your partner is telling the truth and they have changed.

Chapter 38: How to Appreciate Your Partner and Accept Them

In any relationship, we need to be able to accept our partners the way they are no one is perfect and an important thing to remember is that perfection is a myth. No one in this world is perfect, and everyone is flawed. If you come into your relationship thinking that your partner is perfect and that you won't have any issues then this you are setting yourself up for very unrealistic expectations, it's because they didn't realize that chasing perfection doesn't get you anywhere. Instead of trying to make everything perfect, accept your partner how they are, and love them unconditionally.

When we decide to share our life with someone else we've already taken the time to get to know them, and we take the time to understand who they are and what they're about when we take the step to join our lives with them forever we have told them that we accept them for who they are Is after you have gotten in a relationship you find that this is not true anymore than your relationship needs work a relationship cannot work if you do not accept your partner for who they are By that same logic by that same logic your partner and yourself will have bed communication and find that you're unable to communicate as efficiently as you'd like to because you feel that your partner doesn't understand you which can lead to feelings of neglect.

Remember that you don't want your partner to have unrealistic expectations of you so you shouldn't have unrealistic expectations for them either. If you want your relationship to work, then you will need to understand the importance of being able to make sure that you are thinking realistically.

When you become frustrated with your partner, you need to pull back and recognize what it is you're thinking. Is what you are thinking something that your partner really needs to change or is it something that you've built up in your mind because you have unrealistic expectations about what they should be or what you want them to be? Is it something that you need to change with your thought process, or is it something that genuinely needs to be changed in your partner himself? Another question that you should ask yourself is why is it your partner's job to live up to unrealistic expectations? On the opposite side to this, why is it your job to live up to your partner's unrealistic expectations? You need to realize that having the right expectations of yourself, your partner, and your relationship are the best ways that you're going to be able to make this relationship work.

Flexibility is another thing that is going to help you appreciate your partner and make sure that you are accepting them the way they are. It's very easy to think of the world as just black or just white and think that this is wrong, or this is right, and there is no in-between, but that's not realistic. Things don't have to be one way or the other. Instead of labeling your way as the right way or your partner's way is the right way, remember that you need to compromise and understand how things actually are.

Negative thinking is much easier for some people than positive thinking because being negative doesn't require half as much effort as being positive. When a person is being negative and thinking negatively, it's very self-imposed and self-centered behavior. When we think negatively, we are not accepting our partner for who they are, and instead, you see the negative in them because you're focusing on being negative yourself. Being positive instead of focusing on why your partner is the way that he is will cause you to be able to focus on what's amazing about him and why you like him in the first place. This, in turn, is going to lead you to accept him for who he is, and this will lead to you appreciating him for who he is as well. Just as you need the love of your partner to make you happy and whole, your partner needs your love to make him happy and whole as well. He needs you to be here for him as well.

Another helpful hint to appreciating your partner is to force yourself to see things in a different light and put the focus on you. What we mean by this is that you should ask yourself how you would feel if your partner was judging you the way that you're judging them. Another question you should ask is that if they didn't accept you the way that you're not accepting them how you would feel if you thought your partner didn't understand you or love you the way that you needed to be loved and respected? Keeping this in mind, you'll be much more flexible, and you'll be able to understand why you shouldn't treat your partner this way.

You should also strive to remember that the past is gone and there's nothing you can do about it. You can make up for the past. That part is possible, and we're not saying that it is not. What we're saying is whatever happened in the past you can't go back in time and make it so that that didn't happen. There are no do-overs or a reset button on the things you do because life is not a video game. It's here and now and you need to learn that if you make a mistake, you can't undo it, but you can try and fix it and move on from it. You just need to remember that whatever has happened has already happened and there's nothing you can do to change that. We all make mistakes, so instead of focusing on the past, try living in the present and give your partner the gift of understanding that. If you're always comparing things to how they were before or you're always comparing things to the past and bringing up past arguments along with things that can't be changed, the only thing that you are actually doing is hindering your acceptance of your partner and your acceptance of each other. If this continues over time, it could actually end up destroying your relationship because you're not focusing on the future the way that you need to be. The biggest reason that this is an issue that can be so damaging is because when you are doing this, it brings resentment and past pain to the relationship. This, in turn, brings hurt into the relationship, along with fighting and harsh words. To avoid this, you should focus on the present and what you can do in the present to change things to make them better for your partner and yourself.

When we judge others it's often a result of our own personal criticisms that we've had to endure ourselves, but we shouldn't put pressure on ourselves to do things a certain way, and we shouldn't put pressure on our partner to do things that way either. Letting what others have said to you or done to you can affect you and your thought process and the way you treat others, including your partner. This is why people say your past shapes who you are. If your mistreated when your younger or you've had bad relationships, you can unintentionally carry that over into your future relationships even though you don't mean to. The way to get past this is to understand that that is what you've got this issue in the first place and then work on trying to change. In the long run, this will ensure that your heart and spirit are happier and more fulfilled. This will cause your treatment of your partner to get better and make sure that your partner's spirit and heart are happier too.

When you put unnecessary pressure on your partner, the only thing you're doing is pushing them away. Now every relationship has pressure, and every relationship has areas where your partner will be under pressure but what we're saying is instead of judging yourself and judging others understand that everyone has limitations and you can't put too much pressure on someone because they will crack. This may not happen right away, especially if your partner is strong, but eventually, even the strongest person can break eventually if you keep pushing them too hard. If you cause your partner to crack, then your relationship is going to falter immediately because they're going to feel resentment towards you for doing so. When you are happy and fulfilled as an individual you will be less critical and rude to your partner.

Something to remember is that even though your partner can meet your needs, you can meet your own needs as well. You can also meet your partner's needs as they meet yours. In order to fully appreciate your partner and to accept them for who they are, you need to remember that when you are happy with yourself, you'll be happy with everything around you. The same is true if you're unhappy. If you are unhappy with everything around you, you are going to be overly critical of your partner, and you won't appreciate them for who they are.

When you recognize that you're unhappy, you will at least be able to understand that you need to tell your partner in a loving and respectful manner that you're unhappy. Then you can work together on becoming happier so that you can appreciate each other and accept each other the way you need to. Negativity in a relationship is one of the biggest reasons that a relationship can falter because when that happens, it breeds insecurity, painful arguments, and hurt in the relationship that you have. When you're able to understand that you and your partner can meet your needs and that you should apply positive thinking instead of negativity, you'll be able to see your partner as your partner. This is what you should be seeing them as instead of just seeing your partner as someone who's supposed to meet every single need of yours.

Something to remember is that a happy relationship will occur when two people are happy and content. When two people are happy and content with coming together and being together, they realize that their relationship has fewer problems and they are much better at appreciating each other. Many people have heard the expression that their partner completes them, and for many, this is true. For just as many, they feel completely alone and love that that feeling grows with their partner. For many happy couples, they understand that they feel complete already with their partner and with themselves. So, they have the best of both worlds.

Each of us has to be responsible at least in part for our own happiness and because of this happy person in a relationship is able to increase the flexibility and the happiness that you have together as a couple in your relationship. Flexibility is very important when accepting your partner for who he is. This is because when you're able to be flexible is the ability to see that you can converse with your partner freely and without judgment. It also helps your ability to be able to compromise in your relationship.

You never want to hurt your partner or be cruel to them, and you need to remember that this is why you need to remember the tips of empathetic dialogue as well as listening in the same way. The way that we speak with our partners can affect every part of our relationship, and if you want to have your partner feel like you appreciate them for who you are, then you will need to make sure you watch your words.

Chapter 39: Healing from Toxic Relationship

If your spouse was your abuser, you wouldn't necessarily think twice about cutting off contact. In fact, it would likely be the best thing you could do for your life going forward. This doesn't change simply because your abuser happens to be your mother. The same dynamic is involved in both cases: She can't harm you if she can't reach you. The question is, what does that really mean?

It means exactly what it says, no more, no less. It means you don't see your mother. In addition, it means you don't talk on the phone, email, text, or skype. It means no messages through some third party. It means no social media stalking. It means you cut them out of your life, and you do it with as little feeling or sympathy as they have given you over the years.

Sounds cold, doesn't it? It is, and it'll be hard, perhaps the hardest thing you will ever do, but you need to understand that there is a very good reason for you to do it. As the child of a narcissistic mother, you were conditioned to tolerate terrible things and that affected you in ways that are long-lasting, and emotionally and socially crippling. As you recover, as you rebuild your identity, the last thing you need is to be sucked back into that vortex of narcissistic madness. Yes, it is as simple as that. This is your time. You can reconnect at some point in the future when you and your boundaries are stronger and there is far less chance of getting sucked back in. For now, however, you need to take care of yourself.

Blowback

You need to remember that your narcissistic mother is like a junkie. She is always in search of her emotional fix. Up until now, she's had you for that. You were her connection, her narcissistic supplier, and now that you have closed-up shop, her supply has gone and like any good addict, she's going to react. Here are some things you will want to watch out for:

She will not respect your no contact decision. Going no contact is erecting a boundary, and if she was able to respect boundaries in the first place, you would not be doing it. As a result, she is going to contact you regardless of what you say. After all, she sees you as an extension of herself, not as a fully realized human being with rights and needs of your own. As a result, it may be impossible for her to understand why you are doing this. So, she is going to call, text, email, even stalk you on social media. This can be handled by screening your calls and emails. Let her leave voicemail messages, filter her emails into a single folder that you can go through at your leisure, and block her on social media. If she shows up at your door and you answer, which is always a choice, don't allow her inside. At the door, be courteous and professional, don't allow yourself to be drawn into a debate and don't allow her to threaten you. Tell her again why you have walked away from her and end the conversation. After all, as much as she would disagree, this is all about you now, not her.

She will send her flying monkeys. Make a note of who among your family members and friends are trying to get you back in contact with your mother. They will complain that you never talk to Mom, they will demand to know why, and they will try to convince you to re-establish contact. These are her flying monkeys and no matter how well-intentioned they may seem, and regardless of whether they understand what they are really doing, these flying monkeys have come to do her bidding and are ultimately harmful to you. You may need to accept the fact that you will likely have to cut them loose as well. You will be able to recognize them by the way they seem to sympathize with you while not really wanting to hear you out. Instead, they will try to guilt you into relenting.

She will resort to character assassination. Narcissists who can't reach their victims directly, either by themselves or through their flock of flying monkeys, will do so indirectly through the use of smear campaigns and character assassination. You will find yourself at the center of a whirlwind of accusations and innuendo, and the people who confront you about it will be those you thought were either on your side or completely uninvolved. Even worse, when you defend yourself, you are likely to find that Mom has already poisoned the well by painting a convincing portrait of herself as your victim and you as some sort of caricatured monster. So, after years of psychological abuse, you will be the one seen as a liar.

The sad truth is that by going no contact with your narcissistic mother, you may well find yourself being shunned by many friends and members of the family, people who have taken her side in the conflict. It will hurt. That is inevitable and that is alright. Let it. These people are actually doing you a favor, by sorting themselves into your mother's camp, they are letting you know that they are part of the problem and people you will want to avoid anyway until you are ready to reengage. Your number one goal is to move on, and as long as this is going on, then nothing on that end has changed. You cannot control that, but you can control how much of it gets to you. (Lee, 2018)

Other Challenges When Going No Contact

Your plan is only as good as your resolve, and everything from your family, the culture we live in, and your own upbringing is going to challenge that resolve. For example, people won't understand why you have turned your back on your mother. Our culture, after all, venerates motherhood. To do otherwise is to acknowledge that the bedrock of the family isn't as solid as we would like to believe it to be. After all, in an almost religious way, Mom stands as the epitome of all that is good and nurturing, self-sacrificing and protective, and people who were lucky enough not to have had your experience are going to judge you harshly. Never mind the fact that you did not make this choice on a whim, and that it involved years of personal struggle to finally take action, all they will see is that you turned your back on your own mother. More than that, to go no contact with your mother involves a great deal of cognitive dissonance because you have spent a lifetime in that mother venerating culture, you were brought up to believe in that ideal, and there is still a part of you that wishes Mom could have lived up to it. As a result, you are going to have issues that will make maintaining your resolve that much more difficult.

You're likely to second-guess yourself. Setting aside the cultural disapproval you may face, the cost of walking away from your narcissistic mother could be far greater than you might think because you are also walking away from the people who love and side with her, and that will make you question the wisdom of what you are doing, make you wonder if you have done the right thing.

You may even end up making a few trials runs at it, cutting her out of your life for a little while, then going back again. That's alright, it's part of the learning process, part of taking what you know and understand intellectually, that your mother does not love you, or at least she doesn't love you in the way you deserve to be loved by a mother and applying that new emotional knowledge to your emotions. You need to believe in yourself, which after a lifetime of narcissistic abuse is a tall order. It is essential that you understand that you are doing the right thing for yourself.

You're likely to feel very conflicted. Here's that cognitive dissonance again, the knowledge that you are a survivor of abuse and the self-criticism and self-blame for not being able to somehow avoid this decision by fixing the relationship. You may even feel the shame of having to make this choice, made all the worse by the way the rest of the family is treating you as they rally around mother.

This brings us to an interesting question: What do you, as an adult survivor of a narcissistic parent, when Mom gets old and infirm? After all, aren't the children supposed to care for their elderly parents? Isn't that the societal expectation? Aren't they owed something here?

As with so many of these questions, the answer would be easy if you were raised by a normal mother who taught you right and let you develop into your own person. You were not, however, raised by a normal mother with normal and expected maternal instincts. You were raised by a pathological narcissist who used your formative years to twist you into a vessel for her will, who became a seething vortex of need every time you had something of your own going on and exhibited monstrous rage whenever you even questioned her.

The problem is that she really does need you now. She is old and likely sick, and the golden child, your sibling who turned out just like her, sees no reason to get his hands dirty. He has his own life to live, his own conquests to make, and so the responsibility gets dropped on you with a great big helping of guilt to make sure you do the "right thing."

Mom did make some effort to care for you during your early years. That effort may have been minimal of she was the self-absorbed neglectful sort of narcissistic parent, but she still thinks you owe her no matter how poorly she met your needs. If she was the engulfing kind of narcissistic parent, she'll make sure you know how much she did for you, whether you wanted her to or now, all the ways she made your life better, and also how you owe her everything. Regardless, as far as she is concerned you owe her and you're guilty of putting her through the trouble of raising you.

Is she right? No. She is the one who made love conditional. She is the one who left you with a skewed view of relationships. She is the one who meddled in areas she had no right to be, who verbally and emotionally abused you, who made you question your own sanity and denied you the self-esteem and assertiveness to truly take control of your own life and now she thinks she's going to waltz in and park her walker in your home, where she can turn her toxic attentions onto your family, inflicting the same harm on them that she did on you, all because in some twisted way she feels entitled to that for simply expelling you from her birth canal? It's time she begins to understand that this is not how the world works.

Relationships, if you haven't learned this yet, are optional. That goes for all of them. Family is a concept, it's not something written in stone. Just as a home doesn't need to be a house, biology doesn't dictate who your family is. It doesn't matter what society says. It doesn't matter what the church pastor says. It doesn't matter what the therapist says. It doesn't matter what friends say. It doesn't matter what family says, and it certainly doesn't matter what some wrinkled, abusive narcissist says. She has no family claim on you.

Chapter 40: How to Heal from Emotional Anxiety

How to Heal the Scars

One of the hardest things anyone will ever have to do is to end a relationship. Whether it is a family relationship, a marriage, or even just a friendship, every relationship is sacred as it fills a special place in a person's heart. This is why codependent relationships are so devastating. They tear away at a person's heart day by day until there is nothing left but pain and misery. Unfortunately, in order to escape that pain and misery a person may have to end a relationship, no matter how intimate or long-lived it may be. Although the decision to end a relationship can be painful, the act itself doesn't have to be overly devastating.

Recognize the Decision is yours

When it comes to ending a relationship perhaps the most important thing to remember is that the decision is yours. You alone have chosen to remain in the relationship, and you alone are now deciding to bring it to an end. While this may seem to add a significant burden of guilt on your shoulders, especially in the case where the other person appears devastated from the decision, it also adds an element of control that is critically important. More often than not the other person in the relationship will fight to maintain the relationship, thereby maintaining control over you. However, by recognizing that the decision to leave is yours you can prevent them from taking the decision away from you. Once you allow the other person to talk you out of your decision you fall back into the codependency that you are striving to escape. Therefore, it is vital that once you make the decision to end a relationship you stick with it no matter what.

Needless to say, such an act should never be taken lightly, therefore it is important to take the time to carefully weigh all factors involved when reaching this final choice. However, once you have made up your mind to end a relationship the important thing is to trust the decision you are making. If you allow yourself to second guess things, especially in light of any arguments that the other person might have, or of any sympathy you might feel toward them, your resolve will begin to waiver, creating doubt, confusion and even guilt in your heart and mind. These are the tools that a codependent person will use to gain control over another person, therefore you need to protect yourself from them at all costs. Subsequently, once you make the decision to end a relationship you need to trust that you are making the right choice and you need to see the process through to the end. Only then can you regain the control over your life that is necessary for building the healthy and happy life you both desire and deserve.

Have the Conversation

For one thing, it suggests that the other person doesn't deserve a face-to-face conversation in which they can speak their piece. After all, a letter is essentially a one-sided conversation, thus it forces one person's opinion on the other. Therefore, in order to be fair, it is best to have a conversation where both sides can have their say.

Choosing the right location for such a conversation is absolutely critical, as this detail alone can significantly affect the nature of the conversation itself. If you have it in a place where the other person feels in control, they will try to take over the conversation, thereby changing the course of events in their favor. Alternatively, if you place them in a strange environment where they feel out of control it can cause them to become overly defensive, closing off to you in every way. While this may not be the worst thing, especially in the case of ending a relationship, it can still add pain and suffering that can be avoided. The best option is to choose a place that is familiar to both parties but that doesn't give an advantage to either. A place that is both public yet somewhat private, such as a quiet corner in a park or on a beach, may be the perfect choice. Here you can have a private conversation without feeling intimidated, trapped or on display.

This is important since the emotional nature of the event will be so strong that it can easily scramble anyone's mind. The last thing you want to do is stumble over the points you want to make, or even worse, forget many of them altogether. Therefore, it is vital that you write down those points so that you can refer to them in the event that your mind begins to cloud over. That said, you don't have to write a speech as such, reading word for word as if you were holding a press conference. Instead, list the topics you want to cover as though you were writing a grocery list. You can even check off each item as you cover it in order to keep track of the progress of the conversation. In addition to ensuring you stay on point with the things you want to discuss, having this list will also eliminate the stress that trying to remember everything can cause. Now, instead of having to memorize your lines for a performance you can have a flexible conversation, one that allows for heartfelt discussion from all sides and that still ensures you get your points across.

Avoid Placing Blame or Guilt

No one ever ends a relationship for good reasons. You wouldn't end a marriage because you were having too much fun, or you felt too loved. Nor would you end a friendship because your friend was too nice to you. Instead, you choose to end relationships with people who bring pain, suffering and misery into your life. As a result, it can be all too tempting to fill the relationship ending conversation with accusations, blame and guilt, thereby attacking the other person as though they are on trial. While this may seem like a good way to bring closure by releasing all of your anger and frustration it can actually backfire, causing you to feel guilty long after the relationship is ended. Therefore, in order to avoid causing more pain than necessary, both for yourself as well as the other person, it is vital that you avoid placing blame or guilt on the other person in the course of your conversation with them.

A good way to achieve this goal is to avoid from focusing on the past. While it may seem logical to focus on the reasons for ending a relationship, such as the actions and behaviors of the other person that caused you pain and suffering, this will only come across as accusatory in the end. A better approach is to focus on the future. After all, you aren't ending the relationship just to get away from the codependent behaviors that are causing you harm, you are ending the relationship in order to start a fresh, healthy and happy life for yourself. Thus, rather than focusing on the dark past that you are breaking free from you should focus on your future hopes and dreams, those things you are moving toward. This will put a positive spin on the conversation, avoiding the negative aspects of anger, blame and guilt.

You can treat it like you would if you were putting in your notice at work. Anytime you quit a job it's usually because you are unhappy with the job you have. When you put in your notice you can rant and rave about how badly you have been treated, or you can choose to tell your boss that you are ready for new challenges, or that a job you have always wanted has become available. In the end, it is always best to live and let live. Once you end the relationship you will be free from the codependent behaviors and influences that caused you pain, and that is all that counts. Therefore, focus on the positive future rather than the negative past. While the process of ending a relationship will be painful, it doesn't have to be traumatic. By staying as positive as possible you will ensure that the pain and suffering experienced by everyone involved remain as minimal as possible.

Remain Calm and Compassionate

Again, this may not be an easy thing to do, especially if the other person reacts in a highly emotional way. And since they are codependent in nature, this is probably a very safe bet. Fortunately, there are a couple of tricks that can help you to keep your calm even in the worst-case scenario. One is to treat the conversation as a done deal. In other words, this isn't a negotiation in which one side or the other will come out the winner. This is a decision that you have already made, therefore you have already won. The outcome is already decided. The future is already written. Therefore, you don't have anything to worry about. You can't be roped back into the relationship, nor can you be forced to do anything you don't want to do. Those days are in the past. In the here and now you are in control of your life, your destiny, and even your emotions. You don't have to get drawn into an argument as there is nothing to prove or gain as a result. Instead, you just have to deliver the message that you are moving on with your life.

Another trick to help you remain calm and compassionate is to recognize that aggressive behavior is usually a sign of pain. Therefore, if the other person flies off on a tangent, ranting and raving about all of the things you have done or how bad you are as a person, rather than arguing back simply recognize that they are crying out in pain. If you react in an emotionally charged way you will only increase that pain and suffering, making you a monster in the process. You aren't a monster, which is why you want to end your codependent relationships. Therefore, act as the decent, loving person you are and be ever-compassionate no matter what. See this act of love and compassion as the first step toward your newfound happy and healthy life.

Be Firm

Finally, when it comes to ending a relationship it is absolutely vital that you be firm. Stand by your decision, no matter how much the other person argues, begs or even threatens. You have decided to move on with your life, and nothing should undermine your conviction to do so. Therefore, be strong, be confident, and most importantly, be firm in your decision to end the relationship.

Being firm doesn't mean that you have to be mean or aggressive, it simply means that you have made up your mind and you need to stick to the choice that you have made. If you allow yourself to be dissuaded from your decision you can find yourself sliding down the slippery slope that leads back to codependency. The fact of the matter is that you have reached the conclusion that in order to be healthy, happy and strong you need to be out of this particular relationship. While staying in it may benefit the other person it won't benefit you, and you need to start putting yourself first in order to create the life you deserve. Therefore, staying firm isn't about being stubborn or even right, rather it's about doing the right thing for yourself. By now you know that you can't fix other people, however you can fix yourself and that's what you have to do. That process starts with removing yourself from toxic environments, such as codependent relationships, and putting yourself in more positive environments instead, ones that promote healthy, happy relationships as well as a healthy and happy sense of self-worth.

Chapter 41: Managing Stress and Anxiety to Prevent Anger Outbreaks

Often, one of the major reasons why you're anxious and get angry easily is because you're stressed out. When you're anxious and stressed out, your nerve receptors are ultra-sensitive. Trivial things irritate you and make you mad. Thus, you have to manage stress first, to be able to prevent your anger outbreaks and unnecessary anxiety. Below is the list of steps that you can implement.

Identify Your Stressors

Think about the times that you have been stressed. What are the causative agents of your stressful incidents? Be specific. Here are examples:

- You were tasked to submit the weekly sales report of your company and the deadline is the following day
- You were assigned to give the opening remarks in a meeting during the weekend
- A male friend is asking you for a date, but you don't like him
- Your teenage daughter has been staying out late at night and you don't know why

These examples may not stress other people, but for many, they are stressors bound to make them anxious or stressed. And during the span of the day, they get irritated by insignificant things because of these stressors.

If you analyze the examples given, they won't be stressors when you look at them with a positive frame of mind. Although, they are genuine stressors, you can reduce them to ordinary tasks by merely changing the way you think. Yes, it's again based on the way you think. Isn't the mind a powerful tool that you can optimize?

Knowing this fact will help you face your stressors. It's recommended that you confront them head on, and not avoid them, except in extraordinary circumstances when you could be seriously injured. A specific example is when confronting violent bullies.

Avoid or Confront Your Stressors

Experts recommend that you confront your stressors, or that you expose yourself to the stressor until you become desensitized. But, be careful in confronting your stressors without proper planning. You should map out your alternative actions in case some 'accident' happens. Bear in mind that your mind has that power to reduce a stressor to a motivator or to an irrelevant stimulus. Use your mental power to address this concern. Hence, think of your stressors as minor concerns that you can easily resolve.

Psyche Yourself about Your Stressors

You have to psyche yourself every day that they are not stressors but are triggers to develop yourself. Allow the idea to permeate your brain. Your thoughts can turn the events into a stressful situation or a motivational, learning experience. It's entirely up to you.

Focus on Positive Thoughts

After qualifying the events (stressors) as learning experiences, you must continue doing so. Perceive them in a positive way. Again, it's all in your mind. The way you think affects the way you react to incidents. Find the positives in the negatives, and they will become positives. Be optimistic and change the way you think, and you'll get rid of your stressors.

Spend Some Relaxation Time

You need a calming activity to help your de-stress. This is the same with anger. These relaxing activities include meditation, breathing exercises and the like. While you're relaxing, you can continue building your optimism of things around you. These will help you maintain your focus and redirect your thoughts to more positive outcomes. Once you are able to relax and relieve your stress, your anger and anxiety episodes will lessen, or will disappear for good.

Manage Your Thoughts

Your thoughts are the most inspiring power you possess as a human being. Through your thoughts, you process new ideas and cover new horizons in lesser period. Reaching milestones and achieving greatness has always been a function of thoughts, more reason why observation is a primary element of every scientific research.

Identify your thought: unfortunately, most people are ignorant of their thoughts. No one cannot know his or her thoughts only that most people have failed to pay attention to it. To manage your thought, you need to know it; understand its component.

Change your Negative Thoughts: after you have identified your thoughts, the step is to change your thoughts. Wrong thoughts will undoubtedly be on your mind if you are always involved in poorly expressing your anger.

Be Grateful: when events around you do not work out the way you hope they will be grateful for other things that are working the way you have expected. When you feed your mind with reasons you have to be thankful, it takes away your attention from what you are losing and takes it to what you have enjoyed. More so, you have less reason to feel offended toward people even when they offend you; you will remember the good things they can still do, or probably did.

Chapter 42: Overcoming Fear and Anxiety

Fear is one of our strongest emotions. It has an astoundingly strong effect on your mind and body.

From time to time, they can take over your life, affecting your ability to eat, rest, concentrate, travel, enjoy your day, leave the house, or excel at work or school. This can prevent you from achieving the things that you need to do or acquire the things that you need, and may, furthermore, impact your health.

What makes you anxious or restless? Since anxiety is similar to fear, the strategies mentioned above also work well for anxiety. Anxiety occurs when fear is debilitating and endures over a prolonged period of time. It is connected to something that might or will happen in the future, rather than what's happening right now.

What do fear and anxiety feel like? When you feel frightened or nervous, your mind and body react quickly. Your heart may beat more quickly. You may breathe in extraordinarily fast, shallow breaths. Your muscles may feel weak. You may sweat a lot. Your stomach may feel queasy. You may find it difficult to concentrate on anything. You may feel frozen, cemented to the spot. You may not be able to eat. You may have hot and cold sweats. You may get dry mouth. You may get astoundingly tense muscles.

Over time, you may become depressed, experience trouble sleeping, develop headaches, have difficulty working and preparing for the future, have issues having sexual intercourse, and lose self-confidence.

These things happen because your body, detecting fear, is setting you up for an emergency, so it makes the blood in your body flow to your muscles and gives you the mental ability to focus on what your body sees as a threat. Furthermore, it may you elevate blood sugar.

Why do I feel like this when I'm in no real danger? Early humans required the fast, mind-blowing responses that fear causes because they were routinely exposed to physically dangerous conditions; regardless, we do not normally face comparable perils in modern-day living.

Regardless of this, our mind's bodies still work quite similarly to those of our early ancestors, and we have comparable reactions to our modern worries over bills, travel and social conditions. Nevertheless, we can't escape from or physically attack these issues!

The physical assessments of fear can be alarming in and of themselves – especially if you are experiencing them, and you don't have the foggiest idea why, or in case they seem, by all accounts, to be disproportionate to the situation. Instead of warning you about impending danger and setting you up to respond to it, your fear or anxiety can kick in when it perceives very dangerous or slightly dangerous. These situations could be imaginary or minor.

Why won't my fear go away? When will I feel normal again? A small amount of fear is normal when you are faced with something new. Or it could be a faint, slightly intuitive fear about someone or something, even though you can't put your finger on why. Some individuals feel constant fear and anxiety, with no particular trigger.

Understanding Panic Attacks

People who have attacks of nervousness often complain that they have difficulty breathing, and they worry that they're having a heart attack or will lose control of their bodies.

What is a Phobia/Fear?

A phobia is an over-the-top fear of a particular animal, thing, place or situation. People with fears have an amazing need to avoid any contact with a specific explanation behind the cause or fear. Coming into contact with the explanation behind the fear makes such a person with phobia fretful or panicky.

How Can You Help Yourself?

Face your fear if you can.

If you, by and large, avoid conditions that you are afraid of, you may stop achieving the things that you need or want to do. You won't have the chance to determine whether your fears regarding the situation are valid, so you may miss the opportunity to learn how to manage your fears and lessen your anxiety. As a result of being overly cautious, your anxiety may increase, facing your fearful emotions and attacking the underlying causes can be a suitable technique for beating your anxiety.

Know Yourself

Get acquainted with your fear or anxiety. Keep an anxiety diary by jotting down your fearful and anxious thoughts when they occur. You can try setting yourself small, reachable goals for standing up to your fears. You can write down a list of things that you can look at now and again when you are most likely to become frightened or anxious. This can be a feasible technique for observing the beliefs that are behind your anxiety. Keep a record of when it happens and describe what happens.

Exercise

Exercise requires some concentration, and this can take your mind off your fear and anxiety.

Relaxation

Mastering relaxation techniques can help you to deal with the mental and physical feelings of fear. These techniques can help you to relax your shoulders and help you to improve your breathing. You may imagine yourself in a relaxing spot. You can also try alternative methods for relaxation, such as yoga, meditation, and back rubs.

Avoid Excessive Food Intake

Eat lots of fruit and vegetables and avoid consuming too much sugar or sugary foods. Too much sugar consumption increases blood sugar; this can lead to feelings of tension. Try to go without drinking an excessive amount of tea and coffee, as caffeine can increase anxiety levels.

Avoid or Limit Your Consumption of Alcohol

It's normal for some people to drink when they feel fearful. Some individuals call alcohol 'Dutch guts', yet alcohol can make you feel progressively anxious or tense.

Complementary Medications or Alternate Strategies

Some individuals find that complementary medications or exercises, for example, relaxation strategies, meditation, yoga, or tai chi, help them to deal with their anxiety. You can select whichever of these strategies that you prefer to win over your anxiety.

The Link between Excessive Fantasizing and Overthinking

Which one interests you more? Fantasy or reality?

To begin with, we should look even more cautiously at the word's "dream" and "reality." When an adult says that he/she understands the difference between dream and reality, how is she defining each word? By dream, he/she might infer fiction. "Fiction" has a variety of suggestions. Fiction can mean a lie. When someone says that the media doesn't impact him/her since he/she understands the difference between dream and reality, I think he infers by "reality" that people and conditions on TV are made or composed. We know, for example, that the TV show Friends was a story about the associations and experiences of a social event of 20-year-olds. In what ways is the story fictional rather than true? Everything considered, adult observers realize that the people on T.V. are performers who are paid to play parts.

When we watch a TV show, we're essentially imagining that these are real people and these conditions and events are really happening as we watch them unfold. To the extent that we acknowledge these characters and their conditions and associations are possible and significant, we investigate them. To the extent that we become tied up with the fantasy, we are drawn into the show.

So where does reality come in, and what is the critical significance of "reality" in this particular circumstance? The reality of a recounted story isn't about whether it is a dream or a creation; it is about whether it is possible and could actually happen in real life. Paradoxically, the best kind of dreams are the ones that strike us, none way or another, as real or credible. We reflect on how much we would like to manifest incredible dreams in real life, and fiction is a representation of that very reality; it empowers us to envision a situation and to feel as though a particularly captivating or fulfilling story could be legitimate.

I once found two women looking at their dream darlings over coffee. They were discussing their favorite "celebs": celebrating their "hotness", what they love about them, why they would make bewildering darlings, and how amazing that it would be to meet them in person. Some time ago, on the news, I read a journalist's article about a pubescent youth asking a Sports Illustrated supermodel (who was probably his mom's age) to go with him to prom. He was admiring the young man's initiative and how he risked public humiliation to attract the woman of his dreams.

We live in a world where people imagine that they have fallen "in love" with T.V. and film stars, erotic entertainment stars, and supermodels. They are fascinated... from a distance. There is something about these fictional relationships that feel safe for these people. There is something that many people find engaging about connecting with famous people in their own darkened viewing rooms. (These fictional relationships can, of course, also occur in our real lives; people may fantasize about that individual at work that they have never truly chatted with.) Part of the allure is that they can safely (without consequence) project the characteristics and personality traits that they desire onto this person.

But somehow, maintaining a strategic distance from other people makes us need them altogether more. In any case, to really revere, as C.S. Lewis says, is to be unprotected.

However, this isn't just about crushing on Hollywood celebs; fantasy can infiltrate huge parts of our life. However, to dream is to live-in what isn't instead of living in what is. In this way, fantasizing can lead to overthinking: from suggestive amusement to destructive effects.

For example, a married man who constantly fantasizes about his young office secretary and constantly pictures himself in a relationship with her may neglect his own relationship. A single woman who becomes madly in love with a man who she's scarcely spoken with may imagine what their life could be like, choose names for their two children, or mentally furnish their dream house, only to have her heart broken by his disinterest. A housewife who is trapped in the fantasy and passion of her romance novels may surrender her own reality instead of working to improve it.

A young person who spends all his time fantasizing about his football career after he is forced to quite due to injury is escaping the present moment instead of pursuing equally fulfilling but more realistic career options. A miserable college student, surfing the internet for fantasy women, may avoid social opportunities that would permit him to connect with real-life women and experience fulfilling relationships.

Fantasizing about someone who is unattainable in real life may seem, by all accounts, to be a harmless indulgence, but it can lead people to infidelity and prevent people from pursuing meaningful, real relationships. These fantasies could also become a source of stress and inferiority as, by their very nature, our fantasies are unattainable; they could become a source of rumination and overthinking for someone who becomes anxious or depressed when real life does not meet their fantasy-fueled expectations. These expectations could also lead us to project certain qualities onto our prospective partners that are unrealistic and set ourselves up for perpetual disappointment.

Studies have exhibited that if you mix fact with fiction, people tend to be more likely to believe fake information. For example, in one assessment, German students read an episodic story called "The Kidnapping", into which either evident or false information had been implanted. A control group read an identical story without the announcements implanted. One certifiable insistence was that action fortifies one's heart and lungs. The counterfeit assertion was the opposite statement – that action weakens your heart and lungs. Results showed that the participants in the study were interested in the information that was provided to them but paid little regard to whether the information was true or false.

Chapter 43: Effects of Emotions in Your Daily Life

Here are the main types of emotions and how they build our lives by building us or breaking.

Fear

Fear is a powerful emotion experienced by all humans. It alerts us about the presence of danger in our environments. It involves chemical reactions that affect our brains when we come up across certain situations. People have different types of fears regarding personalities. Other fears are caused by trauma, past experiences, or fears of something else like loss of control.

Fear ruins people. It has killed young ambitions, destroyed relationships, killed businesses destroyed faiths, destroyed negotiations, and killing lives. It becomes our obligation to understand our fears and come up with ways on how we can face them and reduce them.

Happiness

Being happy is not only a feeling of feeling good. Various research has shown that happiness does not make us only feeling good but also makes us healthier, nicer to ourselves and other people, and be more productive in our daily activities. Therefore, everyone needs to feel happiness emotion to live a comfortable life.

Living a happy life is not hard. It does not entail denying negative emotions or trying to fake happiness by being joyful at all times.

Love

Love is the heart's emotion. It is a good emotion. It sometimes makes us do crazy things that help us to build our lives, but in other cases, it can cause us to do things we are not proud of and as a result, end up breaking our lives. Everyone wants to be loved or to be in love. It's an emotion of compassion and fullness that we receive from our lovely ones. Love for oneself is also a crucial factor. It leads to the acceptance of ourselves despite our inferiority.

Love emotion plays a major role in our lives, both positively and negatively. It has a major impact on our health systems. Love also creates closer ties with our friends and families, which creates stronger relationships, thereby building our lives greatly.

Love can also greatly break our lives. Currently, it is a major cause of suicides among the young generation from the feeling of not being loved and not accepting yourself. It contributes to depressions between individuals, which results in personal stress, psychological problems, and mental diseases. From the above points, love emotion should be not a bed of roses. Always be cautious with other people's hearts regarding the love that you offer since it greatly affects them positively or negatively by either building or breaking their lives.

Anger

Anger is a powerful emotion characterized by feelings of antagonism, hostility, frustration, and agitation towards other people. It plays a major role in in-flight management. The feelings of the emotion of anger are easily noticeable from an individual.

For example, one can display the emotion by frowning, talking with a strong stance, yelling, and physiological responses such as sweating and turning red or through aggressive behaviors such as throwing objects.

Most individuals perceive anger as a negative emotion which only ruins relationships and break down our lives.

Pride

When we think of deadly sins, pride is arguably one of them. However, pride is not as bad as people think. Sometimes pride helps us to build our lives and also improve the lives of others. It is natural for a person to feel the emotion.

The accomplishment of certain goals and objectives tends to make us feel proud of our own efforts. It is from the pride that we feel motivated and desire to achieve more goals, which help us to build our lives. On the other hand, emotion has led to the downfall of many individuals, families, and dynasties. Pride people are usually arrogant and do not follow instructions set aside. There is even a saying the pride comes before a fall.

Guilt

The feeling of guilt is unique from the emotion of sadness. It combines feelings of humiliation, anxiety, shame, and frustration. The emotion greatly affects us by affecting our sense of self-worth and self-esteem.

The feeling of guilt in an individual can adversely affect a person. It makes us avoid other people due to the fear that we wronged them, which is not necessary. Some people are triggered to punish themselves for sins that they did not commit. It lowers our self-esteem when we try to figure out how the other party perceives us which results in stress and eventually depression. It's therefore good for one to open up to the other party and ask for forgiveness rather than keeping the harmful emotion.

Sadness

Sadness is an emotion that all people experience from time to time. Its characterized by feelings of disappointment, grief, hopelessness, and dampened moods. It is expressed in different methods and the most common ones being crying, withdrawal from others, quietness, and low morale. It is normal for one to feel sad. However, excessive sadness destroys our lives since it leads to stress, which is the mother of many depressions. Sadness is also an important emotion that helps you build your life. When we are sad, we tend to move away from the factor contributing to the sadness, which might be an impending danger.

How Emotions Help You to Survive and Thrive

Emotions guide your lives in numerous ways. Most of you do not understand to which extent emotions drive your thoughts and behaviors. They impact your lives through a million ways, either positively or negatively. According to recent research, emotional intelligence is more important than intelligence quotient since it predicts over 54% of the variation in success, quality of life health, and relationships. They play a significant role in helping you survive and thrive, as shown by the paragraphs below.

Help Build Stronger Relationships

By understanding your emotions, how to manage them, and express them, you can build stronger relationships with your friends. This is because you are able to express your feelings positively to the other party. Emotions also help you to communicate effectively without fear both at work and in personal lives, which aids in building strong relationships with other people. One should try to figure out other individuals' emotions.

They Affect Decision Making

Emotions are the root course of your daily decisions. They affect not only the nature of the decision but also the speed at which you make the decision. Take, for example, the emotion of anger. It leads to impatience in most people, which results in rash decision making. In other cases, if you are excited, one is more likely to make quick decisions, not considering their implications, which could be dangerous. When afraid, the choices that you make could be clouded by uncertainty and might be poor decisions.

They Improve Your Health

There are many physical benefits associated with your emotional well-being. Take, for example, the emotion of falling in love leads to relaxation and contentment and also boosts the growth of new brain cells, which improve your memory capacity. Positive emotions also help you to reduce the chances of contradicting emotion-related diseases like depression and high blood pressure, which are some of the leading sources of death. It's, therefore, becomes vital for people to take care of their emotions to increase their chances of survival and thriving in life.

They Motivate You to Take Actions

When faced by a situation, emotions help you to take steps. Take an example when you are about to sit for an exam, one might feel a lot of anxiety as tom whether they will pass the examination and also how it will affect the final grade. It's from the emotion that one is compelled to study hard to pass, which leads to success. Always consider taking positive actions towards emotions for you to live a comfortable and successful life.

Emotions Help You to Avoid Danger

According to naturalist Charles Darwin, emotions are believed to be adaptations that allow humans to survive and reproduce. They serve as an adaptive role by motivating you to act quickly and take quick actions to increase your chances of survival and success. A good example is when you experience fear as a result of a coming danger like a dangerous animal or a possible threat. You are more likely to free from the threat by running, which increases your chances of survival. When angry, you are more likely to confront the source of the irritation which increases the rate of your survival.

They Help You to Understand Other People

Life without friends could be very much dull and with many problems. You require help from one of your friends since no person can survive independently. Emotions help you to understand the people that you interact with on a daily basis, which plays a significant role in determining the chances of your success. By understanding other people, you learn about their weaknesses, and hence, when interacting and dealing with them, you avoid situations that would hurt them. By understanding other people, you can respond appropriately and build strong and mutual relationships with friends, families, and loved ones. This leads to your success and also helps you to thrive in hard situations.

Enhance Understanding

Your emotions act as a means of communication to the society. When you are interacting, it's always good to express your emotions to them to help them understand you better. For example, somebody's language and signals such as facial expression and body movements aid others in understanding you more. This is an important aspect that increases your chances of survival and success.

They Build You as a Strong Leader

World great leaders and business entrepreneurs are known to have a common trait that is they understand other people's emotions. Understanding others' opinions not only helps an individual to influence others but also, it's a tool that helps to inspire them. It, therefore, becomes possible to build trust among your workers and also develop teamwork among them leading to the success of your organizations.

They Help You to Apologize When Wrong

Many people do not understand the importance of apologizing when faulty. When wrong your emotions of the guilt towards the affected party make you apologize. By apologizing, you can re-establish your dignity to those that you hurt; it helps you to repair the broken relationship with your friends and also helps to let other people know that you are not proud of your actions, but instead, you are sincerely sorry for your actions. It's from your emotions that you apologize. The apologies are a great catalyst to your success in life by the restoration of broken bondages and families.

They Help You to Cope with Difficult Life Situations

Your emotions help you to deal with hard life situations. When a situation like death strikes one of your loved ones, the emotion of sadness and anger falls on you, the emotions make you express your responses through methods such as pushing others away, crying or even blaming yourselves for hard situations.

They Boost Your Creativity

Emotions are usually connected to your thoughts. When in a hard situation, your emotions trigger your brains to take rapid actions to counter the situation. Take an example when attacked by a dangerous animal; the emotion of fear triggers the brain to search for any weapon that would kill the animal. Also, when in an interview, the emotion of anxiety to get the job motivates you to think hard for you to acquire the posts. In many situations, creativity from your emotions leads to your success in the workplace and also at your homes with your families.

They Help You to Accept and Appreciate Yourselves

When you achieve your goals and objective in life, emotions of joy, happiness, pride tend to overwhelm you. The emotions help you to appreciate yourselves more from work well done. Recognizing yourselves motivates you to do more, which results in success in life. Without self-appreciation, it becomes difficult for other people to appreciate you or recommend you to other people who would have helped.

Chapter 44: How to Break the Cycle of Anxiety

Anxiety is described as the act of having persistent and excessive worry. However, the issue with anxiety goes far beyond a single worry. If an individual were to only be dealing with one worry, then it probably would not seem like as big of a deal. Unfortunately, people who have anxiety disorders, more specifically generalized anxiety disorder, tend to be swarmed by one worry that then leads into another worry, then another, and so on. This explains why anxiety is actually a cycle.

Worries are also what keeps that cycle going around and around. Even though a person might be experiencing a worry that could actually be solved, the worry continues on for multiple reasons. The first reason for why is that there are some of a person's worries that can fall under the category of biased thinking. This could mean an individual is giving too much weight to a likelihood that a negative outcome will take place. Biased thinking can also mean a person is exaggerating how bad the negative outcome will end up being.

Some types of worries are actually strengthened by the negative thoughts that a person has about themselves like the person is not capable of coping with any type of negative outcome that could possibly occur.

The second reason why a person might find their worries continuing to take up most of their thoughts is due to the fact that some worries persist because of how certain information in an environment goes about being processed. Someone who suffers from generalized anxiety disorder will sometimes selectively choose to look into the information that will support their worries while ignoring any information that refutes their worrying thoughts.

Memories can also be selective just like a person's worries. In some instances, people who have issues with anxiety have a difficult time remembering any data that portrays a contradiction to the particular worry they are currently dealing with.

The third possible reason for why an individual's worries might be persistent is based on how the person is responding to those worries. Someone who has an untreated anxiety disorder might respond to their fears by trying one of three things. They might attempt to suppress their worries, seek reassurance that nothing negative will actually happen, or they could end up avoiding a situation the triggers their fear.

The greatest downfall to choosing any of those responses is that any of those strategies will make a person feel horrible, which will lead to their worries being reinforced.

However, with the right mindset and the use of some helpful changes in a person's thoughts and behaviors, it is possible for someone to break their cycle of anxiety. A simple example of a negative thought can help to prepare people to begin the process of breaking the cycle of anxiety. The thought "I know that my boyfriend is going to break up with me" is actually an impulsive thought that is extremely normal for a person to have when they are in a relationship with someone. The response could pertain to a particular situation that happens, or it could appear to come 'out of the blue.

Even though that thought may be normal for a person to have, someone who suffers from extreme anxiety would give that thought too much weight and meaning. This ends up leading to the person mulling over all of the possible reasons for why their thought could become true as well as the person will try to lessen their anxiety in the short-term. Unfortunately, when a person tries to reduce their anxiety in the short-term, this only makes that same anxiety stronger in the long-term.

The belief -which in this case is that a person's boyfriend is going to break up with them- becomes that much more significant and is experienced a lot more regularly. The belief will also be much more intense than it would be for someone who does not have an anxiety problem.

The above points are some of the major reasons for why a person should look into overcoming their anxiety by breaking the cycle of it. The first strategy to doing so is for the person to learn how to accept that not every thought a person has warranted an actual reason to become worried. Basically, not every thought that a person has is going to be true.

That being said, rather than trying to battle with one's negative beliefs, they should start focusing on acceptance-based techniques that involve a person identifying the negative thought they are having and putting a label on it. The label might be that the thought is a worry or a judgment. The person should also be trying to show mindfulness to the moment when the belief first comes out as well as at the particular moment when the belief begins to fade from the person's awareness.

It can be difficult and intimidating for a person to learn how to accept and alter a person's negative thoughts so they can be mindful of when the thoughts come up. It is for that reason that is a person may want to consider looking into some support groups, either in person or online, that can help them to work through the process.

The way in which a person goes about doing so is they have to sever the link between their biases created from their thoughts as well as from the information they have gathered. The process that the person will take is called cognitive restructuring, which is the foundation for the treatment approach known as cognitive-behavioral therapy.

Cognitive restructuring gives an individual the opportunity to critically evaluate any possible distorted thought they might be having. The thought "my boyfriend is going to break up with me" is considered a type of distorted thought. The cognitive restructuring comes into play when the individual begins asking themselves a series of questions pertaining to the belief that will result in a more balanced view of all of the relevant facts a person needs to make their thoughts become more rational.

The process of cognitive restructuring will take a bit of time, but the results will be worth it in the end. The first step to restructuring one's thoughts is to learn how to notice when one is having their distorted thoughts. However, it is best to only focus on one type of cognitive distortion at a time. A few examples of distorted thoughts include mindreading, personalizing, underestimated coping abilities, catastrophizing, and entitlement beliefs.

For a week, an individual should focus on their distorted thought, like their entitlement beliefs. The person should look at any moments when they find themselves having those entitlement beliefs. For example, they may notice they are expecting their friends to just pay for their dinner and so they do not offer to pay any money towards the meal.

When the person realizes their cognitive distortion, they should then ask themselves what are some other ways they could think about the situation. With regard to the entitlement beliefs example, the person might ask themselves some other actions they could take rather than not offering to pay their way with the dinner. Three alternative questions that they could consider are: What is the worst possible thing that could happen if they simply offer to chip in some money? What is the best possible outcome that could occur if the person were to pay for their meal? and what is the most realistic outcome that will happen if they pay for their own meal?

The second step to cognitive restructuring is for an individual to begin keeping track of how accurate their thoughts actually are. For example, a person could have a thought about how thinking about their problem will help them to find a solution to said problem.

For that example, a person could write down every time they notice that they are overthinking in one column and then note whether the overthinking leads to any useful problem-solving in the second column.

When the end of the week comes around, the person should then determine what percentage of time their overthinking actually led to them conducting some useful problem-solving moments.

A person could also choose to record the estimated number of minutes they spent overthinking when they are able to take notice of when it occurred. This approach can give a person the opportunity to notice how many minutes of overthinking they did in succession with their useful problem-solving moments.

The third step for the process of cognitive restructuring is for a person to figure out a way to behaviorally test their thoughts. An example of a possible though could be that the person does not have any time to take a break. For one week, the person could go about following their typical routine and by the end of each day, they will rate how productive they were based on a 0-10 scale.

During the second week, the individual is asked to take a five-minute break every hour. They are also asked to do the same rating at the end of each day that week. At the end of the second week, the person will look at the ratings for both week one as well as week two and compare their ratings of productivity for both of the weeks. It is likely that the person will find that they were actually more productive when they took the small breaks every 60 minutes.

For example, if a person has a thought such as, "I will never be capable of getting this done right" they should consider all of the evidence they have that would prove that statement to be true as well as all of the information that has to prove that the statement is not true.

Similar to tracking the accuracy of one's thoughts, the person can write down their objective evidence, which supports the thought that they cannot get something right, in one column and put the objective evidence that supports the idea that their thought is not true in the second column.

Once the individual has done this, they would then want to write out a few balanced thoughts which would accurately reflect their evidence. An example of such a thought could be that the person is aware that they have made poor decisions in the past, but they have also made a lot of good decisions in the past that led to their success.

It is okay for a person to not completely believe in their new thought that proves their original negative thought to be wrong. It is simply important to start experimenting with trying out thoughts that poke holes in their negative thinking.

During this process, a person picks a focus of attention, for example, their breathing. Then, for a certain number of minutes, the person will have to put all of their attention on the sensations they are experiencing while they are breathing, rather than simply thinking about the fact that they are breathing.

Whenever the person finds that they are having any other thoughts other than the sensations that go along with their breathing, they are asked to gently- and without any self-judgment- return their focus back to the sensations they are experiencing while they are breathing.

While mindfulness meditation is not explicitly a tool used for cognitive restructuring, it is, however, a great tool used to train a person to become mindful and aware of when they become too wrapped up in their thoughts. When someone is able to reach mindful awareness about the thoughts they are having, it becomes an essential starting point in the cognitive restructuring process.

The final step to the cognitive restructuring process is for a person to learn how to utilize self-compassion. When a person has self-compassion, that means they are able to talk to themselves in a kind manner, even when they find that they are going through some form of suffering at that moment.

Chapter 45: Treatment for Anxiety

One of the most important questions that someone dealing with anxiousness has to ask is, how do I treat it? This is just as true of someone dealing with their own symptoms as it is of someone dealing with anxiousness in the context of a relationship. Because worry is not a heterogeneous condition, the forms of treatment can take many different forms. The availability of many treatment options is true of many mental health conditions in addition to anxiety, but it is perhaps particularly important in the case of anxiousness because of the many different conditions that can fall under this moniker.

As the reader as seen, the term anxiety is often used to refer to GAD, although this condition is estimated to account for less than half of cases of anxiousness worldwide. In this, the reader will be familiarized with all of the different treatment modalities available for generalized anxiety disorder. At the end, a discussion of treatments for other important disorders like specific phobias and panic disorder. There also will be a discussion of alternative medicine treatments for anxious symptoms.

Treatment for anxiety can be divided into the four main areas listed below:

- Medication
- Therapy
- Dietary changes

- Alternative medicine

This treatment is intended to be used by the reader as a general guide for those treatments that are available. One of the important takeaway points in that anxiety is a condition that the affected individual is dealing with and which the affected individual should find a solution to. The role of the spouse or partner of the anxious person is to provide support for their significant other and to help them navigate the waters of their condition. As much as the spouse or partner of an anxious person may want to guide or steer their partner in the direction they think they should take, it is ultimately the decision of the anxious person what form their treatment should take if they decide to opt for treatment.

When it comes to treatment, there are some differences between anxiety and other conditions of mental health like depression and schizophrenia. In these latter two conditions, the pathways that are believed to contribute to the symptoms of the conditions have been extensively studied. This has led to the development of specific classes of medications intended to treat these conditions. For example, in depression, the role of serotonin in modulating depression has been extensively studied while in schizophrenia, the role of dopamine has been the object of study. Less is understood about anxiousness and the role that neurotransmitters play in modulating it. Anxiousness is often grouped together with depression as anxious symptoms represent a comorbidity that may be seen in as many as 50% of depressed individuals.

They should understand the different types of treatments that are available. They should also understand that not all treatments are effective in all individuals. When it comes to anxiousness, although medication is frequently prescribed, the role that counseling plays in treating the anxious condition is perhaps more significant than it is in other common conditions that affect mental health. This is something that the reader should keep in mind. In some anxious disorders, counseling is considered the first line treatment rather than medication.

Medication Treatment for Anxiety

No discussion of medication treatment for anxiousness would be complete without the serotonin-norepinephrine reuptake inhibitors (SNRIs). These two classes of medications are mainstays in the treatment of depression. Indeed, SSRIs are among the most commonly prescribed medications worldwide, regardless of indication. SSRI antidepressants are a billion-dollar industry and the reader has likely seen television commercials for these medications.

It may come as a surprise that these medications are also prescribed for anxious disorders. When it comes to medication treatment, anxiousness is the little brother of depression. The desire to create drugs that are exclusively designed to treat anxiety has not been pursued the way that antidepressant medication has. This may be because of the inherent heterogeneity that is present in anxiety disorders, or it may be because of the perception that medication treatment for anxious symptoms will always be vying with counseling for primacy. Indeed, there is a perception both in the medical community and among the public that depression can be adequately treated with medication while anxiousness represents a different can of worms altogether.

Be that as it may, there are many medications available for the treatment of anxious symptoms. It has already been stated that nearly all of these medications were produced to treat depression, and this is true for the SSRIs and SNRIs. SSRIs, as the name suggests, work by targeting the serotonin reuptake complexes at the synapse. By blocking these proteins, SSRIs are able to increase the concentration of serotonin present in the synaptic junction. SNRIs work by a similar mechanism, but they increase the concentration of both serotonin and norepinephrine at the synapse. Although the reasons why these medications work is not well understood, studies have shown that these two classes are effective in treating people with depression, anxiety, or both.

SSRIs and SNRIs are not the only medication classes available for the treatment of anxiety. Serotonin agonists like Buspirone and benzodiazepines are also commonly prescribed to treat anxiety. Benzodiazepines have become less popular in recent decades because of the risk of addiction and overdose death. Issues that the reader should keep in mind are that medications can be problematic in older adults because of the prevalence of drug interactions in anxiolytics. As the reader shall soon see, counseling and other treatments have been shown to be very effective in the treatment of anxious symptoms, so if medication is not an option, there are typically other options available.

Therapy for Anxiety

Therapy is considered a first-line treatment for anxiety disorders in contrast to other conditions of mental health. Anxious men and women often have an element of consciousness or agency in their disorder, which makes therapy very effective in treating these conditions. This idea of agency in the context of anxiousness may be difficult to understand, but it essentially means that anxious people are often conscious of their condition and the dysfunction that comes with it in ways that other people with mental health conditions are not. As we have seen, individuals with obsessive-compulsive disorder are very conscious that they have a problem, although they generally have great difficulty in breaking the pattern of obsessions and compulsions that characterizes their conditions.

Perhaps the most popular type of therapy for men and women with anxiousness is cognitive behavioral therapy or CBT. CBT essentially addresses the mental or agency component of the disease process in anxious individuals. CBT is a type of psychotherapy that involves recognizing and targeting dysfunctional thought patterns and regulating emotions. This is an important step for anxious people to engage in. Indeed, some anxious people are able to recognize the importance of ceasing their anxious or obsessive thoughts, even without realizing that they are engaging in what is known as cognitive behavioral therapy. Therapy is particularly effective in conditions like specific phobias and OCD where anxious people can easily become locked into a downward spiral of fear, avoidance, and obsession.

Natural Treatments and Alternative Medicine

There are several effective treatments for anxiousness that fall outside the realm of traditional medications and therapy. These include dietary and lifestyle changes, a subject that is being actively studied. Some foods, such as those that contain caffeine are known to exacerbate anxiety. Indeed, some individuals may develop the symptoms of panic disorder solely because of substances consumed in their diet like caffeine. In the realm of lifestyle change, smoking cessation has been shown effective in the treatment of anxious symptoms in some people.

There are several other important remedies for anxiousness that fall outside of the big two categories of treatment. The other forms of treatment that some men and women with anxiousness have found effective include the following:

- Herbal and traditional remedies
- Transcendental meditation
- Aromatherapy

There are many herbal remedies that men and women have tried to help them deal with their symptoms. Many of these remedies have been used by native and aboriginal groups for hundreds or thousands of years. The list of remedies includes St. John's wort, passionflower, kava, and ayahuasca. Although many herbal remedies are readily available in Western countries like the United States, other forms of treatment like kava and ayahuasca are frequently listed as controlled substances in Western countries. Someone interested in using one of these traditional compounds will have to do their research to determine how they can get their hands on them in the community in which they live.

A quick word about transcendental meditation and aromatherapy. Transcendental meditation has been used as a treatment for many different types of mental illness, including anxiety and depression. This type of treatment may be of particular use in anxiety as it focuses on freeing the individual and their mind from those concerns that way it down and keep it attached to the world. Meditation, therefore, can involve a range of techniques that can relax both the body and the mind. Aromatherapy has been studied in the context of worry secondary to another condition, although there is a belief that it can also be effective in primary anxiety disorders.

Chapter 46: Affirmations for Success

Affirmations are "I" statements that help to reiterate an important point. They will help guide you in establishing positive thoughts and a healthy pattern of thinking. It can be easy to get into the habit of telling ourselves negative affirmations. These might include things such as "I am not good enough" or "I am ugly."

Too much thinking that involves this kind of idea will lead you to feel as though you are not successful. These affirmations are going to take you through the right pattern of thinking to feel positive and have a mindset geared toward fulfilling your biggest fantasies.

Repeat these to yourself daily in order to retrain your brain. Write them down and leave notes around your house. Repeat them more than once and write them down to really reiterate the overall message of these positive affirmations.

Breathe in through your nose and out of your mouth right before reading them in order to clear your mind and relax your body. Read them in a calm place so you can focus on the message the most.

Affirmations for Finding Success

Each of these categories of affirmations can help you with your goals. They have been separated so that you can consistently repeat the ones that are most applicable to your goals. Another breathing method you can try is to breathe in as you count to two, say the affirmation, and breathe out as you count to three. Other than that, simply focus on your breathing while we read these.

Positive Thinking Affirmations

1. Everything I will ever need is something that I already have.

2. I am not afraid of the future because I know that I will be able to get the things that I want.

3. Even things that are challenges to me are things that can teach me something good.

4. I am not afraid of anything bad happening because I know that I have the strength to get through it.

5. I don't hold on to negative experiences and the pain that they bring.

6. I learn from bad things that happen, but I don't allow myself to dwell on them.

7. I understand that letting go of negative thoughts can help me to find a more positive future.

8. I know that not everything will go my way but staying positive will still help me to get through these things.

9. Even when things don't go my way, I believe in my ability to keep moving forward.

10. I am thinking positively because I know that it will help me the most in the end.

11. I am focused on positive thinking because it is the only option I have.

12. There will always be a bright side to even the darkest of things that happen to me.

13. I do not allow myself to become stressed by the unexpected. I take every new opportunity as one to learn from.

14. I am open to the idea of positive thinking because it is an attitude that can spread.

15. There will always be a chance to start over for me.

16. It is never too late to achieve my dreams.

17. Giving up is not in my vocabulary.

18. Ending something will always be out of my own intuition because I know what is best for me.

19. I am appreciative of all that surrounds me.

20. I am lucky to have the things that I do.

21. I am happy about the things in my past that I've experienced. Even the bad things have helped me create the person that I am now.

22. I am always open-minded because I know this will help me to find success.

23. I am willing to take new risks because I know that my positive mindset will help me push through even if things don't go my way.

24. It is exciting to try new things.

25. I am appreciative of every moment I have alive.

26. Even the bad experiences will help me to learn something about myself.

27. I reward myself when I work hard and achieve something that I wanted.

28. I am not too hard on myself if I don't achieve a goal that I had initially wanted to.

29. I set realistic goals for myself.

30. I am enthusiastic about the hard work that it will take to achieve these goals.

Confidence Affirmations

1. I am attractive.

2. I am beautiful.//

3. I am strong.

4. I am smart.

5. I am powerful.

6. I have everything that I already need that helps to create the beautiful and individual person that I am.

7. I have unconditional love for myself.

8. I love myself because this is the only body that I have. It is the only mind that I have.

9. I deserve to be happy.

10. I deserve to have confidence.

11. There is nothing wrong with loving myself.

12. I am my own best friend.

13. I like the person that I am.

14. I like the way that I think.

15. I know that I have flaws, but they are things that I either embrace or try to improve.

16. Other people love the person that I am.

17. Others love me for my flaws.

18. I deserve to be loved by other people.

19. I don't let anyone else treat me negatively.

20. I know what I deserve. I understand my worth. I recognize my value.

21. I do not need others to validate the person that I am.

22. I do not need others to give me the confidence needed.

23. I have all the confidence I will ever need in my own mind already.

24. I lead myself because I know what I am worthy of.

25. I take care of myself because I deserve it.

26. I love myself because that is the most important person needed to love me.

27. I do not doubt myself. I have the confidence to know that the decisions I make are right.

28. I do not have regrets. I simply learn from my past mistakes.

29. I do not allow myself to feel guilty over the things I've done. I take these situations as opportunities to learn from myself and grow.

30. Everything about me is something that I am proud of. I am confident with the person that I have become.

31. Even when I am feeling down about myself, I know what I need to do in order to feel better and more confident.

32. No matter which challenges I might face, I always know the things I need to do in order to push through.

33. There is nothing that will stop me from getting the things that I want.

34. There is nothing that someone else can say that will make me feel bad enough about myself to want to give up.

35. I know that I have enough worth and value.

Dedication and Hard Work Affirmations

1. I work hard because I deserve to get the beneficial things that come along with my strong work ethic.

2. Through my work, I act with confidence to prove my dedication.

3. I focus on what is most important and do not allow other distractions to stop me.

4. I know that it is better to get the work done now than to push it off.

5. I know when not to force myself too hard and encourage rest in order to keep me rejuvenated and focused.

6. I take action in order to get the results that I want.

7. I know how to turn my attention toward something productive even when I am feeling very distracted.

8. I am committed to finishing tasks even when I want to give up.

9. I take criticism well and appreciate feedback because it helps me to grow.

10. I am worth all of the hard work I put in toward making a better life for myself.

11. I focus on relaxing in order to keep me working in a healthy direction of success.

12. I am observant and detail-oriented, so I can understand the whole picture and recognize all the things that need to be done in order to keep moving forward toward success.

13. I have the enthusiasm needed to achieve the things that I want.

14. I am excited about the work obstacles I will face because I know that it will make me stronger.

15. The ups and downs throughout my journey just make this adventure more exciting.

16. I embrace my failures and mistakes and use them to my advantage to accelerate forward.

17. I keep my mind relaxed when it needs to be and energized when it is most beneficial.

18. I am aware of my strengths and weaknesses and adjust the things I do accordingly to these so that I am

aware of the best way possible to achieve the things I want.

19. I don't let the things in my past affect how I will work moving forward.

20. I understand my limits, so I know how to have the highest level of self-discipline.

21. My mind keeps me disciplined so that I am able to follow through with my goals.

22. I am dedicated to getting the things that I want, and I know that I have the most control overachieving these things.

23. I control my impulses to stay focused on the things I need to do.

24. I have strong willpower.

25. I know when I need to say no and when I need to say yes.

26. I won't give up even when things take longer than I would have expected.

27. Finishing projects is faster than starting a bunch and never completing them.

28. It is natural for me to know when to start and stop something.

29. I know how to create a plan and follow through with it so that I can better achieve my goals.

30. My will is unbreakable.

31. I am dependable and can trust myself to finish the things that I want.

32. Other people depend on me and trust me to finish things as well.

33. I have entire control over the decisions that I make.

34. I manage my emotions so that they do not negatively affect my work.

35. I work to create a better life for myself and a better world for those around me.

36. I find passion within my work to help drive me through the challenging parts even when it might be work that I don't like.

37. I am grounded in reality and understand the reality of the work that I do.

38. I make sure that my time is spent in the healthiest way possible, which is working toward something positive.

39. I work for security so that I always have something to fall back on if any of my ventures don't work out the way I expected.

40. I stand up for myself and make sure that I get what I deserve in a working environment.

41. I understand the things that I can and cannot control with my work.

42. I trust that everything will turn out as it should, even when work is especially stressful.

43. I have created a working life that I love, and I'll never stop improving it.

44. I am my best self when I am disciplined and working toward something hard.

45. I work hard to bring abundance within my life.

46. When I work hard at my job, it will bring me even more abundance in my life.

47. The harder I work, the more I will gain.

48. The more I gain, the more I learn.

49. My work is that I am proud of and helps me create a better life.

50. I will always be dedicated to working hard for the things that I desire most.

Chapter 47: Practicing Cognitive Behavioral Therapy

We will show you how to overcome the disorders and improve your relationships. In recent decades we have seen an increase in the growth of competency-based, collaborative methodologies to help clients. CBT has shifted its focus from what's amiss with the patients to what's right with them, as well as from what's not functioning to what is. An important initial step in dealing with a psychological problem is learning more about it, also known as "psychoeducation." This form of learning about the difficulty gives you the relief of knowing that you are not alone and that other individuals found useful methods to overcome it. You may find it useful as well for your friends and family to learn more regarding your problem. Some individuals find that having a proper understanding of their worries is a hugely positive step towards recovery.

Axing Anxiety and Depression

To the extreme, you may find out that anxiety restricts your interaction with others, stops you from going outside your house, or prevents you from working as expected. Some people become anxious following distinguishable traumatic events. Mostly, however, anxiety would slowly grow without you being able to do anything about it. You may have identified symptoms of an anxiety disorder or your psychiatrist or doctor may have diagnosed you with it.

Beliefs That Keep away Fear

To say the least, anxiety can be quite uncomfortable. We in no tend to invalidate your personal experiences, physical symptoms, or disturbing thoughts, but we would like to encourage you to ensure that you put on some anti-fear attitudes. Think of these nervous feelings as a bully that is trying to persuade you that he is tougher, bigger, and more dangerous than he is. You need to bring this kind of intimidation to an end! Anxiety involves the below ways of thinking:

- Overemphasizing the chance of a negative event/threat occurring.
- Overemphasizing how bad it will be if the negative event/threat did occur.
- Underrating your ability to surmount or cope with the negative event/threat.

Overcome your anxiety and fears by using below ways of thinking as your weaponry:

- Be realistic on the chances of the negative event/threat occurring: 'It might happen, but it is not as probable as I imagine'.
- Bring the badness of the negative event/threat into perspective. This tactic is known as anti-awfulizing: 'It is bad but not awful, unfortunate but not terrible, tough but not horrid, hard but not tragic'.
- Give yourself credit for the coping abilities so far. Hold a high-endurance philosophy: 'It is not comfortable, but

I can tolerate it', 'it is hard to endure with, but I can do it', 'it is difficult to bear, but it is still bearable'.

Exposing Yourself

At this point, one needs to do exposure exercises. Exposure exercises involve identifying your worries and fears and planning to face them. Facing one's fears in a deliberate and planned manner is the best way one knows to overcome anxiety disorder. Although facing fear is not fun, it is efficient. Think about how unhappy you became because of your anxiety disorder. Have you had enough of living life through a veil of fear? Would you consider going through temporary pain doing exposure exercises is worth it for a lasting gain of overcoming anxiety? The following list is important for implementing effective exposures:

- Make the exposures adequately challenging to be uncomfortable but not so devastating that you would unlikely stick to the technique.

- Continue exposing yourself to dreaded situations/events frequently and each time make them gradually more challenging. One-time isn't enough. As a rule, keep on exposing yourself to these fears often until you become desensitized or habituated to them.

- For the exposure sessions to work, ensure that they are long enough. Remain in the situation/event until your anxious sensations reduce by approximately 50 percent.

- Try avoiding or controlling aspects of your anxiety by taking note of the things you do. During the exposure sessions, try as much as possible to resist any safety behaviors/actions.

- Remind yourself of the acronym FEAR in CBT. It is a terminology that means Face Everything and Recover!

- Believe that you can tolerate, accept, and cope up with discomfort brought about by anxiety. You do not have to love it, but you can endure it.

- Record your exposure works and keep them so that you can trend and track your development and progress.

Preparing Your Exposure Plan

You will now need to transform your intention into action. Many people delay starting exposures unless they create time for it. Honestly, exposing oneself to fears is not a walk in the park, hence quitting is easier than maintaining it. Quitting exposure sessions in the present can as well mean putting up with fear and anxiety in the future. Often exposures are not as bad as one may think it is. The more often one doe's exposure exercises, the faster they tend to overcome their anxiety disorder. For instance, one may record things such as answering phone calls, going to the supermarket, and sitting in her garden as her first 3 exposure activities. These become the first goals of specific exposure events to confront. Now resolve exactly the day and the time you will do your preliminary exposure session. Commit yourself to a particular time aids you to do it. Also, assign times to redo the same exposure session as repetition is key to overcoming anxieties. Do not leave a gap of more than a day between two repetitions if possible. The more often the exposure sessions the better. The time one should spend in an exposure work is likely to vary but the rule of thumb remains in the situation till the anxiety has meaningfully diminished (by about 50%).

Being Realistic on the Likelihood of Bad Events

When individuals suffer from any anxiety problem, they fear bad things occurring and are inclined to assume that they are very probable to occur. Whether one worries about becoming sick, harm coming to them or loved ones, having a panic attack, or being socially rejected, he/she overestimate the probability of the bad things occurring. Anxiety can affect how you reason and think to a notable degree.

Bringing Bad Activities Back into Perspective

Anxiety often leads one to make a dreaded event more awful in their mind than it is in actual life. When pierced with anxiety one tends to blow negative/bad events out of proportion and often decide that they are unbearable, awful, and world ending.

Fortunately, events are rarely this terrible. Mostly one would cope with their feared event no matter how difficult and uncomfortable it may be. Ways of thinking that are anti-anxiety in nature involve increasing beliefs in our ability to handle unpleasant events and sensations. Tell yourself always that you can and that you will cope with the anxiety – although it is not an easy thing to do. Remember that you have been through episodes of panic and fear before, and despite finding it very uncomfortable, you have survived. You can also try developing improved attitudes on the likelihood of other individuals negatively judging you. Do not attach too much importance on what other people may be thinking of you as it might lead you to feel even more worried and anxious. Instead remind yourself and always have an attitude like 'it is unfortunate if people think negatively about me, but it is not unbearable or terrible'. Keep in mind that no matter how embarrassing your symptoms of anxiety may be; others may be more understanding and compassionate than you would expect.

Surfing Physical Sensations

Anxiety and depression come with so many mental and physical sensations. The sensations can be frightening and intense. If you have experienced panic attacks, you are possibly not a stranger to numerous of the symptoms

It is all too easy for you to mistake your physical feelings as serious or dangerous signs of bad health. If you do not recognize your mental and physical sensations as part of anxiety, you are likely to mistakenly think that you are going crazy, having a heart attack unable to breathe, passing out, or even dying.

It is fathomable that one may wish to halt their symptoms and try to control them. Regrettably, these efforts to fight against the bodily sensations of anxiety nearly always have an absurd effect. One ends up freaking about their anxious sensations and by trying to control or eradicate them, he/she actually worsens and perpetuates them. The attempts to stop, avoid, or reduce physical feelings are as well termed as safety behaviors.

See your psychiatrist if you have a real health problem that requires medical investigation. It is always very important for you to get a clean bill of health before getting yourself into the exposure exercises, this may assist you to standardize your irritating physical symptoms of anxiety.

Walking away from wearisome worry

When one has an anxiety disorder the probability that one becomes worried is high. Mostly, every individual gets worried from time to time. To avoid worrying all together you would have not to care about anything. Nonetheless, there is a huge difference between unhealthy anxiety and healthy concern. The initial involves unproductive fear and worry. Worry that takes up lots of our time as well as energy, is unproductive and triggers anxiety.

If you realize that your present most persistent worries do recur repeatedly even though in somewhat different forms and means, then you have some definite worry themes. This can mean that you perhaps worry about these spheres of your life excessively, even when there nothing wrong going on. The most common worry themes include relationships, finances, health, and other's opinions about you. If you have been worrying over a long time, chances are that you may not comprehend that you can train your mind to be free from the worrying thoughts and feelings. Worrying is a dangerous habit and with perseverance and tenacity, you can overcome it. Breaking it needs a lot of sacrifices and hard work, but the outcome is worth it. One tends to feel vulnerable and strange when they start resisting their worry habit. But in a matter of time, you will get accustomed to the sweet reprieve of not being a constant worrier anymore. Do not give yourself so much time to be worried. Engross yourself in events and activities to redirect your attention from worrying thoughts.

Pick activities that need concentration like doing accounts, listening to others, or solving puzzles. In so many ways, exercise can be of great value to you and can aid in 'sweating out' your worries.

Relaxation Strategies

Getting to learn how to relax one's body can be a very useful part of therapy. Shallow breathing and muscle tension are both linked to anxiety and stress. So, it is vital to be aware of the bodily sensations and to frequently practice some exercises to help in learning how to relax. Calm breathing involves deliberately slowing down one's breath. Whereas Progressive Muscle entails methodically tensing and relaxing diverse/different muscle groups. Just as it is with any other skill, the more the relaxation strategies are done, the more quickly and effectively they work. Other useful relaxation strategies include meditation, massage, yoga and listening to calm music. However, it is important to note that the aim of relaxation is not to eliminate or avoid anxiety (since anxiety is not completely dangerous) but making it somehow easier to endure the feelings.

Chapter 48: The Solution to Relationship Anxiety

When you're still standing in the dark of your attachment-related fear, there are two ways in your relationships you can find happiness — and even stable attachment "earn." One way is with an attachment figure who is caring, supportive, and constantly available. It may be but not always a romantic partner. This person may also be a member of a family, a relative, a clergyman, a therapist, a counselor or even God. It can really be someone you like you can turn to for help.

The other approach is by what I call compassionate self-awareness — a self-awareness from the viewpoint of having a concern for your own pain, and a desire to alleviate it. Happiness seeps in endlessly in both cases to console you and remind you that you are deserving of it. Finally, you must be open to love from an emotionally accessible attachment figure and be open to being compassionately self-aware to receive a stable attachment.

Fortunately, a truly loving partner can help you build compassionate understanding of yourself; and compassionate self-awareness can help you become more accessible to a truly loving partner. Both of these will build on the other — a little bit at a time — to make you feel worthier of love, see your partner in a more optimistic light, and work with your partner to promote a happier, safe relationship. They can also help you build a sense (or, more accurately, a mental representation) of your partner — and ultimately yourself — that you can take with you wherever you go, that can support and encourage you in times of distress. The belief that finding the right partner will help you feel loved and happy is what makes you dream-and romantic stories. You should understand it intuitively. But a conscientious understanding of oneself requires some clarification.

Self-Awareness

To strengthen your interpersonal relationships, you need to look at your role in causing issues — or what you are doing to discourage relationships from even starting out. And, as I have explained, the prejudices of people continue to blind them to those insights. And it can be difficult to develop self-awareness and make good use of that.

But if you succeed in noticing your propensity to affirm your own and your partner (or future partner) pre-conceptions, you will begin to see such prejudices more readily and more clearly. You will be more able to make meaningful improvements not to misinterpret assumptions as absolute reality anymore.

It's helpful to think of self-knowledge as composed of emotional awareness, thinking awareness, and metallization — all of which I'll explain below.

Awareness of Emotions

Emotions have a wealth of knowledge which would be absent from a solely intellectual life. For example, it's the difference between thinking a new love interest on paper is a good match for you, and actually feeling on cloud nine.

Individuals may also recognize values or perceptions by opening up to feelings that they were previously unaware of, or that they didn't know the intensity of. For example, a woman may realize that she is in love with a friend only after feeling somebody else's envy about his dating. Another example is a woman who knows she wants to spend time alone, but only discovers how important it is when her new boyfriend gets clingy. Not only do feelings breathe life into existence; they also give us knowledge to act upon.

In addition to being in contact with their feelings, people need to be able to self-regulate — or control them so they don't get overwhelmed. They're trying to do this in a variety of ways, many of which fail — and some of which you can relate. They may be attempting to hide, ignore or numb distressing emotions, for example. But when such methods are used too often, the emotions are likely to go deep, only to come out later — and with vengeance, sometimes making people nervous, frustrated, or angry. A particular approach is when people ruminate, analyzing the causes and effects of an issue repeatedly as they try a solution. But when there is no real or straightforward solution to the question, they stay caught up in a loop of feeling frustrated and depressed, attempting to solve problems to alleviate their anxiety, struggling to resolve their question, and then becoming more depressed. Or they get so rattled that all their feelings feel like one large boulder firmly fixed on their heads.

In comparison, people who successfully self-regulate are able to manage their feelings and embrace them. They may be using the coping mechanisms I described above, but they do so without other means of working against themselves. For example, while at work they may suppress their emotions but allow themselves to get upset at home and speak to their partners and others about their feelings. We don't protect themselves too strongly against it because they don't feel overly threatened by their distress. This helps them to become more completely aware of themselves. As a result, instead of feeling like they drown in them, they are able to ride the wave of their emotions.

To help explain, imagine someone who grieves over a close friend's death. If this person is afraid or wants to escape his grief, he may shut down his emotions, leaving him trapped in emotional numbness (although shielded from pain) and unable to really communicate in a meaningful way with others. By comparison, someone who embraces sadness more is usually willing to share it with loved ones and maintain close interpersonal relationships. While it's still difficult to deal with negative feelings, those who can successfully self-regulate don't experience emotional anguish (distress over their distress) as much as people battling their feelings.

Many people believe that acknowledging a tough situation means they have to either commit themselves to it or act upon it. They try to dismiss their experience, although they are not prepared to do so. So, in the end, without a way to fix it, they remain depressed.

Distinguishing Thoughts and Emotions

Understanding the difference between the thoughts and feelings is important. You may be shocked to hear that a lot of people are misunderstanding them. For instance, saying, "I feel like I was too quiet on that date" wouldn't be unusual for anyone to say. It, of course, is a thought and not feeling. Emotions are a mixture of being excited in a specific way and the significance that we impose on that excitement. And you can feel ashamed not to say anything on a date.

When people misinterpret their emotional thoughts, their true feelings remain unexplored. Recognizing this mistake easily and then focusing on emotions often leads people to view themselves in a more emotional way. For example, once you know you feel ashamed, you can also understand that you fear being judged. And then you may seek reassurance or support; or you can realize that there's no need for your fear.

Awareness of Thoughts

Your way of thought influences how you view yourself and your convictions about yourself. For example, when you repeat beliefs like "Danny doesn't really love me you reinforce self-doubts and low self-esteem. Only because he feels bad for me, he remains with me. "These feelings also activate emotions, such as depression and fear of rejection.

If you know it or not, all through your day you have a running subtext of thoughts. This can be immensely beneficial to introduce the subtext to the consciousness in discovering how you maintain unhappiness within yourself and your relationship. You too have an opportunity to work on change with that awareness. Often only the very consciousness itself is necessary to promote progress.

Metalizing

The third and final aspect of self-awareness is metallization, a method popular with psychoanalyst Peter Fonagy and his colleagues (Fonagy, Gergely, Jurist, & Goal, 2002; Slade, 2008).

They explained this as a process in which people through their minds experience themselves and the world. This allows them to take a reflective stance — thinking about the psychological reasons for their own behavior and those of others. Metalizing often includes being emotionally linked and at the same time maintaining the positive mindset. Many who have a good metalizing ability know that by thinking about them differently they can alter the very essence of their experiences.

Metalizing necessarily implies that people have common experiences. As described by researcher Kristin Neff (2008), this common humanity naturally gives people a sense of connection and under-representation to themselves and to others. For those in pain they can feel empathy and sympathy because they can relate.

All too often, however, people who are anxiously attached do not feel fully that they are part of that common humanity. As a result, while they may understand why other people do and feel as they do (it's just human), they don't apply to themselves that same understanding. And while they have compassion towards others, they view themselves as flawed in a way that makes them feel incapable of compassion — and more often tend to blame themselves towards issues with relationships. Nevertheless, over time, their repeated experience of feeling rejected — even if their partners don't mean rejecting them — leads them to respond by attacking their partners.

Metallization can sound complicated; and it is so in some ways. Yet when you understand your feelings when you think about why you do what you do, or why others do what they do, you already experience it in your life.

Self-Compassion

Self-knowledge — which involves emotional awareness, thinking comprehension, and metallization — is a powerful resource, but by itself it can't help you. So, let's look at the other half of the recipe for positive, sustainable change — self-compassion.

Individuals are not simply knowing themselves or possessing feelings or thinking thoughts; they are linked to certain experiences. It is normal for people to treat themselves with empathy and to respond to themselves with self-compassion as they embrace themselves and others with their emotions. Also, if people don't speak much about self-sympathy, they do speak about sympathy, how you feel for someone else in pain. This means putting yourself in the shoes of someone else, or showing empathy, and trying to relieve their pain. Compassion for oneself is actually taking the same approach with yourself.

Researcher Kristin Neff (2008) is at the forefront of discussing compassion for oneself and its implications. She describes it as having three key components: self-kindness, shared morality, and concern.

Self-Kindness

This is exactly how it sounds — to be kind to yourself. People who accept this quality are gentle when they experience discomfort, loss or insufficiency. In these circumstances they respond with empathy and gentleness rather than being angry with or critical of themselves. We have a willingness to treat themselves well, not only to achieve instant gratification, but to be safe, happy, long-term people. And, though at the moment they are loving and embrace themselves, they are inspired to improve for the better, too.

The above are extremely significant. Some people are afraid that self-kindness could lead to laziness or complacency, or too easily letting them off the hook. Yet real self-compassion — like general compassion — is not just a search of instant gratification. Find some well-known humane men that you currently respectfully think of Buddha, Gandhi, Christ, Martin Luther King Jr. Nelson Mandela and Mother Teresa. Their deep kindness encouraged them to persistently strive to help others feel a greater sense of well-being — and this could be part of achieving ambitious goals. Similarly, self-compassion will inspire you to seek inner development, naturally.

Conclusion Part 2

Well done!

We have looked at love and the pleasure it brings to the heart. Ameer, a Malaysian medical doctor, said "love does not hurt, only the person who does not know how to love hurts you". You must understand that love and the fear of love are the most topics on earth because of its complexity. Most of the fears that make you suffer can be controlled and resolved. Those fears that haunt your life daily were only learned and can be unlearned. You can control them whenever you want to.

It is just a matter of you gearing up, making up your mind, and taking action. Face your demons. Sometimes fear poses as a big mountain you cannot go past, you do not have a clue of what to do, but soldier yourself up, face it and you will realize it was not as terrifying as you thought it was. When you are afraid, master the ways of overcoming the fears and many more others and you will be able to overcome your fear for love.

Mental habits may seem laughable, but they are dangerous if not taking care of. Every mental habit drives its imagination, which can end up manifesting into reality. Let us look at a mental habit of imagining of betraying him with someone else. At first, it will be in the mind but if you keep thinking about the same thing over and over again, then you will end up executing the imagination. Mental habits instill fear that in the end causes havoc in your life.

How we can be able to overcome our fears in the relationship. In as much as fear is learned and can be unlearned, it is always good for one to take it easy and slow while trying to overcome it. Rushing it may bring more disaster than before. It can make you land on wrong remedies that may worsen the situations.

Not every remedy of overcoming fear works for everyone. There are different types of fear thus different solutions are used. Just like when you are sick. If you are suffering from a bacterial infection, you cannot go to the pharmacy and buy cancer medicine, this won't work. You must administer the right medication for the disease to disappear.

While overcoming your fear, it is not a must that you resist your fears. Sometimes resisting your fears makes it worse. You can learn to surrender to your fear and come out stronger than before. When you come out stronger, you are able to push further, and you will find that the fear is leaving.

The problem arises when one tries to hold on his fears and does not want to let them go or does not want to surrender to them and use them as a steppingstone. If you cannot let your fear go or if you can't master a way of overcoming them, you will never be free mentally, socially and psychologically, where all this will have a negative impact on your relationship and life as a whole.

However, not everybody that faces their fears is able to overcome their fears at an expected or specified speed. There is nothing wrong when you take your time to overcome your fears. Everything has its own time, and your fears have time, and when it reaches you will be able to fight them.